BRITISH SOCIAL ATTITUDES 28

NatCen Social Research is an independent, non-profit social research organisation. It has a large professional staff together with its own interviewing and coding resources. Some of *NatCen Social Research's* work – such as the survey reported in this book – is initiated by *NatCen Social Research* itself and grant-funded by research councils or charitable foundations. Other work is initiated by government departments or quasi-government organisations to provide information on aspects of social or economic policy. *NatCen Social Research* also works frequently with other institutes and academics. Founded in 1969 and now Britain's largest social research organisation, *NatCen Social Research* has a high reputation for the standard of its work in both qualitative and quantitative research.

The contributors

Glen Bramley
Professor of Urban Studies at Heriot-Watt University, Edinburgh

Elizabeth Clery
Research Director at *NatCen Social Research* and Co-Director of the *British Social Attitudes* survey series

John Curtice
Research Consultant at *ScotCen Social Research*, part of *NatCen Social Research*, and Professor of Politics at Strathclyde University

Geoffrey Evans
Official Fellow in Politics, Nuffield College and Director of the Centre for Research Methods in the Social Sciences, University of Oxford

Sonia Exley
Lecturer in Social Policy at the London School of Economics and Political Science

Anthony Heath
Professorial Fellow and University Professor of Sociology at Nuffield College, Oxford University

Lucy Lee
Researcher at *NatCen Social Research* and Co-Director of the *British Social Attitudes* survey series

Rachel Ormston
Research Director at *ScotCen Social Research* and Co-Director of the *Scottish Social Attitudes* survey

Alison Park
Research Group Director at *NatCen Social Research* and Co-Director of the *British Social Attitudes* survey series

Miranda Phillips
Research Director at *NatCen Social Research* and Co-Director of the *British Social Attitudes* survey series

Alice Sullivan
Director of BCS70 and Senior Lecturer at the Institute of Education

Eleanor Taylor
Researcher at *NatCen Social Research* and Co-Director of the *British Social Attitudes* survey series

James Tilley
University Lecturer in Quantitative Social Science at Jesus College, University of Oxford

David Utting
Independent writer, researcher and policy consultant

Anna Zimdars
Lecturer in Higher Education at King's College London

Editors:
Alison Park, Elizabeth Clery
John Curtice, Miranda Phillips
and David Utting

2011–2012 Edition

BRITISH SOCIAL ATTITUDES 28

NatCen
Social Research that works for society

Los Angeles | London | New Delhi
Singapore | Washington DC

First published 2012

SAGE Publications Ltd
1 Oliver's Yard
55 City Road
London EC1Y 1SP

SAGE Publications Inc.
2455 Teller Road
Thousand Oaks, California 91320

SAGE Publications India Pvt Ltd
B 1/I 1 Mohan Cooperative Industrial Area
Mathura Road
New Delhi 110 044

SAGE Publications Asia-Pacific Pte Ltd
3 Church Street
#10-04 Samsung Hub
Singapore 049483

Library of Congress Control Number: 2011941713

British Library Cataloguing in Publication data

A catalogue record for this book is available from the British Library

ISBN 9781446252581

Printed by MPG Books Group, Bodmin, Cornwall

Contents

3   Private education

**Private schools and public divisions: the influence
of fee-paying education on social attitudes**
Geoffrey Evans and James Tilley **37**

4   School choice

Parental freedom to choose and educational equality
Sonia Exley **53**

List of tables and figures

Table conventions

1. Figures in the tables are from the 2010 *British Social Attitudes* survey unless otherwise stated.

2. Tables are percentaged as indicated by the percentage signs.

3. In tables, '*' indicates less than 0.5 per cent but greater than zero, and '–' indicates zero.

4. When findings based on the responses of fewer than 100 respondents are reported in the text, reference is made to the small base size.

5. Percentages equal to or greater than 0.5 have been rounded up (e.g. 0.5 per cent = one per cent; 36.5 per cent ≈ 37 per cent).

6. In many tables the proportions of respondents answering "Don't know" or not giving an answer are not shown. This, together with the effects of rounding and weighting, means that percentages will not always add to 100 per cent.

7. The self-completion questionnaire was not completed by all respondents to the main questionnaire (see Appendix I). Percentage responses to the self-completion questionnaire are based on all those who completed it.

8. The bases shown in the tables (the number of respondents who answered the question) are printed in small italics. The bases are unweighted, unless otherwise stated.

Introduction

Last year's *British Social Attitudes* report saw Britain at a political crossroads. A year on, events suggest we're now a nation in trouble. Three years after the global banking crisis started we're scarcely out of recession. Turbulent financial markets, falling growth forecasts, public spending cuts and rising unemployment all loom large. Playing to an often sceptical and disengaged audience, political leaders across the spectrum trumpet fairness. They do so in the context of impassioned debate on welfare, education and housing, all areas which are facing spending cuts to tackle the deficit. Only the National Health Service remains avowedly protected. Yet despite satisfaction with the NHS riding high, as we reported last year, it too is controversially on the brink of yet more organisational change.

Amid all this, in August 2011, the rules changed on the streets of several major English cities, which experienced riots of a scale and intensity not seen for 30 years. The shocking spectacle of masked rioters in running battles with police, upturned vehicles, burning buildings and mass looting prompted a bout of national soul-searching. Declarations by some that the riots were the work of a "feral underclass", resulted in a clamour of voices in every direction. The Prime Minister, David Cameron, spoke – as he had in opposition – of a need to "mend" and "strengthen" British society.

Every year since 1983, *British Social Attitudes* has given the public a voice so as to shed light on how British society looks and feels. By providing an understanding of what people really think about the issues that affect their daily lives and how their views are changing, it has created an invaluable resource for policy makers and commentators. The findings described in this report are based on interviews carried out a few months after the 2010 election that ended 13 years of Labour government and resulted in a Conservative-Liberal Democrat administration. And so this year's report sits on a cusp: reflecting people's experiences of Britain under Labour, but also informed by their hopes, fears and expectations of life under the Coalition. No one was predicting riots at the time of the survey, but the findings still provide valuable clues as to some of the key questions now confronting our society. How do people respond to prolonged economic uncertainty? Do people think we're generally cohesive and optimistic? Or are we beset by the kind of fragmentation and pessimistic inclinations that the Prime Minister has memorably decried as "can't-do sogginess"?

This year's report sits on a cusp: reflecting people's experience of Britain under Labour but also informed by their hopes, fears and expectations of life under the Coalition

Democracy under pressure

Voter turnout figures in the 2010 general election suggest democratic engagement remains under pressure. An increase in turnout to 65 per cent, following the low points of 59 per cent in 2001 and 61 per cent in 2005, offered some comfort – especially given the loss of trust in politicians we reported last year following the MPs' expenses scandal. But the stark fact is that this was the third successive election where turnout was low: after all, it did not once fall below 70 per cent in the seven preceding decades. And the 2010 election did nothing to persuade young people to return to the ballot box, an issue that has been particularly evident since 2001. Just under a half (47 per cent) of 18–34 year olds said they voted in 2010, down from nearly three-quarters (73 per cent) in 1997 (and far lower than the rate found among older groups). As our Political engagement chapter shows, neither the internet, nor television debates between the party leaders – the innovation of the 2010 campaign – did much to engage voters beyond those already interested in politics.

Education and 'educational apartheid'

Critics across the political divide have condemned "the apartheid between our private and state schools". So our Private education chapter examines how far the values and opinions of former pupils of fee-paying schools are in any way separate, or symptomatic of a divide between society's governors, who disproportionately attended private schools, and the governed. Not only do we find that distinctions exist (for example, in people's political views and how they assess their own social status), but also that they cannot only be explained by advantages conferred by family background, educational attainment or occupation and income. So differences in schooling appear to exert their own influence over attitudes, something which also emerges in our School choice chapter. This finds the privately educated to be among the most supportive of a parent's right to choose their child's secondary school. The chapter also finds strong public support for both school choice and educational equality, suggesting little apparent recognition of the tension that exists between the two.

Delving deeper into politically disputed territory we find greater acceptance over time of a shift from state funding of higher education to tuition fees and student loans. At the same time, support for the continued expansion of university places has reached an historic low, as explored in our Higher education chapter. Most interesting, is the discovery that existing graduates are more likely to oppose the continued expansion of higher education, thus protecting the value of their investment in it, while those in manual occupations and without a university degree are more likely to want to reduce barriers to participation.

A paler shade of green

Coincidentally, the views of graduates stand out in our assessment of attitudes towards the environment; but that is because, in this instance, they have proved less susceptible to increased public scepticism regarding climate change. Willingness to make financial sacrifices to protect the environment has also declined, amid indications that growing scepticism is linked to economic concerns as well as the 'climategate' row over the evidence for global warming (as explored in the Environment chapter). Our Transport chapter examines attitudes to car use and finds an accompanying ambivalence about matching green intentions with everyday behaviour.

Growing confidence and the NHS

If anyone supposed that views about the environment were symptomatic of more general public cynicism, they would be hard-pressed to draw the same conclusion from attitudes towards the National Health Service – so popular that it's been repeatedly referred to in the media as a national religion. At a time when the government is preparing to introduce service commissioning by GP consortia, our NHS chapter shows that public satisfaction with the NHS (which stood as low as 34 per cent in 1997) is running even higher than the record 65 per cent reported a year ago, at 70 per cent. We also see that expectations about waiting times for hospital treatment have risen dramatically over 25 years: people now expect to be treated promptly. As we warned last year, politicians who expect their reforms to improve efficiency as well as patient care will find that the bar for maintaining public confidence in the NHS has been set high. From the public's perspective, it is perhaps little wonder the pathway to reform has been so fraught.

Division or cohesion?

Some of the societal divisions we identify – notably private and higher education – perhaps echo traditional class differences rather than more modern manifestations of self-interest. However, the report also focuses on other topics that touch more directly on some of the concerns raised in the context of riots and Britain's economic woes, including attitudes towards childhood, child poverty and housing.

The context for our Childhood chapter is the reports from recent years suggesting that children's well-being is not safeguarded as equitably in Britain as in many other developed countries. Somewhat reassuringly, we find that most people think Britain is a good country to grow up in and that a majority agree that most young people are responsible and well-behaved. They also think children have better educational opportunities than 10 years ago. Even so, when we ask people to compare childhood today with the past, only a minority believe that children are as well behaved or are happier nowadays.

However, the Child poverty chapter shows that people are not optimistic that Britain will improve in this respect in the next decade. Eight out of ten anticipate that child poverty will actually increase (51 per cent) or stay the same (29 per cent). Most people see tackling child poverty as an important task for government. Yet it's noticeable that the explanations people most often adopt to explain why they think British children live in poverty relate to perceived poor parenting – family breakdown and parents abusing drugs and alcohol, not wanting to work or lacking education – rather than government failings. It's perhaps here where the public's views resonate with those of David Cameron when he talks of "troubled families" and a "broken society".

 Public satisfaction with the NHS is running even higher than the record 65 per cent reported a year ago, at 70 per cent

Our Housing chapter explores the implications of an increasingly acute division, between those already on the housing ladder and those who aspire to join them but cannot afford to. Here we find some confusion between self-interest and recognising wider social needs. Not only do those who oppose new housing in their locality outnumber those who support it, but opposition is strongest in the south of England, where housing shortages are most acute.

Old certainties on the wane

As policy makers extend their search for measures that might strengthen society, old certainties are in increasingly scarce supply. Low voter turnout, falling identification with political parties and a steady decline in religious affiliations all feature. As our Religion chapter describes, as many as half the public say they do not belong to any particular religion, compared with a third only a generation or so ago in the 1980s. More specifically, the proportion who identify with the Church of England has halved from 40 to 20 per cent. And the loss of certainty isn't confined to spiritual or political matters: the increased scepticism we observe regarding threats to the environment also seems to reflect some loss of faith in science and scientists too, with over a third (37 per cent) now thinking that many claims about the environment are exaggerated.

Such shifts in people's fundamental beliefs are reflected elsewhere. Examining attitudes to social morality in England and Scotland, for example, we find there have been remarkable changes of view over time on issues such as same-sex relationships and bringing up children outside marriage; all of them moving away from traditional faith doctrines.

Politically, attitudes can always be expected to fluctuate, not least with the economic cycle. Even so, our Devolution chapter describes a decline in what might broadly be considered social democratic values in the past 10 years. A modest fall in concerns about different aspects of economic inequality is accompanied by greater acceptance of the better off using their incomes to buy better health and education. More dramatically, support for government increasing taxes and spending more on health, education and social benefits has halved from a peak of 63 per cent nine years ago, to just 31 per cent in the latest survey. Views on tax and spend are 'thermostatic' – that's to say they need to be interpreted in the content of fluctuations in actual spending levels. However, it's striking that support for 'tax and spend' policies has reduced to a level last seen in 1983 in the aftermath of recession and continuing 'stagflation' in the economy.

Each to their own?

The *British Social Attitudes* survey began almost 30 years ago just a couple of years after Britain had similarly been shaken by urban riots and recession. Changing social attitudes since then mean that political leaders looking for ways to strengthen society now will find they are on much more fragile ground with fewer obvious levers to pull. The problem it seems is more complicated than 'broken' suggests – the message from this year's study is more nuanced than that. The signs are of a more fragmented society no longer underpinned by old certainties. Our democracy is under pressure with no strong signs of recovery, picking up strongly on the plummeting levels of trust in our big institutions we reported last year. For some, this will be compounded by the fact that religious belief is on the decline.

Last year we reported that continuing concern about the gap between rich and poor wasn't matched by support for welfare and redistribution. This year that trend is confirmed. The democratic and religious ties that used to bind continue to creak. We're living in a society where a sceptical public appear unconvinced by our current collective responses to key social issues like welfare, inequality, housing or the environment. And although people do see child poverty as something for government to tackle, it is seen as rooted in poor parenting. Less engaged or willing to make sacrifices for the common good during challenging times, the British public perhaps increasingly sees it as the responsibility of the individual to get through. If that's true, what hope for the Big Society?

 The signs are of a more fragmented society no longer underpinned by old certainties

Acknowledgements

British Social Attitudes could not take place without its many generous funders. A number of government departments have regularly funded modules of interest to them, while respecting the independence of the study. In 2010 we gratefully acknowledge the support of the Departments of Health, Work and Pensions and Education (previously the Department for Children, Schools and Families) as well as the Departments for Business, Innovation and Skills, Communities and Local Government, and Transport. Thanks are also due to the Economic and Social Research Council (ESRC) and the Hera Trust.

The Economic and Social Research Council (ESRC) continued to support the participation of Britain in the *International Social Survey Programme* (ISSP), a collaboration whereby surveys in over 40 countries administer an identical module of questions in order to facilitate comparative research. Some of the results are described in our Environment chapter.

We are also grateful to Professor Richard Topf of London Metropolitan University for all his work in creating and maintaining access to an easy-to-use website that provides a fully searchable database of all the questions that have ever been carried on a *British Social Attitudes* survey, together with details of the pattern of responses to every question. This site provides an invaluable resource for those who want to know more than can be found in this report. It is located at www.britsocat.com.

The *British Social Attitudes* survey is a team effort. The report editors could not do their job without the invaluable editorial support provided by the two *British Social Attitudes* researchers, Lucy Lee and Eleanor Taylor. The survey is heavily dependent too on staff who organise and monitor fieldwork and compile and distribute the survey's extensive documentation, for which we would pay particular thanks to Pauline Burge, Emma Fenn, and their colleagues in NatCen's administrative office in Brentwood. Thanks are also due to the fieldwork controllers, area managers and field interviewers who are responsible for all the interviewing, and without whose efforts the survey would not happen at all. We are also grateful to Sandra Beeson in our computing department who expertly translates our questions into a computer assisted questionnaire, and to Roger Stafford who has the unenviable task of editing, checking and documenting the data. Meanwhile the raw data have to be transformed into a workable SPSS system file – a task that has for many years been performed with great care and efficiency by Ann Mair at the Social Statistics Laboratory at the University of Strathclyde. Many thanks are also due to Natalie Aguilera and Imogen Roome at our publishers, Sage, and BergHind Joseph who have worked with us to design a new format for the report.

Finally, we must praise the people who anonymously gave up their time to take part in our 2010 survey. They are the cornerstone of this enterprise. We hope that some of them might come across this volume and read about themselves and the story they tell of modern Britain with interest.

1. Political engagement
Bridging the gulf? Britain's democracy after the 2010 election

Turnout increased somewhat in the 2010 election (up four points from 2005, to 65%), but was still relatively low by historical standards. This was despite, among other things, the introduction of televised leaders' debates and much greater use of the internet in political campaigning. This chapter examines the health of Britain's democracy in the wake of these developments, looking in particular at whether politicians were more effective in 2010 at reaching out to those who are least engaged in politics.

The small rise in turnout in 2010 masks some deeper problems concerning people's motivation to vote.

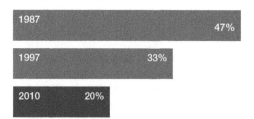

1987	47%
1997	33%
2010	20%

18%

Say it's not worth voting

Only 20% **trust British governments** to put the interests of the nation above those of their own political party at least most of the time, down from 33% in 1997 and 47% in 1987. One in five (18%) now say it is **not worth voting**, up from 3% in 1987.

There is no consistent evidence that those with least motivation to vote were particularly likely to return to the ballot box. At 33 points, the difference in turnout between those with most and least **interest in politics** was still much higher than in 1997 (20 points).

....

While relatively popular, the innovations of the 2010 election campaign – televised leaders' debates and more online campaign activities – were not particularly successful at reaching out to the less engaged.

51% watched the televised leaders' debates

Half (51%) watched the **televised leaders' debates**, making them one of the most popular ways of following the campaign. However the debates appealed primarily to those interested in politics, 74% of whom watched compared with 26% of those with little or no interest in politics.

Three in ten (31%) took part in some form of **digital election campaign activity**, up from just 13% in 2005. However the increase was much greater (from 34% to 65%) among those interested in politics than it was among those without much interest (from 9% to 21%).

31%

took part in digital election campaign activity

Author: John Curtice*

Britain's democracy has been a source of concern in recent years (see for example, Power Inquiry, 2006). A gulf has seemingly opened up between rulers and ruled. During the last 20 years or so, there have been numerous allegations of 'sleaze' and of financial irregularities committed by politicians, culminating in the MPs' expenses scandal of summer 2009 that, among other things, forced the resignation of the Speaker of the House of Commons and resulted in three MPs being sent to prison. In response the public withdrew what little willingness to trust politicians they already had (Curtice and Park, 2010; Committee on Standards in Public Life, 2011). Meanwhile, some voters became inclined to shun the democratic process entirely. Whereas, between 1922 and 1997 turnout in general elections had never fallen below 70 per cent, in 2001 it fell to just 59 per cent, and thereafter recovered only slightly, to 61 per cent, in 2005. Younger voters in particular seemed especially inclined to stay at home (Curtice and Bromley, 2002; Clarke *et al.*, 2004).

Unsurprisingly, these developments have been accompanied by a concern to find ways to reconnect voters with the democratic process. Such a concern was at least part of the motivation for the considerable programme of constitutional and regulatory reform introduced by the 1997–2010 Labour government (Curtice, 2011). That concern has also helped foster interest in the potential of the internet to increase levels of trust and participation in politics, both by making it easier to access information about what government is doing and by making it easier for people to get politically involved and organised (Negroponte, 1995; Dertouzous, 1997; Bimber, 2002). Certainly in the 2010 election campaign both parties and candidates made much greater use of the internet both to disseminate information and to try and get more people involved in their campaigns (Kavanagh and Cowley, 2010; Wring and Ward, 2010). Although scepticism has also been expressed about whether the internet can promote participation (Margolis and Resnick, 2000; Davis, 2005), its ability to do so nowadays would seem all the greater following not only the widespread use of broadband, but also the explosion of social networking sites and the spread of mobile 'smart phones' that provide unprecedented ease of access to the digital world.

Yet in practice during the 2010 election campaign it was a very familiar and long-established technology – television – that was the focus of greatest interest. Although commonplace in many countries, a UK general election campaign had not previously been graced by a televised debate between the leaders of the main parties, largely because incumbent Prime Ministers have felt such debates would be of greatest benefit to their rivals. However, way behind in the polls, in 2009 the then Prime Minister, Gordon Brown, agreed to participate in three debates with his two main rivals. Not only were the rhythm and tempo of the campaign heavily influenced by the three jousts that were held on the three Thursdays prior to polling day (Kavanagh and Cowley, 2010), but the first debate, watched by over 10 million people and widely agreed to have been won by the Liberal Democrat leader, Nick Clegg, was followed by a dramatic surge in the popularity of the Liberal Democrats in the opinion polls. As a result, much of the focus of the ensuing campaign was on what deal the Liberal Democrats might strike with whom in the event that the party held the balance of power in the new parliament.

* John Curtice is Research Consultant at *ScotCen Social Research*, part of *NatCen Social Research*, and Professor of Politics at Strathclyde University.

However, despite the drama and speculation of the campaign, together with the greater use of 'new' technology, in the event there was no more than a modest increase in turnout. Just 65 per cent cast their vote, up four points on 2005 but still considerably less than what had once been regarded as the floor level of 70 per cent. Apparently the gap between politicians and voters was still rather wide.

In this chapter we examine the health of Britain's democracy in the wake of the 2010 election. We consider two questions in particular. First, what conclusions should be drawn from the no more than modest increase in turnout? Does it represent evidence of a continuing and deep-seated failure on the part of politicians to secure the interest and attention of voters, or does it herald at least a partial return to what might be considered a healthier pattern of electoral participation? Second, in what ways did people follow or get involved in the election campaign? How successful were the leaders' debates in reaching out to a wide audience? And is there any evidence that the internet enabled people to become more involved? In our conclusion we consider whether the relationship between Britain's politicians and people looks to be any stronger after the 2010 election or not.

Turnout

There are broadly two main influences on whether or not people go to the polls (Bromley and Curtice, 2002). One set comprises the motivations that voters bring to an election. Do they feel they have a duty to vote? How much interest do they have in politics? And do they have a strong sense of attachment to a political party they are keen to express on polling day? Those who do not feel they have a duty to vote, have little interest in politics and do not feel a sense of attachment to a political party are less likely to go to the polls than those who do.

The second set of influences on turnout comprises the context in which an election takes place – or rather voters' perceptions of the choice that they are being asked to make (Heath and Taylor, 1999). Voters are more likely to go to the polls if they feel the outcome of an election might make a difference. They would, in turn, seem more likely to think the outcome could matter if they feel the parties are presenting very different policy positions – though the impact of such a perception might be reduced if voters feel that parties and politicians cannot be trusted. Voters might also be thought more likely to vote if the outcome of the election appears to be close.

Context is, though, likely to matter more to some voters than to others. Those who are strongly motivated to vote can be expected to cast a ballot irrespective of the circumstances of a particular election. In contrast, for those with little motivation to vote, their propensity to go to the polls may well depend significantly on whether they feel that voting might actually make a difference. Thus when the context of a particular election fails to offer a strong stimulus to vote, turnout is likely to fall most among those with a weaker motivation to participate. As a result, existing differences in

10m

10 million people watched the first leaders' debate

electoral participation between those, say, with little interest in politics and those with a great deal, are widened.

Our previous research has suggested that such a pattern was in evidence in 2001 and 2005 (Bromley and Curtice, 2002; Curtice et al., 2007). At both elections voters were less likely to feel there was a great deal of difference between the Conservatives and Labour than at any previous election since 1964 – and this was particularly true of those with a weaker motivation to participate in the first place. The 2001 and 2005 elections were also ones in which there seemed to be little prospect of any outcome other than the re-election of the incumbent government. And turnout fell most heavily among those with little interest in politics and those without any sense of attachment to a political party.

But what of the context in which the 2010 election was held? In many respects it is one that we might expect would have encouraged more people to vote. When translated into seats at least, many opinion polls pointed to the possibility that no single party would win an overall majority, while the surge in the Liberal Democrats' poll ratings after the first of the leaders' debates added to the apparent excitement and uncertainty of the contest (Kavanagh and Cowley, 2010; Pickup et al., 2011). At the same time, the election took place in the wake of the most serious financial crisis and recession since the 1930s. Not only might this have awakened public interest in how the economy was to be managed in the next few years, but also the parties disagreed about how to tackle the large public sector deficit.

Yet there was also one very large cloud hanging over the election – the scandal over MPs' expenses that dominated the newspaper headlines in the summer of 2009. This served to reinforce the perception many people already held that politicians were more concerned to advance their own interests than the public good. Trust in politicians descended to yet another new low (Curtice and Park, 2010). And a distrustful electorate is often thought to be reluctant to go to the polls (Almond and Verba, 1963; Crozier et al., 1975; Wolfinger et al., 1990; Pattie and Johnston, 2001).

So there are two important questions to ask of the pattern of turnout in 2010 and how it relates to people's motivations and attitudes. First is there evidence of a decline in people's motivation to vote that suggests that it may continue to prove more difficult to persuade voters to go to the polls in future, however exciting and polarised an election might be? Second, in so far as there was a recovery in turnout at the election is there any evidence that the less strongly motivated were particularly more likely to make it to the polls this time, and that therefore, to some degree at least, politicians had rather greater success than in 2001 and 2005 in reaching out to the less 'engaged' section of the electorate?

 In many respects the 2010 election is one that we might expect would have encouraged more people to vote

Motivation

Certainly one motivation to vote remains as strong – or as weak – as it has been at the time of previous elections. When asked how much interest they "generally have in what is going on in politics", in recent years consistently around a third have said they have "a great deal" or "quite a lot" of interest, one third indicated they have "not much" or no interest at all, while one third have fallen somewhere in-between (see Table 1.1). Evidently, only a minority take a deep interest in the nation's political affairs, but equally only a minority affect not to have any interest at all.

Table 1.1 Trends in interest in politics, election years between 1997 and 2010

	1997	2001	2005	2010
How much interest in politics	%	%	%	%
Great deal/quite a lot	30	31	34	31
Some	33	35	34	34
Not much/none at all	37	34	32	34
Base	*1355*	*3287*	*4268*	*1081*

In contrast, as has often been noted (Crewe and Thomson, 1994; Clarke et al., 2004), there has been a long-term decline in the proportion who feel a strong sense of attachment to, or identification with, a political party.[1] Table 1.2 shows that the proportion who say they identify "very" or "fairly" strongly with a political party is 10 percentage points lower now than it was at the time of the 1987 general election, at which point the decline was already well in train. Half a century ago the party partisan was commonplace in Britain. Now he or she is a rarity. And in so far as a strong sense of attachment does help bring voters to the polls, there is no doubt that today's politicians have a harder task securing the engagement of the electorate than their predecessors did.

Table 1.2 Trends in strength of party identification, election years between 1987 and 2010

	1987	1997	2001	2005	2010
Strength of party identification	%	%	%	%	%
Very strong	11	10	7	7	7
Fairly strong	35	27	29	28	29
Not very strong	40	46	49	46	41
None	8	10	12	13	16
Base	*2847*	*1355*	*3282*	*4268*	*3297*

However, there is not that marked a difference between the position now and that at the time of the 1997 election, when turnout was still above the 70 per cent mark – indeed the proportion of "very" and "fairly" strong identifiers together has barely changed since then at all. All that has happened is that there has been a six point increase in the proportion who say they have no party attachment at all, with a commensurate fall among those whose identification is "not very strong" anyway. To that extent at least, it is not immediately obvious that voters were markedly more difficult to get to the polls in 2010 than they had been at other recent elections.

But what of the third and perhaps most powerful motivation of all, the feeling that one has a duty to vote? We ascertained this by asking:

Which of these statements comes closest to your view about general elections?
In a general election...

> *...it's not really worth voting*
> *...people should vote only if they care who wins*
> *...it's everyone's duty to vote*

In our 2008 survey we found that there had been a noticeable decline in the proportion of people who felt that there was a duty to vote, a decline that was largely replicated a year later (Butt and Curtice, 2010; Curtice and Park, 2010). Table 1.3 shows that at 61 per cent, the proportion who say that, "it's everyone's duty to vote" is in fact five percentage points higher now than it was in 2008, suggesting that by the election at least civic duty had recovered somewhat. Yet if we look at all three readings obtained between 2008 and 2010 and compare them with earlier measures, the level is consistently lower than the 65 per cent or so mark that was the norm during the previous decade. Moreover, the proportion who give the most negative response – that "it's not really worth voting" at all – remains at the all time high of 18 per cent, first recorded in 2008. All in all, it appears that there was some erosion of the sense of civic duty during the course of the last parliament.

There was some erosion of the sense of civic duty during the course of the last parliament

Table 1.3 Trends in civic duty, 1987–2010

	87+	91	94	96	98	00	01	04	05	08	09	10
	%	%	%	%	%	%	%	%	%	%	%	%
It's not really worth voting	3	8	9	8	8	11	11	12	12	18	17	18
People should only vote if they care who wins	21	24	21	26	26	24	23	27	23	23	23	20
It's everyone's duty to vote	76	68	68	64	65	64	65	60	64	56	58	61
Base	3413	1224	970	989	1654	2008	2795	2609	1732	990	1017	921

+ *Source: British Election Study*

So there are some signs that voters' motivation to go to the polls was weaker in 2010 than it had been even just a decade previously. However, the changes since 1997, when turnout was still above the 70 per cent mark, have not been dramatic. It would not seem impossible for turnout to have returned to that level once more – if the election had been regarded as sufficiently exciting and important.

Context

We have suggested that one reason why voters might have regarded the 2010 election as relatively important was if they felt there was more difference between the parties than in 2001 or 2005. To assess this we asked respondents:

Now considering everything the Conservative and Labour parties stand for, would you say that there is a great difference between them, some difference, or, not much difference?[2]

As Figure 1.1 illustrates, at 23 per cent, the proportion who felt there was a great deal of difference between the two largest parties in 2010 was 10 percentage points higher than it had been five years earlier. However, the level in 2010 was still at least 10 points lower than it had been at any previous election between 1964 and 1997, and certainly was nowhere near the peak of 88 per cent seen in 1983.[3] By historical standards then, the two largest parties were still regarded as relatively indistinct from each other.[4]

Meanwhile, there was the question of trust, which had fallen to an all time low in 2009 in the immediate wake of the MPs' expenses scandal. Table 1.4 reveals that trust had been restored somewhat by the time the 2010 election had concluded. Now 20 per cent said that they "trust British governments of any party to place the needs of the nation above the interests of their own political party" at least most of the time, four points up on 2009. At the same time, the proportion saying they "almost never" trust them fell seven points to 33 per cent. Indeed both figures were very similar to the equivalent figures in 2006, obtained long before the MPs' expenses scandal broke.

Figure 1.1 Percentage saying there is a great difference between Conservative and Labour, election years 1964–2010

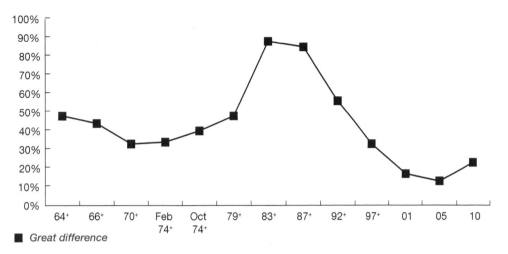

■ Great difference

The full data on which Figure 1.1 is based can be found in the appendix to this chapter
⁺Source: British Election Study

Table 1.4 Trends in political trust, 1987–2010

	87 (1)	87⁺ (2)	91	94	96	97 (1)	97⁺ (2)	98	00
Trust government	%	%	%	%	%	%	%	%	%
Just about always/most of the time	37	47	33	24	22	25	33	28	16
Only some of the time	46	43	50	53	53	48	52	52	58
Almost never	11	9	14	21	23	23	12	17	24
Base	*1410*	*3413*	*1445*	*1137*	*1180*	*1355*	*3615*	*2071*	*2293*

	01	02	03	05	06	07	09	10
Trust government	%	%	%	%	%	%	%	%
Just about always/most of the time	28	26	18	26	19	29	16	20
Only some of the time	50	47	49	47	46	45	42	45
Almost never	20	24	31	26	34	23	40	33
Base	*1099*	*2287*	*3299*	*3167*	*1077*	*992*	*1143*	*1081*

⁺Source: British Election Study
Columns that are shaded indicate they are taken from surveys conducted shortly after a general election

However, on closer inspection of Table 1.4, we can see that levels of trust are always higher after an election than they are immediately beforehand (Curtice and Jowell, 1997). This can be seen most clearly in the two entries for 1987 and 1997. In each case the first of these readings was taken shortly before a general election was held, while the second (which, like all the post-election election readings in the table, are shown in a shaded column) was taken in the weeks immediately afterwards. Both pairs of readings reveal that the proportion that trusted governments at least "most of the time" was eight to ten points higher after the election in question than beforehand. Similar spikes in the level of trust are also to be found in the post-election readings for 2001 and 2005.

What we should then compare is the level of trust in 2010 with the position after other previous elections. It is clearly lower. In 2005 the level of trust was already below what it had been after the 1987, 1997 or 2001 elections; indeed it had fallen consistently from one election to the next. But in 2010 the proportion that trusted governments at least "most of the time" was another six points lower, while the proportion that "almost never" trusted them was seven points higher. The parties may have been thought to be a little further apart, but at the same time their policies were, thanks perhaps to the continuing fallout from the expenses scandal, also being met with a considerable air of scepticism. And importantly, those voters who say that they do not trust governments at all are noticeably less likely to vote; only 59 per cent said that they did so in 2010, compared with 75 per cent of those who trust governments at least "some of the time". So it seems that the marked increase since 2005 in the proportion who do not trust governments at all did help to depress turnout in 2010.

Trends in turnout
Against this decidedly mixed backdrop perhaps it was remarkable that turnout increased at all in 2010. Maybe the excitement of the contest brought some voters to the polls. In so far as it did, is there any evidence that the increase in turnout occurred primarily among those with a weaker motivation to vote, thereby helping to narrow the gap in levels of turnout between the 'engaged' and the 'disengaged' that had become noticeably wider in 2001 and 2005? Table 1.5 shows that in one respect at least this does appear to have happened. At 86 per cent, turnout in 2010 among those who do feel a sense of civic duty to vote was much the same as it was in 2001 and 2005. In contrast, between 2005 and 2010, turnout increased by seven points among those who feel it is not worth voting at all, and by 10 points among those who say that people should only vote if they care who wins. Even so, the level of participation among these two groups, and especially those who say that people should only vote if they care who wins, was still notably down on 1987.

31%
of people who say "it's not really worth voting" turned out to vote

Table 1.5 Turnout, by civic duty, 1987–2010

	1987[+]	Base	2001	Base	2005	Base	2010	Base
% who voted								
It's not really worth voting	36	109	24	317	24	210	31	157
People should only vote if they care who wins	75	697	49	644	50	379	60	169
It's everyone's duty to vote	92	2586	85	1798	85	1122	86	579

[+] *Source: British Election Study*

In any event, the picture of an apparent narrowing of the gap between the 'engaged' and the 'disengaged' in 2010 is not replicated when we look at the relationship between turnout and political interest. Table 1.6 suggests that, if anything, turnout increased primarily (by four points) among those with most interest in politics. Indeed, at 86 per cent turnout in this group returned to its level in 1997 (87 per cent). In contrast, turnout changed little between 2005 and 2010 among those with less interest in politics, with the consequence that the difference in turnout between those with more and less interest in politics remains much wider than it was in 1997. Meanwhile, much the same is also true of the relationship between turnout and the degree to which people feel a sense of attachment to a political party (not shown). Although turnout increased most (by eight points) among those with no party identification at all, the difference in the level of turnout between this group and those with a "very" or "fairly" strong sense of attachment was still much bigger than it had been in 1997.

Table 1.6 Political interest and electoral participation, 1997–2010

	1997[+]	Base	2001	Base	2005	Base	2010	Base
% who voted								
Interest in politics								
Great deal/quite a lot	87	939	81	1009	82	1422	86	333
Some	81	1066	72	1107	72	1484	71	369
Not much/None at all	67	901	51	1171	52	1362	53	365

[+] *Source: British Election Study*

The lessons of 2010

Despite the modest increase in turnout in 2010, there are still some question marks about the health of Britain's democracy so far as electoral participation is concerned. People's motivation to participate has continued to weaken. In addition to a long standing, continuous decline in partisanship, there now also seems to have been some decline in people's sense of civic duty. Meanwhile, following the MPs' expenses scandal, trust in politics and the political system has been eroded yet further.

And although rather more voters felt there was something of a difference between the parties, and even though the election may have generated somewhat greater excitement, it is far from clear that this did a lot to close the gap between politicians and those with relatively little motivation to vote. The gulf between ruler and ruled in Britain has, it seems, still to be bridged.

Following the election campaign
The leaders' debates

Of course, turnout is just one key measure of the health of a nation's democracy. Also often regarded as important is whether or not voters are sufficiently well informed to be able to cast a meaningful vote (Bartels, 1996; Milner, 2001; Luskin *et al.*, 2002). And voters would seem more likely to be adequately informed if they have read something about what the parties are saying and followed some of the campaign coverage in the media. They might also have refined their opinions through discussions about the election with friends and family.

The advent of televised leaders' debates might have been thought to have helped in that regard. Broadcast live at prime television viewing time, the degree to which the media focused their attention on the debates might have been expected to have ensured that they attracted the attention of voters too, and perhaps in particular the attention of those who otherwise take little or no interest in politics. On the other hand, with plenty of other programmes to watch, perhaps those voters with little interest in the election opted to give a 90 minute diet of undiluted politics a miss.

The 2010 column in Table 1.7 shows the proportion of our respondents who said they watched one of the leaders' debates, and demonstrates how that compares with their reported level of involvement "during the campaign in the run up to the general election" in other kinds of 'conventional' political activity – by which we mean activities that did not involve the use of email or the internet (to which we turn below). As we can see the debates certainly had a wide reach – around half (51 per cent) say they watched. However, people were no more likely to watch at least one of the debates than they were to undertake many other conventional campaign activities. Even though they have long since ceased to be the centrepieces of the campaign, just as many people watched a party election broadcast (52 per cent) as watched a leaders' debate. Equally more or less as many did something even more traditional – read a leaflet published by a party or candidate (50 per cent). Meanwhile only slightly fewer read about the election in a newspaper (42 per cent) or watched some other kind of television programme about the election (41 per cent).

Table 1.7 also shows how many people undertook the same activities (other than, of course, following a leaders' debate) in 2005. This reveals there is no sign either that the leaders' debates helped increase the overall proportion of people who engaged in some kind of conventional campaign activity. Indeed, at 80 per cent, the proportion who undertook at least one of the activities listed in the table was actually slightly less than the 83 per cent who did so in 2005. A number of those activities proved to be somewhat less popular in 2010 than they had been in 2005, including most notably watching or listening to an election programme other than a leaders' debate.

Table 1.7 Conventional campaign activities, 2005 and 2010

	2005	2010
	%	%
Undertook at least one 'conventional' activity	83	80
Watched party election broadcast	56	52
Watched/listened to leaders' debate	n/a	51
Read party/candidate leaflet	56	50
Discussed election with friends/family in person or by phone	46	45
Read newspaper election articles	47	42
Watched/listened to (other) election programme	51	41
Contacted by party/candidate in person or on phone	15	14
Tried to persuade someone how to vote by phone	5	7
Contacted party/candidate in person/by phone/letter	4	6
Attended election meeting	2	3
Wrote to/phoned media	1	1
Base	*3167*	*1081*

n/a = not asked

However, although the leaders' debates may not have increased the proportion who did something conventional to follow the campaign, perhaps they were particularly successful at reaching out to the politically uninterested and less engaged section of the electorate? To assess this Table 1.8 shows the proportion of those with different levels of political interest that watched one of the debates and how that pattern compares with following the election campaign in other ways. The analysis fails to support our speculation. Only around a quarter (26 per cent) of those with little or no interest in politics watched a leaders' debate, while three-quarters (74 per cent) of those with at least "quite a lot" of interest did so. Indeed, watching the debates seems, if anything, to have been particularly the preserve of the politically interested; in the case of the other ways of following the campaign shown in the table, the difference between the politically interested and uninterested in their reported level of involvement was consistently less than it was for the debates. If we bear in mind also that no less than 96 per cent of those who watched a leaders' debate also reported undertaking at least one of the other activities listed in Table 1.8, it seems safe to conclude that the leaders' debates proved primarily to be yet another way in which

Watching the debates seems, if anything, to have been particularly the preserve of the politically interested

those who were already inclined to follow or even become involved in the election campaign opted to pursue their interest.

Table 1.8 How people followed the 2010 election campaign, by political interest

	Degree of political interest		
	Great deal/ quite a lot	Some	Not much/ none at all
	%	%	%
Watched/listened to leaders' debate	74	55	26
Read party/candidate leaflet	68	50	30
Watched party election broadcast	68	50	27
Read newspaper election articles	64	44	21
Watched/listened to other election programme	58	44	22
Base	333	369	365

Using the internet

But if the leaders' debates did not succeed in reaching out to a wider, more politically disengaged section of the electorate, perhaps the internet did? As we noted earlier, one of the hopes set out for the internet was that it might help to reach out to groups conventionally disengaged from British politics because it would be easier for people to get involved. If so, perhaps that potential was finally realised in 2010 now that usage has exploded. On the other hand perhaps those who used the internet to follow the campaign proved largely to be much the same kind of people who get involved in conventional activity (Norris, 2006; Norris and Curtice, 2008).

To ascertain which of these perspectives is correct we first of all asked our respondents about their involvement in various 'digital' election campaign activities, such as looking at websites, reading a blog or tweet, and using email or the internet to contact parties, candidates, the media or friends and family about election issues (see Table 1.9). We had also asked much the same question in 2005. The comparison reveals that far more used the internet to follow or get involved in the 2010 election campaign than did so five years previously. Overall, nearly one in three people (31 per cent) undertook one of the 'digital' activities in the table compared with one in eight (13 per cent) in 2005.[5] In part this reflects the fact that more people had access to the internet in their own home than was the case five years previously; that proportion now stands at 78 per cent, an increase of 16 percentage points. But at the same time, those with access to the internet were nearly twice as likely to use it to follow or get involved in the campaign in 2010 compared with 2005. Two in five (40 per cent) home internet users undertook a digital campaign activity compared with just over one in five (21 per cent) in 2005.

That of course still leaves use of the internet to follow the election campaign trailing a long way behind the more conventional activities we detailed in Table 1.7. However, the balance of activities undertaken digitally appears to be different from those undertaken conventionally. In line with some of the claims that have been made on behalf of the medium, people were more likely to use digital technology to interact with others rather than be the passive recipients of information; the single most popular activity for which the internet and email were used was to discuss the election with family and friends. Nearly one in five (18 per cent) of all voters, or nearly one on four (24 per cent) of those with access to the internet at home, used the internet in that way.

Table 1.9 Digital campaign activities, 2005 and 2010

	2005	2010
	%	%
Undertook at least one 'digital' activity	13	31
Discussed election with family/friends	7	18
Looked at non-party website for election information	6	14
Looked at party/candidate website	6	13
Read blog/twitter about election	1	7
Contacted by party/candidate	1	6
Tried to persuade someone how to vote	1	3
Contacted a party/candidate	1	2
Contacted media	*	1
Base	3167	1081

Less than 0.5 per cent

So the 2010 election saw the internet begin to become part of the regular fabric of the way in which voters follow and become involved in an election campaign. But is there any evidence that the internet is helping politicians to reach the less politically interested in a manner that we have already seen more conventional forms of campaign activity fail to do?

Table 1.10 shows how far involvement in both 2005 and 2010 in any form of conventional and any form of digital campaign activity varied according to people's level of political interest. In the case of digital activities our proportions are based only on those with access to the internet at home. The results suggest that, if anything, those less interested in politics are relatively less likely to get involved in a digital activity than a conventional one, and that this was even more clearly the case in 2010 than in 2005. For example, those with "some" interest in politics were almost as likely (in both 2005 and 2010) to have been involved in at least one conventional activity as were those with at least "quite a lot" of interest. In contrast the most politically interested were almost twice as likely as those who only have "some" interest to have engaged in at least one digital activity; in 2010, for instance, the relevant figures are 65 per cent and 36 per cent respectively. Meanwhile, at 31 percentage points, the increase between 2005 and 2010 in the proportion of the politically interested engaging in a digital activity was far greater than the equivalent 12 point increase among those with little or no interest in politics.[6]

Table 1.10 Involvement in conventional and digital campaign activity, by political interest, 2005 and 2010[7]

% involved in any...	Degree of political interest		
	Great deal/ quite a lot	Some	Not much/ none at all
2005			
...conventional activity	94	89	64
...digital activity	34	17	9
2010			
...conventional activity	94	89	62
...digital activity	65	36	21

The question on "digital activity" is only asked of those who use the internet for their work or for any other reason

Political interest is, of course, far from being the only factor that influences whether people use the internet to follow or get involved in an election campaign. Age also matters. Exactly half of those under 35 with access to the internet at home used the internet for that purpose compared with only around a third (34 per cent) of those who were 35 or older, whereas younger people were just as likely as their elders to undertake at least one conventional activity. But that does not mean the internet is helping to engage a generation that might otherwise be lost politically. Turnout continued to be particularly low in 2010 among younger people – only 47 per cent of those under 35 voted, far lower than the 73 per cent who did so in 1997.[8] Rather, the internet is a medium that is enabling both younger and older voters who already have a strong motivation to become involved in politics to pursue that interest further. No less than 99 per cent of those who engaged in any digital political activity in 2010 also undertook at least one conventional activity.[9] Rather than helping to reduce inequalities in participation the advent of the internet is, so far at least, serving, if anything, to widen them.

We perhaps should not be surprised at this. Leaflets come through people's doors uninvited and may secure at least a glance. A party election broadcast may appear just before a favourite programme is about to start. A newspaper may be bought for its sports coverage, but then its political front page catches the reader's eye. In contrast, much of what people see and read via the internet is what they themselves have sought out. Consequently, internet campaigning is less likely than more conventional communications to secure the attention and involvement of those for whom politics is not a passion.

Conclusions

The 2010 election has secured its place in history because of what happened immediately thereafter – the formation of Britain's first coalition government since 1945. There has been much speculation about how well this arrangement would work and its possible consequences for the future of British politics (Bogdanor, 2011). As a result, perhaps, relatively little attention has been paid to the question of how many people and who participated in the election in the first place.

Our evidence suggests the question of who participates in British elections remains a pressing one. Although overall turnout in 2010 was four points higher than in 2005, by long-term historical standards at least, once again an awful lot of people failed to cast a ballot for any of the options before them – even though the election was clearly more closely contested than any since 1992. Although popular, the introduction of leaders' debates did not prove to be an effective way of reaching out to the uninterested, while increasing use of the internet as a way of following and participating in politics has done little to ensure that Britain's politicians reach out to all voters rather than just those with a mind to listen.

It thus perhaps should not come as much of a surprise that in the event the politically uninterested again stayed at home in particularly large numbers. Meanwhile, beneath the electoral surface there are signs that the notion that people have a duty to vote is being eroded while trust in politicians has continued to be worn away. How Britain is governed may now have changed, but the by now all too familiar gulf between politicians and the electorate remains.

Notes

1. The *direction* of someone's party identification is ascertained via a sequence of questions as follows. First, all respondents are asked:

   Generally speaking, do you think of yourself as a supporter of any one political party?

   Those who do not name a party in response are then asked:

   Do you think of yourself as a little closer to one political party than to the others?

   Those who still do not name a party are then asked:

   If there were a general election tomorrow, which political party do you think you would be most likely to support?

   The *strength* of party identification as reported in Table 1.2 is then ascertained by asking all respondents who named a party in response to any of the above three questions:

   Would you call yourself very strong (party), fairly strong, or not very strong?

   where 'party' refers to the name of the party with which the respondent identifies.

   The row labelled 'none' in that table refers to those who did not name a party in response to any of the first three questions above.

2. Between 1964 and October 1974 the question read, "Considering everything the parties stand for would you say there is a good deal of difference between them, some difference or not much difference?"

3. The 1983 figure comes from that year's British Election Study, as quoted in Crewe *et al*. (1995).

4. There also seems to be little doubt that voters were more likely to be expecting a close result in 2010. A poll conducted by Populus just before polling day found that as many as 47 per cent thought the result would be a 'hung' parliament in which no single party won an overall majority (Populus, 2010). In 2005 the same company's eve of poll survey reported that only five per cent were anticipating a hung parliament (Populus, 2005).

5. We would note that although our two sets of questions are worded very differently, this estimate of the degree to which people used the internet to follow the campaign is very similar to the 33 per cent figure reported by Gibson et al. (2010), thereby lending weight to the apparent robustness of our figure.

6. It might be thought this picture is a result of the fact that our list of digital activities contains a somewhat different mix of activities than our list of conventional activities. Perhaps the activities in our digital list are ones that appeal more to the politically interested irrespective of the medium via which they take place? However, much the same result is obtained if we look specifically at discussion about the election with family and friends, a relatively popular activity that appears on both lists. Using the internet to conduct such a discussion is close to being the exclusive preserve of the politically interested. As many as 41 per cent of those with at least "quite a lot" of interest in politics used the internet in that way compared with just 17 per cent of those with "some" interest and 13 per cent of those with little or no interest at all. In contrast, while those with "some interest" (41 per cent) are less likely than those with at least "quite a lot" of interest (65 per cent) to discuss the election by conventional means, they are still clearly more likely to do so than those with little or no interest at all (24 per cent).

7. Bases for Table 1.10 are as follows:

	Great deal/ quite a lot	Some	Not much/ none at all
2005			
conventional activity	1044	1104	1019
digital activity	681	705	465
2010			
conventional activity	333	369	365
digital activity	295	376	239

8. As the following table illustrates, the difference in turnout between those aged less than 35 years and those 65 years and over remained as large as it was in 2005 – and much bigger than it was in 1997.

% voted	1997+	Base	2001	Base	2005	Base	2010	Base
Age group								
18–34	73	770	50	793	49	957	47	236
35–64	85	1403	71	1734	74	2313	74	555
65+	88	508	82	755	85	996	88	286

+ Source: British Election Study

9. Equally, as many as 78 per cent of those who used the internet to discuss the election also discussed the election either face to face or on the phone. In contrast only 41 per cent of home internet users who did not use the internet to discuss the election did discuss the election via more conventional means.

References

Almond, G. and Verba, S. (1963), *The Civic Culture: Political Attitudes and Democracy in Five Nations*, Princeton, N.J.: Princeton University Press

Bartels, L. (1996), 'Uninformed Votes: Information Effects in Presidential Elections', *American Journal of Political Science*, **40**: 194–230

Bimber, B. (2002), *Information and American Democracy*, New York: Cambridge University Press

Bogdanor, V. (2011), *The Coalition and the Constitution*, Oxford: Hart Publishing

Bromley, C. and Curtice, J. (2002), 'Where have all the voters gone?', in Park, A., Curtice, J., Thomson, K., Jarvis, L. and Bromley, C. (eds.), *British Social Attitudes: the 19th Report*, London: Sage

Butt, S. and Curtice, J. (2010), 'Duty in decline? Trends in attitudes towards voting', in Park, A., Curtice, J., Thomson, K., Phillips, M., Clery, E. and Butt, S. (eds.), *British Social Attitudes: the 26th Report*, London: Sage

Clarke, H., Sanders, S., Stewart, M. and Whiteley, P. (2004), *Political Choice in Britain*, Oxford: Oxford University Press

Committee on Standards in Public Life (2011), *Survey of Public Attitudes towards Standards of Conduct in Public Life 2010*, London: Committee on Standards in Public Life

Crewe, I., Fox, A. and Day, N. (1995), *The British Electorate, 1963–1992*, Cambridge: Cambridge University Press

Crewe, I., and Thomson, K. (1994), 'Party Loyalties: Dealignment or Realignment?', in Evans, G. and Norris, P. (eds.), Critical Elections: *British Parties and Voters in Long-Term Perspective*, London: Sage

Crozier, M., Huntington, S., and Watanuki, J. (1975), *The Crisis of Democracy: Report on the Governability of Democracies to the Trilateral Commission*, New York: New York University Press

Curtice, J. (2011), 'Rebuilding the bonds of trust and confidence? Labour's constitutional reform programme', in Diamond, P. and Kenny, M. (eds.), *Reassessing New Labour: Market, State and Society under Blair and Brown*, Oxford and Chichester: Wiley-Blackwell

Curtice, J., Fisher, S., and Lessard-Phillips, L. (2007), 'Proportional representation and the disappearing voter', in Park, A., Curtice, J., Thomson, K., Phillips, M. and Johnson, M., *British Social Attitudes: the 23rd Report – Perspectives on a changing society*, London: Sage

Curtice, J., and Jowell, R. (1997), 'Trust in the Political System', in Jowell, R., Curtice, J., Park, A., Brook, L., Thomson, K. and Bryson, C. (eds.), *British Social Attitudes: the 14th Report – The end of Conservative values?*, Aldershot: Ashgate

Curtice, J. and Park, A. (2010), 'A tale of two crises: banks, the MPs' expenses scandal and public opinion', in Park, A., Curtice, J., Clery, E. and Bryson, C. (eds.), *British Social Attitudes: the 27th Report – Exploring Labour's Legacy*, London: Sage

Davis, R. (2005), *Politics Online: Blogs, Chatrooms and Discussion Groups in American Democracy*, New York: Routledge

Dertouzous, M. (1997), *What Will Be: How the New Information Marketplace will Change our Lives*, San Francisco: Harper

Gibson, R., Cantijoch, M. and Ward, S. (2010), 'Citizen Participation in the E-campaign', in Gibson, R., Williamson, A. and Ward, S. (eds.), *The internet and the 2010 election; putting the small 'p' back in politics?,* London: the Hansard Society

Heath, A. and Taylor, B. (1999), 'New Sources of Abstention?', in Evans, G. and Norris, P. (eds.), *Critical Elections: British Parties and Voters in Long-Term Perspective*, London: Sage

Margolis, M. and Resnick, D. (2000), *Politics as Usual: The Cyberspace Revolution*, Thousand Oaks: Sage

Kavanagh, D. and Cowley, P. (2010), *The British General Election of 2010*, Basingstoke: Palgrave Macmillan

Luskin, R., Fishkin, J. and Jowell, R. (2002), 'Considered Opinions: Deliberative Polling in Britain', *British Journal of Political Science*, **23**: 455–87

Milner, H. (2001), *Civic Literacy: How informed citizens make democracy work*, Hanover, N.H.: University Press of New England

Negroponte, N. (1995), *Being Digital*, New York: Knopf

Norris, P. (2006), 'Did the Media Matter? Agenda-Setting, Persuasion and Mobilization Effects in the 2005 British General Election Campaign', *British Politics*, **1**: 195–221

Norris, P. and Curtice, J. (2008), 'Getting the Message Out: A two-step model of the role of the internet in campaign communication flows during the 2005 British General Election, *Journal of Information Technology and Politics*, **4**: 3–13

Pattie, C. and Johnston, R. (2001), 'A Low Turnout Landslide: Abstention at the British General Election of 1997', *Political Studies*, **49**: 286–305

Pickup, M., Scott Matthews, J., Jennings, A., Ford, R. and Fisher, S. (2011), 'Why did the polls overestimate Liberal Democratic support? Sources of Polling Error in the 2010 British General Election', *Journal of Elections, Public Opinion and Parties*, **21**: 179–209

Populus (2005), Political Attitudes – Final Election Poll, available at www.populus.co.uk/the-times-political-attitudes-final-election-poll-030505.html

Populus (2010), *The Times* Final Pre-election Poll – May 2010, available at www.populus.co.uk/the-times-the-times-final-preelection-poll-may-2010-050510.html

Power Inquiry (2006), *Power to the People: The Report of Power: An Independent Inquiry into Britain's Democracy*, York: The Power Inquiry

Wolfinger, R., Glass, D. and Squire, P. (1990), 'Predictors of electoral turnout: An international comparison', *Policy Studies Review*, **9**: 551–74

Wring, D. and Ward, S. (2010), 'The Media and the 2010 Campaign: the Television Election?', *Parliamentary Affairs*, **63**: 802–17

Appendix

The data on which Figure 1.1 is based are shown below. The figure simply shows the proportion saying "great difference", while the table gives the relevant statistics for all responses.

Table A.1 Perceived difference between the parties, 1964–2010

	64[+]	66[+]	70[+]	Feb 74[+]	Oct 74[+]	79[+]	83[+]	87[+]	92[+]	97	01	05	10
	%	%	%	%	%	%	%	%	%	%	%	%	%
Great difference	48	44	33	34	40	48	88	85	56	33	17	13	23
Some	25	27	28	30	30	30	10	11	32	43	39	43	43
Not much	27	29	39	36	30	22	7	5	12	24	44	44	34
Base	1699	1804	1780	2391	2332	1826	3893	3776	1794	2836	1076	1049	1035

[+] *Source: British Election Study. Figures for 1964–1992 as quoted in Crewe et al. (1995). Note that exceptionally in this table, those who said "Don't know" or "Refused" to answer the question have been excluded from the base*

2. Devolution
On the road to divergence? Trends in public opinion in Scotland and England

Scotland is often portrayed as more social democratic in its outlook than England. It also has a distinctive religious heritage that might be thought to result in greater social conservatism. But are these claims accurate? And now that devolution is in place and Scotland can debate and decide many policies for itself without reference to England, are the differences between the two countries growing wider – thereby perhaps making it increasingly difficult for Anglo-Scottish relations to be managed within the framework of the United Kingdom?

As evidenced by their attitudes towards economic inequality, people in Scotland are generally a little more likely than those in England to express social democratic views. However, this difference has not widened since the advent of devolution. Rather, opinion in both countries has moved in a somewhat less social democratic direction.

78%

In Scotland 78% say that the **gap between those on high and those on low incomes** is too large, while in England 74% do so. In both cases these figures are six points down on what they were in 1999.

In Scotland 43% agree that the **government should redistribute income** from the better off to the less well off, compared with 34% in England. In Scotland this represents a seven point drop since 2000, and in England a four point one.

Scotland
43%

England
34%

Scotland is not more socially conservative than England, as indeed it was not a decade ago. Meanwhile on some issues opinion in Scotland has become more liberal, in tandem with a similar trend in England.

2000 Scotland	66%
2000 England	67%
2010 Scotland	69%
2010 England	69%

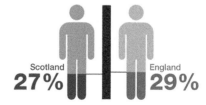

Scotland
27%

England
29%

Exactly the same proportion in both countries, 69% now agree that it is all right for a couple to **live together without getting married**. The figure was much the same – 66% in Scotland and 67% in England – a decade ago.

In both countries only just over a quarter now say that **same-sex relationships** are always or mostly wrong (27% in Scotland, 29% in England). In 2000 that proportion – in both cases – was nearly a half (48% in Scotland, 46% in England).

Authors: John Curtice and Rachel Ormston*

Public policy is not made in a vacuum. It emerges from debate within and between political parties, think tanks, civil servants, pressure groups, together with members of civil society. Debates about health policy, for example, will usually involve the health spokespersons of the political parties, other politicians with a particular interest in the subject, civil servants in relevant departments, think tank and academic researchers with particular expertise in health, and those pressure groups with a professional interest in the health service. These participants interact regularly with each other, and as a result they come to form an informal community of interest or 'policy community' in a particular policy area (Richardson and Jordan, 1979; Rhodes and Marsh, 1992).

The shape of these communities is, however, influenced by the structure of government. Since the introduction of devolution in 1999, health policy in Scotland has been determined by a different government body (the Scottish Government) from the one that decides health policy in England (the UK government). As a result of that change two largely separate health policy communities, populated by different actors and interests, have emerged in the two countries. Indeed across all those policy areas for which responsibility in Scotland has been devolved to the Scottish Parliament, relatively distinct 'territorial policy communities' now exist on the two sides of the border (Keating, 2009).

Different participants can mean different arguments. The balance of views expressed in Scotland's policy communities is certainly often different from that in England. After all, the Conservatives are much weaker north of the border, while the country's distinctive nationalist party, the SNP, are avowedly social democratic (Lynch, 2002; Hassan, 2009). Consequently arguments for a centre-right approach to the role that the state should play in the economy and in the pursuit of greater economic equality are less likely to be heard in Scottish debates than in English ones. At the same time, since devolution there has been a tendency for elites in Scotland to claim that their proposals are consistent with 'Scottish values', and that those values, unlike England's, are social democratic ones (Keating, 2009; Mooney and Pole, 2004; Scott and Mooney, 2009). Scotland's current SNP First Minister, Alex Salmond, has, for example, referred to 'our Scottish social democracy' and 'our social democratic contract with Scotland' (Salmond 2005; 2007). In short, to be a social democrat is often portrayed as part of what it is to be Scottish.

Another area where the policy debate often seems to be different in Scotland is in respect of social and moral issues, such as sexual orientation, family structure and abortion. These, of course, are all subjects on which religious institutions typically take a conservative stance, and especially so the Catholic Church. Historically, levels of attendance at religious services have been higher in Scotland than in England, as has professed adherence to Catholicism (Park, 2002). As a result, statements by religious leaders in Scotland, and especially those uttered by members of the Catholic Church, tend to secure greater media interest and publicity than those of their counterparts in England (see, for example, Puttick, 2008).

....

* John Curtice is Research Consultant at *ScotCen Social Research*, part of *NatCen Social Research*, and Professor of Politics at Strathclyde University. Rachel Ormston is a Research Director at *ScotCen Social Research*.

If policy is not formed in a vacuum, neither is public opinion. It is shaped and influenced by elite level debates (Carmines and Stimson, 1989; Curtice, 2010; Zaller, 1992). So if Scotland now has different territorial policy communities that express different views, views that are then disseminated through the country's distinctive media structure, perhaps as a result public opinion north of the border has begun to diverge from that in England too?

That could create strains on the Union. The more that people in Scotland have different policy preferences from those in England, the greater the pressure for different policies to be pursued on the two sides of the border. And different policies may require different levels of funding, thereby putting pressure on the financial arrangements that currently tie changes in the level of funding made available to the devolved institutions in Scotland to changes in the level of funding of the equivalent departments in England. Moreover, there is no guarantee that any Scottish appetite for different policies will be confined to those policy areas that have been devolved (Mitchell, 2004). In short, growing attitudinal divergence could set in train a process that caused people to look once again at Scotland's constitutional relationship with the rest of the United Kingdom.

Yet perhaps this is too apocalyptic a view. Scotland may have developed its own distinctive policy communities, but this does not mean that the Scottish public are wholly isolated from debates and developments in England. Although Scotland has its own distinctive media, people north of the border have easy access to UK-wide (and inevitably English dominated) media too, a media in which, as one of the two largest parties at Westminster, the centre-right voice of the Conservative party is regularly heard. Similarly, debates about specifically English policies, such as how the NHS in England should be organised, are conveyed across the border by the UK-wide media as well.

Meanwhile, Scotland has experienced many of the same social changes as England that have fostered a long-term trend towards more liberal views on social and moral issues, such as a decline in religious adherence and an expansion of university education (Park, 2002; Evans, 2002). Perhaps these forces have proved more powerful than any prominence given to the statements of religious leaders in Scotland. So perhaps, all in all, the advent of devolution may not have set in train a process that is likely to bring about greater attitudinal divergence – and thus perhaps potential for conflict – between Scotland and England after all.

This chapter examines which of these perspectives is correct. First we consider whether since the advent of devolution Scotland and England have diverged in their attitudes towards the issues that lie at the heart of the left-right divide in Britain, that is how much economic equality should there be and what action government should take to reduce inequality (Evans and Heath, 1995). Then, we turn to social and moral issues. Our analysis is made possible by the inclusion of a set of questions on these two topics on both the 2010 *British Social Attitudes* survey and the 2010 *Scottish*

Growing attitudinal divergence could cause people to look again at Scotland's constitutional relationship with the rest of the United Kingdom

Social Attitudes survey. The former provides us with a sample of respondents resident in England, the latter a systematically comparable sample of people resident in Scotland. All the questions had previously been included on both surveys in the early years of devolution, making it possible to compare trends in attitudes on the two sides of the border since that time.

Equality

Our test of whether Scotland has become more social democratic in outlook than England since devolution focuses on attitudes towards economic equality. Relative to opinion in England, has the Scottish public become, first, more concerned about inequality and, second, more favourable towards government action to reduce it?

The gap between rich and poor

Table 2.1 shows views about income inequality that people in Scotland and England have expressed since the advent of devolution in 1999, when asked:

*Thinking of income levels generally in Britain today, would you say that the **gap** between those with high incomes and those with low incomes is too large, about right or too small?*

In 1999 the vast majority in both Scotland (84 per cent) and England (80 per cent) agreed that levels of income inequality were too large. By 2010 both these proportions had fallen somewhat – but at four points, the difference between them remained exactly what it had been 11 years earlier. So although during the intervening period people in Scotland have, 2009 apart, consistently shown themselves a little more concerned about income inequality than those in England, there is no evidence of opinion in the two countries growing apart.

Table 2.1 Trends in perceptions of income inequality, Scotland and England, 1999–2010

	99	00	01	04	06	09	10
Scotland	%	%	%	%	%	%	%
Too large	84	85	85	82	78	77	78
About right	11	10	10	13	16	16	15
Too small	2	2	3	1	2	2	2
Base	*1482*	*1663*	*1605*	*1637*	*1594*	*1482*	*1495*
England	%	%	%	%	%	%	%
Too large	80	82	79	72	74	78	74
About right	14	15	15	22	22	17	22
Too small	3	2	1	2	1	3	1
Base	*1798*	*1932*	*2761*	*1798*	*913*	*1932*	*913*

Source for Scotland: Scottish Social Attitudes
Base for England: British Social Attitudes respondents living in England

A similar picture emerges when we look at perceptions of the distribution of wealth rather than income (see Table 2.2). People were asked whether they agreed or disagreed that:

Ordinary working people do not get their fair share of the nation's wealth

In 2000, the first year this issue was addressed by both the Scottish and the British surveys, as many as 71 per cent of people in Scotland agreed that wealth was distributed unfairly, compared with 61 per cent in England. In subsequent years the Scottish public appears (with the sole exception once again of 2009) to have consistently been a little more concerned than people in England about wealth inequality. But the difference between the two countries has not widened. In fact in 2010 it was just a statistically insignificant three points.

Table 2.2 Trends in perceptions of the distribution of wealth, Scotland and England, 2000–2010

Working people not get fair share	00	02	04	05	06	07	09	10
Scotland	%	%	%	%	%	%	%	%
Agree	71	64	63	56	56	62	55	59
Neither agree nor disagree	18	22	23	26	29	22	29	28
Disagree	9	11	12	15	13	14	13	11
Base	*1506*	*1507*	*1514*	*1409*	*1437*	*1312*	*1317*	*1366*
England	%	%	%	%	%	%	%	%
Agree	61	61	53	55	54	58	58	55
Neither agree nor disagree	23	23	28	27	29	26	25	28
Disagree	13	13	17	17	14	13	14	15
Base	*2515*	*2419*	*2185*	*3005*	*3195*	*3057*	*2495*	*2360*

Source for Scotland: Scottish Social Attitudes
Base for England: British Social Attitudes respondents living in England

Indeed, far from diverging, together Tables 2.1 and 2.2 suggest that Scotland and England have actually experienced much the same trend during the last decade – a slight decline in the levels of concern about economic inequality. In both countries the proportion thinking the level of income inequality is too large is six percentage points below its 1999 level. Setting aside an unusually high level of concern about inequalities of wealth in Scotland in 2000, there has been a similar reduction in both countries in the proportion agreeing that ordinary people do not get their fair share of the nation's wealth.

However, perhaps public opinion in Scotland appears more distinctive when asked about one of the possible consequences of income inequality – that richer people are able to buy better health care and education for their children. We would certainly expect those of a broadly social democratic outlook to state that such a consequence is unjust when asked:

Is it right or wrong that people with higher incomes can...

    ...buy better health care than people with lower incomes?

    ...buy better education for their children than people with lower incomes?

People in Scotland do indeed appear to have distinctive views on this subject. Table 2.3 shows that they are 17 percentage points more likely than those in England to say it is wrong that people with higher incomes can buy better health care, and 13 percentage points more likely to do so in the case of education. Moreover, in both cases these differences are rather bigger now than they were in 1999 (when they were 10 and seven percentage points respectively).

Table 2.3 Attitudes towards people on higher incomes being able to buy better services, Scotland and England, 1999 and 2010

	Scotland		England	
	1999	2010	1999	2010
Buy better health care	%	%	%	%
Right	28	31	41	43
Neither	23	25	20	30
Wrong	47	41	37	24
Buy better education	%	%	%	%
Right	31	32	44	45
Neither	21	23	17	24
Wrong	44	41	37	28
Base	*1169*	*1350*	*1169*	*773*

Source for Scotland: Scottish Social Attitudes
Base for England: British Social Attitudes respondents living in England

However, this widening of the gap has not occurred because the Scottish public has become *more* social democratic in its outlook, in contrast to the position in England. On the contrary, the percentage of people who think that it is wrong that people can pay for better health care or education has *fallen* in both countries. The gap between them has only grown wider because the move away from a social democrat stance on this issue has been less marked in Scotland than in England. This is, at most, limited evidence of the emergence of an increasingly distinctive strand of opinion in Scotland.

Government action on inequality

If there is little evidence of a widening gap in concern about economic inequality north and south of the border, perhaps we may find more difference in people's attitudes to what should be done about any such inequality. In particular, what matters more, so far as public policy is concerned, is what role people believe government should play in trying to reduce inequality, not least through redistribution of wealth. Attitudes towards such an approach were tapped by asking people whether they agreed or disagreed that:

Government should redistribute income from the better-off to those who are less well off

In most years since 2000, people in Scotland have been keener on redistribution than their counterparts in England (see Table 2.4). So in 2010, 43 per cent of people in Scotland supported such action compared with 34 per cent in England. However, there is no consistent evidence that the gap between the two countries has grown any wider; in 2000 someone in Scotland was 12 percentage points more likely than someone in England to agree that government should redistribute income, while in 2010 the gap was nine points. Instead what is apparent in both countries is a modest decline in support for such a policy.[1]

Very similar results are found if we consider some of the more specific policies that a government might pursue in pursuit of a more equal society. Although not all taxation and government spending has a redistributive impact, a government that was intent on achieving a significant level of redistribution would certainly be expected to

Table 2.4 Attitudes towards government action to redistribute income, Scotland and England, 2000–2010

Government should redistribute income	00	02	04	05	06	07	09	10
Scotland	%	%	%	%	%	%	%	%
Agree	50	45	40	31	39	37	37	43
Neither agree nor disagree	24	25	30	29	26	25	30	28
Disagree	24	27	28	37	33	36	31	26
Base	*1506*	*1507*	*1514*	*1409*	*1437*	*1312*	*1317*	*1366*
England	%	%	%	%	%	%	%	%
Agree	38	37	31	32	34	32	36	34
Neither agree nor disagree	24	25	28	27	26	29	27	27
Disagree	36	35	39	40	38	37	35	37
Base	*2515*	*2419*	*2185*	*3005*	*3195*	*3057*	*2495*	*2360*

Source for Scotland: Scottish Social Attitudes
Base for England: British Social Attitudes respondents living in England

pursue relatively high levels of taxation and spending. Both the *British* and the *Scottish Social Attitudes* surveys have regularly asked their respondents to consider the following proposition:

Suppose the government had to choose between the three options on this card. Which do you think it should choose?

*Reduce taxes and spend **less** on health, education and social benefits*

*Keep taxes and spending on these services at the **same** level as now*

*Increase taxes and spend **more** on health, education and social benefits[2]*

As Figure 2.1 illustrates, during the course of the last decade people in Scotland have more often than not – though not invariably – been somewhat more likely than people in England to favour higher levels of spending and taxation. Typically support for greater taxation and spending has been at least five points higher in Scotland than in England. Against that standard, the fact that in 2010 the gap was as much as 10 points might be thought to be evidence of divergence. However, in the absence of any supportive evidence of such a trend in any other more recent year, that would seem to be an unwarranted interpretation. In contrast, what is not in doubt is that since the beginning of the decade there has been a sharp decline in support for more spending and taxation in both countries. The proportion stating there should be more taxation and spending has fallen since 2001 from 63 per cent to 40 per cent in Scotland, and from 61 per cent to 30 per cent in England. Both publics have evidently reacted strongly against the sharp increases in public spending that occurred on both sides of the border during this period (Curtice, 2010).

Figure 2.1 Support for increasing taxes and spending on health, education and social benefits, Scotland and England, 1999–2010

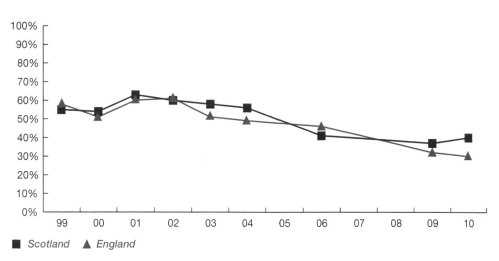

■ *Scotland*   ▲ *England*

The data on which Figure 2.1 is based can be found in the appendix to this chapter

One of the most direct ways in which government can reduce income inequality is through paying benefit to those who are unemployed. When asked which comes closer to their view, that:

*Benefits for unemployed people are **too low** and cause hardship, or,*

*Benefits for unemployed people are **too high** and discourage them from finding jobs?[3]*

people in Scotland have consistently been more inclined than people in England to state that benefit levels for the unemployed are too low (see Figure 2.2). Thus in 2010, for example, 30 per cent of people in Scotland expressed that view compared with 23 per cent in England. But again there is no consistent evidence of this gap between countries widening over time. Rather, once more there has been a tendency for public opinion in both countries to move away from what might be regarded as the social democratic point of view.

Figure 2.2 Agreement that benefits for unemployed people are too low and cause hardship, Scotland and England, 1999–2010

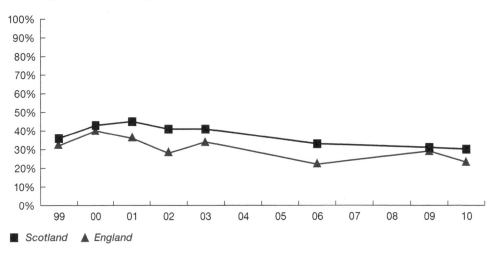

■ *Scotland* ▲ *England*

The data on which Figure 2.2 is based can be found in the appendix to this chapter

So we have failed to uncover any evidence that Scotland has become more social democratic, while England has become less so. People in Scotland are somewhat more likely to be concerned about inequality and to favour government action that might be thought to counteract it. However, they are no more distinctive in that respect now than they were a decade ago, when devolution was first introduced. Meanwhile, Scotland has shared in what seems to have been something of a Britain-wide drift away from a social democratic outlook during the course of the last decade. Scotland may have had its own debates about policy since devolution has been in place, and done so against a public mood that is somewhat more social democratic than that in England, but on issues of economic inequality, at least, this development does not seem to have encouraged people north of the border to become increasingly inclined to come to a distinctive conclusion about the direction that public policy should take.

Social and moral issues

The second area where we suggested attitudes in Scotland might have grown apart from those in England was social morality. Given the greater prominence of religious organisations, not least the Catholic Church, in Scottish policy debates, we wondered whether attitudes towards social morality might have become more conservative in the wake of devolution relative to the position in England. To investigate this possibility we compare trends in opinion in Scotland and England on relationships and parenthood outside marriage, same-sex relationships and abortion.

Relationships outside marriage

Cohabitation has become increasingly common in both countries (Haskey, 2001). This has led to debates about whether or not some of the legal protections and rights afforded to married couples should also be extended to cohabiting couples who are not married, a subject for which responsibility in Scotland is now devolved to the Scottish Parliament (Barlow, 2002; Barlow *et al*., 2001; 2008; Law Commission, 2007). In part, at least, people's views about this issue will depend on whether they regard it as morally acceptable for a couple to live together without getting married in the first place.

When people in the two countries are asked whether they agree or disagree that:

It is all right for a couple to live together without intending to get married

the pattern of responses is almost identical. In both cases, just over two out of three people (69 per cent) agree that cohabitation is acceptable, while only nine per cent in Scotland and 11 per cent in England disagree. The same was true a decade earlier in 2000 when 66 per cent in Scotland and 67 per cent in England agreed, while 13 and 14 per cent respectively disagreed. Both countries have, in other words, remained relatively liberal on this issue, as indeed they have in their attitudes towards sexual relations outside marriage in general.[4]

When it comes to people having children outside marriage, however, opinion is not quite so liberal. As Table 2.5 shows, in both countries more people agree than disagree with the statement that:

People who want children ought to get married

At the same time, however, (and in contrast to the position on relationships outside marriage) opinion in both cases is more liberal now than it was 10 years ago. In 2000,

69%

in both countries agree that cohabitation is acceptable

over half (55 per cent in Scotland and 54 per cent in England) agreed with the above proposition, whereas now the figure stands at 36 per cent and 42 per cent respectively. But this of course means that here too there is no evidence that Scotland has developed a different, more conservative outlook than that pertaining in England.

Table 2.5 Attitudes towards children and marriage, Scotland and England, 2000 and 2010

	Scotland		England	
	2000	2010	2000	2010
People who want children ought to get married	%	%	%	%
Agree	55	36	54	42
Neither agree nor disagree	22	32	19	24
Disagree	21	29	26	31
Base	1506	1366	2515	773

Source for Scotland: Scottish Social Attitudes
Base for England: British Social Attitudes respondents living in England

Same-sex relationships
The lack of divergence in attitudes towards cohabitation and marriage may perhaps seem relatively unsurprising – these are areas where public opinion has been moving in a more liberal direction over a number of decades now. During the last decade, however, same-sex relationships have been the subject of far more public debate and controversy than heterosexual relations outside marriage. Some of that debate and controversy appeared to be particularly contentious in Scotland. This was especially true of the moves to repeal a clause in the 1986 Local Government Act that barred local authorities (and therefore schools) from promoting homosexuality, which north of the border occasioned a conservative inspired private referendum that recorded an overwhelming majority against the move. Thus perhaps on this topic at least people in Scotland may have been especially influenced by the views of their country's religious leadership.

Our findings suggest that nothing could be further from the truth (see Table 2.6). People in Scotland have become much more liberal when asked whether "sexual relations between two adults of the same sex" are "always wrong", "mostly wrong", "sometimes wrong", "rarely wrong" or "not wrong at all". Only a quarter (27 per cent) now say that sexual relations between two adults of the same sex are "always" or "mostly" wrong,

When it comes to people having children outside marriage, however, opinion is not quite so liberal

compared with 48 per cent in 2000 and 40 per cent in 2005. Moreover, this change of opinion is in line with a similar trend in England. Moves such as the introduction of civil partnerships for same-sex couples and giving such couples the right to adopt may have been opposed by many clerics, but in practice these changes have reflected, and perhaps indeed helped bring about, quite a remarkable change of attitude towards same-sex relationships on both sides of the border.

Table 2.6 Attitudes towards same-sex relationships, Scotland and England, 2000, 2005 and 2010

Same-sex relationships	2000	2005	2010
Scotland	%	%	%
Always/mostly wrong	48	40	27
Not wrong at all	29	35	50
Base	*1663*	*1549*	*1495*
England	%	%	%
Always/mostly wrong	46	40	29
Not wrong at all	34	37	44
Base	*2887*	*1794*	*913*

Source for Scotland: Scottish Social Attitudes
Base for England: British Social Attitudes respondents living in England

Abortion

Another moral issue of particular concern to many religious organisations, including not least the Catholic Church, is abortion. On this subject too, however, there is little evidence that a distinctive public opinion has emerged north of the border. This is reflected in the answers that people give when presented with the following questions:

Do you personally think it is right or wrong for a woman to have an abortion...

> *...if there is a strong chance of a serious defect in the baby?*
> *...if the family has a very low income and cannot afford any more children?*

They are asked to state whether they consider a termination in such circumstances to be "always wrong", "almost always wrong", "wrong only sometimes" or "not wrong at all".

For many the circumstances do indeed matter (see Table 2.7). People are nearly twice as likely to feel there is nothing wrong at all about having an abortion if there is a strong chance of a serious defect in the baby than they are to say the same if a termination is sought on grounds of low income. But in both cases the balance of opinion is very similar in both Scotland and England and in neither country has it changed much during the past decade.

Table 2.7 Attitudes towards abortion, Scotland and England, 2000 and 2010

	Scotland		England	
	2000	2010	2000	2010
Have abortion if strong chance of serious defect in baby	%	%	%	%
Always/almost always wrong	16	16	13	15
Not wrong at all	52	50	58	52
Have abortion if family cannot afford any more children				
Always/almost always wrong	38	34	36	35
Not wrong at all	28	29	31	28
Base	1506	1366	2515	773

Source for Scotland: Scottish Social Attitudes
Base for England: British Social Attitudes respondents living in England

In summary then, Scotland shows no discernible signs of developing a distinctive culture on social and moral issues such as relationships outside marriage, same-sex relationships or abortion. Rather than becoming more conservative than England on these subjects during the last decade, opinion in Scotland has either remained unchanged or else become more liberal. Moreover, in each case the trend in opinion – or lack thereof – has been much the same on both sides of the border.

Conclusions

During the last decade or so Scotland has sometimes seemed like a different country socially and politically. The country has continued to reject a Conservative party that in England has experienced a revival in its fortunes. The devolved administration has introduced policies such as free personal care and the abolition of university tuition fees that are often presented as evidence of the country's distinctive adherence to 'social democratic' values. Meanwhile, the country's clerics have seemed to have been more vocal and thus, perhaps, influential.

Yet it seems that Scotland is not so different after all. Scotland is somewhat more social democratic than England. However, for the most part the difference is one of degree rather than of kind – and is no larger now than it was a decade ago. Moreover, Scotland appears to have experienced something of a drift away from a

1in3 in both countries say having an abortion is wrong if done because a family cannot afford to have more children

social democratic outlook during the course of the past decade, in tandem with public opinion in England.

At the same time there is little sign that Scotland's distinctive religious heritage means that nowadays the country is more conservative than England on social and moral issues – or that the country has moved recently in a more conservative direction. Rather we have observed that in respect of one topic at least, same-sex relationships, Scotland has in fact exhibited a dramatic shift in a more liberal direction, again in line with a similar development in England.

So despite the apparent danger that devolution might see Scotland increasingly diverge from England in its attitudinal outlook, it would seem that the task of accommodating the policy preferences of people in both England and in Scotland within the framework of the Union is no more difficult now than it was when devolution was first introduced. Despite the differences in their politics, their political structures and indeed their sense of national identity (Ormston and Curtice, 2010), the two countries continue to bring much the same outlook to many of the key questions that confront governments today. Whether that similarity will prove sufficient glue to keep the Union together remains to be seen.

Notes
1. Further support for this claim comes from a question in which people are asked whether "income and wealth should be redistributed towards ordinary working people". In Scotland the proportion agreeing fell from 68 per cent in 1997 to 63 per cent in 2010. In England the equivalent figures were 59 per cent and 53 per cent respectively.

2. Full data for the three options can be found in the appendix to this chapter.

3. Full data can be found in the appendix to this chapter.

4. In 2010 65 per cent of people in Scotland and 61 per cent in England said that there was nothing wrong at all if "a man and a woman have sexual relations before marriage". In 2000 the equivalent figures were 60 per cent and 62 per cent respectively.

References
Barlow, A. (2002), 'Cohabitation and Marriage in Scotland: Attitudes, Myths and the Law', in Curtice, J., McCrone, D., Park, A. and Paterson, L. (eds.), *New Scotland, New Society?*, Edinburgh: Polygon

Barlow, A., Duncan, S., James, G. and Park, A. (2001), 'Just a Piece of Paper? Marriage and cohabitation', in *British Social Attitudes: the 18th Report*, London: Sage

Barlow, A., Burgoyne, C., Clery, E. and Smithson, J. (2008), 'Cohabitation and the law: myths, money and the media', in *British Social Attitudes: the 24th Report*, London: Sage

Carmines, E. and Stimson, J. (1989), *Issue Evolution: Race and the Transformation of American Politics*, Princeton NJ: Princeton University Press

Curtice, J. (2010), 'Thermostat or Weathervane? Public reactions to spending and redistribution under New Labour', in *British Social Attitudes: the 26th Report*, London: Sage

Evans, G. (2002), 'In search of tolerance', in *British Social Attitudes: the 19th Report*, London: Sage

Evans, G. and Heath, A. (1995), 'The measurement of left–right and libertarian– authoritarian values: a comparison of balanced and unbalanced scales', *Quality and Quantity*, **29**: 191–206

Haskey, J. (2001), 'Cohabitation in Great Britain: past, present and future trends – and attitudes', *Population Trends*, **103**: 4–25

Hassan, G. (ed.), (2009), *The Modern SNP: From Protest to Power*, Edinburgh: Edinburgh University Press

Keating, M. (2009), 'The Territorialisation of Interest Representation: The Response of Groups to Devolution', in Curtice, J. and Seyd, B. (eds.), *Has Devolution Worked?*, Manchester: Manchester University Press

Law Commission (2007), *Cohabitation: The Financial Consequences of Relationship Breakdown*, LC307, London: Law Commission

Lynch, P. (2002), *The SNP: The History of the Scottish National Party*, Cardiff: Welsh Academic Press

Mitchell, J. (2004), 'Scotland: Expectations, Policy Types and Devolution', in Trench, A. (ed.), *Has Devolution Made a Difference?*, Exeter: Imprint Academic

Mooney, G. and Poole, L. (2004), '"A Land of Milk and Honey"? Social Policy in Scotland after Devolution', *Critical Social Policy*, **24**: 458–83

Ormston, R. and Curtice, J. (2010), 'Resentment or contentment? Attitudes towards the Union 10 years on', in *British Social Attitudes: the 27th Report*, London: Sage

Park, A. (2002), 'Scotland's Morals', in Curtice, J., McCrone, D., Park, P. and Paterson, L. (eds.), *New Scotland, New Society?*, Edinburgh: Polygon

Puttick, H. (2008), 'Debate on sexual health 'closed down' by Catholic Church', *The Herald*, 28 April 2008, available at www.heraldscotland.com/debate-on-sexual-health-closed-down-by-catholic-church-1.879463

Rhodes, R. and Marsh, D. (eds.) (1992), *Policy Networks in British Government*, Oxford: Clarendon Press

Richardson, J. and Jordan, G. (1979), *Governing under Pressure: The Policy Process in a Post-Parliamentary-Democracy*, Oxford: Martin Robertson

Salmond, A. (2005), Speech to SNP Conference, 13 October 2006, available at www.snp.org/node/8199

Salmond, A. (2007), Speech to SNP Conference, 18 March 2007, available at www.snp.org/node/8201

Scott, G. and Mooney, G. (2009), 'Poverty and Social Justice in the Devolved Scotland: Neoliberalism meets Social Democracy', *Social Policy & Society*, **8**: 379–89

Zaller, J. (1992), *The Nature and Origins of Mass Opinion*, Cambridge: Cambridge University Press

Acknowledgements
This research was made possible by a grant to the *National Centre for Social Research* from the Economic and Social Research Council (Grant no. RES-000-22-4108). Funding for some of the questions on the *British Social Attitudes survey* that are analysed here was provided by the Department for Work and Pensions (DWP). The views expressed are those of the authors alone.

Appendix
The data for Figures 2.1 and 2.2 are shown below:

Table A.1 Attitudes towards taxation and spending, Scotland and England, 1999–2010

	99	00	01	02	03	04	06	09	10
Scotland	%	%	%	%	%	%	%	%	%
Reduce taxes and spend less on health, education and social benefits	3	4	3	3	3	5	6	5	7
Keep taxes and spending on these services at the same level as now	38	39	30	32	34	35	45	53	49
Increase taxes and spend more on health, education and social benefits	55	54	63	60	58	56	41	37	40
Base	*1482*	*1663*	*1605*	*1665*	*1508*	*1637*	*1594*	*1482*	*1495*
England	%	%	%	%	%	%	%	%	%
Reduce taxes and spend less on health, education and social benefits	4	5	3	3	7	6	6	8	9
Keep taxes and spending on these services at the same level as now	35	39	34	32	38	42	44	56	57
Increase taxes and spend more on health, education and social benefits	58	51	60	61	51	49	46	32	30
Base	*2718*	*1932*	*2761*	*2897*	*2734*	*1798*	*2775*	*967*	*2795*

Source for Scotland: Scottish Social Attitudes
Base for England: British Social Attitudes respondents living in England

Table A.2 Attitudes towards unemployment benefit, Scotland and England, 1999–2010

	99	00	01	02	03	06	09	10
Scotland	%	%	%	%	%	%	%	%
Benefits for unemployed people are too low and cause hardship	36	43	45	41	41	33	31	30
Benefits for unemployed people are too high and discourage them from finding jobs	33	28	26	31	32	39	42	43
Base	*1482*	*1663*	*1605*	*1665*	*1508*	*1594*	*1482*	*1495*
England	%	%	%	%	%	%	%	%
Benefits for unemployed people are too low and cause hardship	32	40	36	28	34	22	29	23
Benefits for unemployed people are too high and discourage them from finding jobs	44	37	38	48	41	55	51	55
Base	*2718*	*2887*	*2761*	*2897*	*2734*	*2775*	*967*	*2795*

Source for Scotland: Scottish Social Attitudes
Base for England: British Social Attitudes respondents living in England

3. Private education
Private schools and public divisions: the influence of fee-paying education on social attitudes

Senior figures within the state apparatus such as politicians, judges and civil servants are disproportionately educated at private schools. Some claim private schooling perpetuates a form of social segregation; this chapter explores and contributes to this debate by examining whether being educated privately affects people's political attitudes and values.

There are differences between the views of the privately and state educated that cannot be explained by differences in where they come from (for example parental income) and where they are now (for example current income).

Privately educated	63%

State educated	24%

63% of the privately educated **see themselves as middle or upper middle class** compared with only 24% of the state educated. Even when we account for upbringing and current income and occupational status, the privately educated are nearly twice as likely as their state counterparts to describe themselves as middle class.

60% of the state educated think there is **"one law for the rich, and one law for the poor"**, compared with 44% of the privately educated. These differences are reduced, but cannot wholly be explained by family background and current social status.

| Privately educated | **44%** | **60%** | State educated |

Since 1986, **support for the Conservatives** has averaged 51% among the privately educated, but only 29% among the state educated.

Going to university seems to reduce some of these differences. The gap between the views of the state and privately educated is smaller among graduates than among non-graduates.

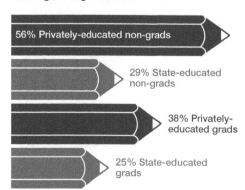

56% Privately-educated non-grads

29% State-educated non-grads

38% Privately-educated grads

25% State-educated grads

Since 1986, **support for the Conservatives** has averaged 56% among privately-educated non-graduates, compared with 29% among state-educated non-graduates. Among graduates the gap is much smaller; 38% of the privately educated support the Conservatives, compared with 25% of their state-educated counterparts.

Authors: Geoffrey Evans and James Tilley*

> What marks England out is the degree to which its schools segregate
> the socially advantaged from the rest. (Adonis and Pollard 1997: 37)

Democracy as exercised in Britain carries no particular expectation that those who run the country will constitute a demographically matched sample of the people they represent or administer. One of the most obvious instances of the way this works in practice is the disproportionate number of people in positions of power and influence who have been educated in private school. When the coalition government took power in 2010, for example, it was led by a Prime Minister educated at Eton College, a Deputy Prime Minister who attended Westminster School and a Chancellor of the Exchequer who went to St Paul's School, while across government as a whole two-thirds of Ministers were privately educated. The proportion of Members of Parliament who went to private schools is lower at 35 per cent, but still up to five times the seven per cent found among the general population (The Sutton Trust, 2010). Nor is it only among politicians that we find a preponderance of privately-educated people at the top: studies in the past decade have found that more than half of all senior civil servants attended private schools (Wilson and Barker, 2003) and that the vast majority of senior judges are privately educated (S.J. Berwin, 2005).

In theory, social exclusivity need not result in unrepresentative government: a man can, in principle, share the concerns and values of a woman, just as a middle-class person can understand those of someone who is working class. But for this to work in practice there has to be some basis of shared values and experiences to allow a proper understanding of the lives and concerns of other people. If the education system – as the moulding social influence on the lives and minds of young people – enshrines the kind of separate development where the future leaders of society are educated apart from the people they will later govern or judge, then warning bells should probably sound.

But does the prominence in power of people who were privately educated really mean that we live in a 'them and us' world more readily associated with the ruling establishment of 50 years ago (Boyd, 1973) than the 21st century? Or might an examination of their attitudes reveal that people who have experienced a fee-paying education share values and views that are little different to those of their state-educated peers?

In this chapter we seek to shed new light on whether or not people who have attended private schools differ in their perceptions, attitudes and political choices from the majority who went to state schools. Before setting about this task, however, we should mention how two technical issues have been resolved to help ensure that the results of our analysis carry real meaning. Firstly, we know that between 10 and 12 per cent of respondents in any *British Social Attitudes* survey will normally have been privately educated at some stage in their school careers.[1] This means the overall number surveyed in any one year is too small for the kind of analyses we need to carry out. However, by pooling the data obtained in different surveys that have asked

* Geoffrey Evans is Official Fellow in Politics, Nuffield College and Director of the Centre for Research Methods in the Social Sciences, University of Oxford. James Tilley is University Lecturer in Quantitative Social Science at Jesus College, University of Oxford.

the same, relevant questions we can assemble samples of up to 8,900 privately-educated people.[2] Secondly, we want to know how likely it is that any differences we find between private and state-school students are explained by their educational experiences, as opposed to other factors in their family backgrounds – or their circumstances at the time of interview. For example, the privately educated will tend to come from more affluent backgrounds than others (Sullivan and Heath, 2003), and have distinctive aspirations and strategies of advancement they endorse for their children, as shown in our chapter on school choice. We need to know whether any differences we find reflect these factors rather than their education. To do that, we use methods that allow us to take account of, or 'control for' a person's background and current circumstances. A more technical description of this can be found in the appendix at the end of this chapter.

The picture that we paint has had to include broad brush strokes. We do not, for example, have information on which private schools our respondents went to or for how long they attended. Yet we might suspect that people educated in the most exclusive and expensive institutions live lives that have less in common with the rest of society than those who are educated in less prestigious private schools. The same might be thought about those educated outside the state system throughout the years of compulsory schooling, compared with those who only attended a private secondary school. So while we include all privately-educated respondents in our reference group for this chapter, it is possible that this results in our underestimating the social exclusivity experienced by those in positions of power who first attended elite preparatory schools followed by the likes of Eton or Harrow.

Who are the privately educated?
The standard question from *British Social Attitudes* surveys that we use to identify people who were privately educated is:

Have you ever attended a fee-paying, private primary or secondary school in the United Kingdom?[3]

Using the responses, we first examine how privately-educated people compare with the general population in terms of jobs, education, income, ethnicity, sex, where they live and social background. How different demographically are they? Interestingly, when we look at the relevant data from different years spread over a quarter of a century, we find little or no change over time in the social characteristics of the privately educated. Using data pooled from a number of different years, we highlight the following findings:

- *Social background:* 34 per cent of privately-educated people have fathers whose jobs were professional or managerial, compared with 14 per cent of those who were state-educated.[4]

55%
of people who were privately educated have a professional or managerial job compared with 29% who were state educated

- *Occupational class:* 55 per cent who were privately educated have a professional or managerial job compared with 29 per cent who were state educated.

- *Income:* one in five people (22 per cent) who attended fee-paying schools are placed in the top 10 per cent ('decile') of the income distribution.

- *Education:* 30 per cent who were privately educated have a degree compared with 12 per cent who went to state schools.

- *Location:* 38 per cent of people who attended private schools live in London or south east England compared with 27 per cent of former state-school students.

- *Ethnicity/sex:* there are few differences in educational background that relate to ethnicity or sex. Ethnic minorities and women are as likely to have been privately educated as men and those not from an ethnic minority.

From this we can see how people who have attended fee-paying schools are relatively privileged in terms of their background and their current lives. But does the evidence also suggest that this advantage is transmitted through families across generations?

Private schooling as 'social apartheid'?
The quotation at the start of this chapter comes from a book published in 1997 intended to debunk the myth of Britain as a classless society. According to its authors – one of whom became an education minister under Labour – the segregation between private and state schooling amounts to a form of "social apartheid" (Adonis and Pollard, 1997). Emotive though that description may be, it has been used more recently by Anthony Seldon, Master of Wellington College, who describes independent schools as "detached from the mainstream national education system, thereby perpetuating the apartheid which has so dogged education and national life in Britain since the Second World War" (Seldon, 2008). So how far do the accumulated data from *British Social Attitudes* surveys bear out such strong claims of separate social development?

Family continuity
We first examine the degree to which there is continuity within families when it comes to private education. Do people educated at fee-paying schools tend to have parents who were also privately educated? In forming their own families are they disproportionately likely to choose a privately-educated partner? Are they more likely than others to send (or want to send) their own children to private schools? Using the responses to questions that have been asked in a number of different years,[5] we again find little evidence of change over time:

- 43 per cent of the privately educated who have children have sent them to private schools, nearly five times the rate for parents who went to state schools (nine per cent).

- Among married individuals, 41 per cent of the privately educated are married to a privately-educated person, compared with six per cent of those who are state educated.

- Finally, of those who are married with children, 65 per cent who went to private schools and whose spouses were also educated privately have sent a child to a fee-paying school, compared with only six per cent of parents who both attended state schools.

These findings point to a striking degree of generational continuity within families when it comes to private schooling, as well as the impressive extent to which individuals who are privately educated tend to marry people from the same educational background. However, to test the claims made about 'social apartheid' we also need to consider how far private schooling is associated with a distinctive set of social attitudes. Do the former students of fee-paying schools express views and political preferences that distinguish them from their state-educated peers? Do they really think of themselves as 'a class apart'?

Social class

We start by looking at where people place themselves in terms of social class. In a number of years between 1983 and 1996,[6] *British Social Attitudes* respondents were told that "Most people see themselves as belonging to a particular social class" and were asked which social class they would say they belonged to, using a card with the categories "upper middle", "middle', "upper working", "working" and "poor".

Looking at Table 3.1 we can see that most state-educated respondents regard themselves as "working class" with less than a quarter (24 per cent) describing themselves as "middle class" or "upper middle class". By contrast, nearly two-thirds (63 per cent) of privately-educated respondents think of themselves as "middle class' or "upper middle class".

Table 3.1 Perceived social class, by educational background[7]

	State educated	Privately educated
	%	%
Upper middle	1	7
Middle	23	56
Upper working/Working/Poor	76	37
Base	*15569*	*2007*

The sense of high social status that this reveals among privately-educated respondents might simply reflect people's proper sense of their circumstances: such as better educational qualifications and higher incomes. However, by controlling our data to take statistical account of background factors and current circumstances we can see whether they alone explain these differences, or whether a private education is more than a 'marker' or 'proxy' for the sense of class superiority being expressed.

Table 3.2 shows what happens to the data on social class perceptions when statistical 'controls' are applied for a number of background factors (specifically: father's occupation, gender, birth cohort and race). The table then shows what happens after taking into account both background and people's current circumstances (specifically: their household income, current occupational social class, educational qualifications and regional location).

Table 3.2 Perceived social class by educational background, taking into account social background and current circumstances[8]

	Controlling for background only		Controlling for background and current situation	
	State educated	Privately educated	State educated	Privately educated
	%	%	%	%
Upper middle	2	6	2	5
Middle	22	47	22	37
Working/Upper working/Poor	76	48	76	57
Base	1360	240	1360	240

Comparing the results from this analysis with those in Table 3.1, we can see that the proportion of privately-educated respondents who identify themselves as "middle" or "upper middle" class after controlling for their background circumstances is 10 points lower at 53 per cent. This suggests that the class identities of people educated at fee-paying schools are, as we suspected, influenced by their privileged family backgrounds. Looking at the other half of the table, which shows the results after our analysis controlling for background and current circumstances we can see the proportion is even lower at 42 per cent, suggesting that the tendency for people who are privately educated to credit themselves with high social status is also related to their levels of income, educational attainment and current occupation. Nevertheless, after taking into account all of these possible explanations for the way respondents view themselves, we see that the class differences between people who have been privately educated and those who attended state schools remain robust and substantial.

Indeed, the estimates shown in Table 3.2 tell us that the privately educated are still roughly *twice* as likely to see themselves as being "middle" or "upper middle" class after all the statistical controls have been applied. This is much higher than we would expect if people who went to fee-paying schools were simply assessing their social class on the basis of their current circumstances. The difference we identify could be characterised as a 'sense of superiority bonus' that comes from attending a private school. While there is no doubt that people who are privately-educated tend to obtain better qualifications and higher status jobs than others, they also appear to acquire the social confidence to place themselves higher in the social pecking order than their state-educated peers.

Attitudes concerning pay, inequality and social justice
The next stage of our investigation is to establish if there are other ways in which the social perceptions of people who attended private schools are distinct. In particular, we examine their views on a number of issues relating to fair treatment and social justice; starting with the responses to questions asked in 2009 about appropriate rates of pay for different types of job. The replies we have analysed concern pay for "a shop assistant" and "an unskilled worker in a factory", for "the chairman of a large national corporation" and "a cabinet minister in the UK government".

After an opportunity to say what they think people doing those jobs actually earn, respondents were asked:

*...what do you think people in these jobs **ought** to be paid – how much do you think they **should** earn **each year before taxes**, regardless of what they actually get?*

Table 3.3 shows the average salaries people thought appropriate, divided between state-educated respondents and those who went to fee-paying schools. Given we have data for fewer than 100 people who have been privately educated, caution must be applied in interpreting the findings outlined below. We can see that views about pay for people in the two low-skilled jobs are similar – and even more so after controlling the data for family background and current circumstances. However, when it comes to assessing the right level of pay for the chairman of a big national corporation or a cabinet minister, those who were privately educated take a much more generous view.[9] The average figure of £237,000 a year suggested for the company chairman by respondents who attended private school is £88,000 higher than the average level proposed by people who went to state schools. The gap between the equivalent assessments of what a cabinet minister should earn is £28,000 a year. And while the differences between the average amounts proposed by privately and state-educated respondents are reduced by controlling for background and current circumstances, they are by no means removed.

We note that the really big differences of view between people educated at private and state schools concern the two jobs at the top end of the pay scale where privately-educated people are more likely to be – or aspire to be – themselves. It may be that those who went to fee-paying schools are merely more realistic about salaries at the highest level than their state-educated counterparts. But we might also suspect that at least some people who were privately-educated have adopted a principle that 'people like us' deserve more. This would be a more convincing possibility if the tendency to value the work of 'top people' more highly than others was accompanied by views suggesting a more general endorsement of social inequality.

To examine this we draw on questions asked by *British Social Attitudes* designed to explore social and political divisions. These have been asked regularly over a quarter

The class differences between people who have been privately educated and those who attended state schools are robust and substantial

of a century, and we again find that there have been few, if any, changes over time in the balance of replies between those who were privately and state educated. Once again, therefore, we are able to base our analysis on pooled data from several years between 1987 and 2009.

Table 3.3 Average perceptions of what people in different jobs should be paid, by educational background, 2009[9]

Type of job	Mean annual pay level suggested by...	
	...state-educated respondents	...privately-educated respondents
	£	£
Chairman of national corporation	149,000	237,000
Controlled for current/background factors	152,000	205,000
Base	685	81
Cabinet minister	69,000	98,000
Controlled for current/background factors	70,000	86,000
Base	676	83
Shop assistant	19,000	18,000
Controlled for current/background factors	19,000	17,000
Base	686	82
Unskilled factory worker	19,000	20,000
Controlled for current/background factors	19,000	19,000
Base	690	83

All figures are rounded to the nearest £1,000

The survey invites respondents to consider three statements about aspects of social justice. These are:

Ordinary working people do not get their fair share of the nation's wealth

There is one law for the rich and one for the poor

Management will always try to get the better of employees if it gets the chance

Respondents were asked to say whether they "agree strongly", "agree", "neither agree nor disagree", "disagree" or "disagree strongly". The questions relate inequality and injustice to social class in order to gain an impression of how far people subscribe to a class-based account of the issues. In Table 3.4 we show the balance of opinion between respondents who attended fee-paying schools and those who are state educated. Combining the data for "agree strongly" and "agree" we present the proportions who agree with each statement, followed by the results after applying statistical controls for family background factors and current circumstances.

Table 3.4 Concern with social inequality, by educational background[10]

	State educated	Privately educated
% agreeing that...		
...there is one law for the rich, and one law for the poor	60	44
Controlled for current/background factors	59	52
Base	*5061*	*716*
...ordinary working people do not get their fair share of the nation's wealth	63	46
Controlled for current/background factors	63	54
Base	*5041*	*714*
...management will always try to get the better of employees if it gets the chance	61	42
Controlled for current/background factors	60	51
Base	*5053*	*712*

We can see that people who went to private schools are substantially less likely than those who attended state schools to agree with the three statements.[11] While 60 per cent of the latter think that "there is one law for the rich and one law for the poor" only 44 per cent of those who were privately educated agree with them. The 16 percentage point gap is, however, more than halved by controlling the data for past and present circumstances – suggesting that family background and current social status go some way to explain the headline difference of view. Very similar patterns can be seen in the percentages agreeing that "ordinary working people do not get their fair share of the nation's wealth" and that "management will always try to get the better of employees if it gets the chance". Even so, the analysis does suggest that a private education exerts an influence on people's views that is independent of other factors. This may not seem

81%

of the state educated agreed there should be "stiffer sentences", compared with 66% of the privately educated altogether surprising given our previous findings that demonstrate the robust effect of private education on self-perceived class and views about top people's pay.

The distinctively conservative nature of the positions taken by privately-educated respondents on social inequality is further emphasised by analyses of other sorts of social attitudes. On questions about law and order, when people were asked how much they agreed or disagreed that "People who break the law should be given stiffer sentences" or "For some crimes, the death penalty is the most appropriate sentence" privately-educated respondents were not more conservative, if anything they were more liberal. While 81 per cent of state-educated people agreed there should be "stiffer sentences", 66 per cent of privately educated did so. And while 61 per cent of state-educated people agreed that the death penalty should be brought back, 47per cent of privately-educated did.[12] While the differences between two groups are reduced by controlling for background and current circumstances, they are not removed.

Support for political parties

The questions we have used to compare attitudes to inequality and social justice deliberately include a class-based dimension that reflects one of the classic ideological divisions between supporters of the political 'left' and 'right'. The responses are a long way from suggesting that people who are state educated and those who went to private schools occupy two separate and ideologically-opposed camps. They show an overlap of views in both cases. But knowing that proportionately fewer people who were educated at fee-paying schools agree with our three statements about social inequality, we can expect to see corresponding differences in their party political affiliations. And while we may anticipate that these will relate mainly to support for Labour and the Conservatives, it will also be interesting to see how privately and state-educated respondents view the more 'centrist' Liberal Democrats. If people who went to private school tend to support one political party more than another, we also need to know whether this is more attributable to their background and current circumstances, including qualifications, occupation and pay, rather than their schooling. Once again, we use statistical methods to control for these factors, including, as with all the other tables, year of survey to account for any changes in overall party support from year to year, which is known to vary substantially.

The *British Social Attitudes* survey asks people if they think of themselves as "a supporter of any one political party" or, if not, whether they are "closer to one political party than to the others". Those who answer "yes" to either question are invited to say which party they incline towards. Table 3.5 shows that the differences between privately and state-educated respondents in their party political affiliations are among the strongest we have seen.

The gap of 22 percentage points between 51 per cent of privately-educated respondents who say they incline towards the Conservatives and 29 per cent of those who went to state schools is very large by survey standards. Average support for Labour (20 per cent) is conversely weaker among the privately educated, for whom the Liberal Democrats (19 per cent) represent an almost equally appealing choice. Put another way, if this was a 'snapshot' opinion poll among people who attended fee-paying schools, the Conservatives would hold a 31 point lead over Labour. Conversely, Labour would lead the Conservatives by 10 points among state-educated respondents.

Table 3.5 Party identification, by educational background[13]

	State educated	Privately educated
% Conservative	29	51
Controlled for current/background factors	30	43
% Labour	39	20
Controlled for current/background factors	41	28
% Liberal Democrat	14	19
Controlled for current/background factors	15	17
% No party affiliation	18	10
Controlled for current/background factors	14	13
Base	*4833*	*682*

People who have been privately educated are also less likely to say they have no party political affiliation (10 per cent) than those who went to state schools (18 per cent). This is the only distinction that all but disappears once we control for other background circumstances and people's current situation. It suggests that where people were schooled does not, of itself, exert much influence over whether they identify with a party or not. However, when it comes to declared party affiliations, we can see that while the data controls result in a narrowing of the gap, the distinctions are still a long way from being explained away by other factors. Private schools, it seems safe to conclude, tend to produce Conservative partisans.

The influence of a university education

So far we have seen that a range of social issues distinguish the attitudes of people who have been privately educated from the views of people educated in state schools. These distinctions almost always persist after we take account of other factors in people's family backgrounds and current circumstances that could potentially explain the differences we observe. We have yet, however, to consider one further influence that is potentially important: that of a university education.

Although the chances of attending university are greater for students at private schools than for those attending state schools (around three times in our samples), there are still a considerable number of privately-educated people who have not been to university. In 2010, for example, less than 40 per cent of the privately-educated adults were graduates. Research has suggested that universities provide an opportunity for students from different social backgrounds to mix, and thereby foster an increased acceptance of social diversity (Hyman and Wright, 1979; Evans, 2002; Pascarella and Terenzini, 2005). We may, therefore, suspect that the views of privately-educated adults who have not been to university will be more distinctive than the opinions held by privately-educated graduates. Conversely, we might expect a university education to lead to a weaker political divide between private and state-educated graduates.

To test this hypothesis, we compare the views of state and privately-educated people according to whether or not they graduated from university. In particular, we examine responses to the three class-based statements about inequality and social injustice and also the educational backgrounds of people who are inclined to support the Conservatives. As Table 3.6 demonstrates, our analysis supports the idea that graduates from fee-paying and state-school backgrounds will tend to be less divided in their views than non-graduates.

The difference between graduates and non-graduates in support for the Conservatives is particularly striking. While 56 per cent of privately-educated people without university degrees express a political preference for the Conservative Party, this falls to 38 per cent among privately-educated graduates. The differences between privately-educated graduates and non-graduates are less marked when it comes to our three statements about social inequalities, but nevertheless non-trivial. For example, 45 per cent of graduates who attended fee-paying schools agree that "there is one law for the rich, and one law for the poor" compared with 51 per cent who went to private

Table 3.6 Views on social inequality, plus support for the Conservative Party, by educational background[14]

	State educated	Privately educated
% agreeing that "there is one law for the rich, one law for the poor"		
Graduate	49	45
Non-graduate	67	51
Base	*53206*	*7037*
% agreeing that "ordinary working people do not get their fair share of the nation's wealth"		
Graduate	56	46
Non-graduate	66	50
Base	*53086*	*7020*
% agreeing that "management will always try to get the better of employees if it gets the chance"		
Graduate	43	35
Non-graduate	63	44
Base	*54378*	*7193*
% Conservative supporter		
Graduate	25	38
Non-graduate	29	56
Base	*62454*	*7947*

school, but did not graduate from university. Although we do not include the results in the table, our analysis applying statistical controls for background and current circumstances does not, again, account fully for the association between people's views and their schooling.[15]

The findings are clear: when private education is followed by university the differences between the privately educated and the state educated in support for Labour versus Conservatives, and associated attitudes towards social inequality, are not eliminated, but they are reduced. The most distinctive attitudes, even after controlling for numerous other differences, are for those who left school at 18 or before. Interestingly, the attitudes that change most are those of state-educated people, who become more like those of the privately educated: integration works in both directions. Whether the growth of university education helps to bridge the social divide created in the school room remains to be seen, though our evidence at least suggests this possibility.

Gender differences
Throughout the analyses undertaken in this chapter we have found that the differences we have highlighted apply to women who were privately educated as well as men. Perceptions and attitudes among those who went to fee-paying schools are very similar irrespective of gender. As opportunities for women to obtain top positions in society are expanding, through efforts to promote women in the boardroom and the court room and the cabinet, the likelihood is that many of these, too, will come from privately-educated backgrounds. Ironically, rather than blurring the boundaries of 'social apartheid', it is quite possible that increasing gender equality will simply augment the privately-educated elite that already exists in positions of power.

Conclusions
In recent decades some commentators have argued that we are witnessing a return to Edwardian levels of social inequality and the exclusion of disadvantaged people from the levers of power (National Equality Panel, 2010). In this chapter we have examined the idea that private schools provide the vehicle for a form of 'social apartheid' at a time when social inequalities risk becoming more polarised. To do this, we looked at the way that adults who were privately educated define their social class and found that they tend to see themselves as more middle or upper middle class than others, even allowing for their generally higher qualifications and employment status. We have seen that their assessments of appropriate pay for cabinet ministers and company chairmen are much higher than those made by people who went to state schools; we have also found them more likely to disagree with statements about the existence and possible injustice of class-based inequalities. Unsurprisingly, the privately educated also tend to align themselves with the Conservatives rather than Labour or the Liberal Democrats. At the same time, while the privately educated may express less egalitarian attitudes than others in their attitudes towards social inequality we do not find evidence that they are more conservative on questions concerning law and order.

 The differences we have highlighted apply to women who were privately educated as well as men

We have also seen evidence that a university education tends to narrow the gap between the views held on social inequality and party politics by people who attended private schools and those who were state educated. Over time, perhaps, the expansion of university education may work to reduce the differences in views that we find are linked to schooling. However, this assumes that all universities are held equal and that we will not see an increasing level of 'social apartheid' where students choose to attend a particular institution as a consequence of being privately or state educated. In this context, we may note the disparity that already exists between Oxbridge – where around half the undergraduates come from private schools – and institutions such as Bolton University, where 99 per cent come from state schools.

Of course, people who have been privately educated tend to be richer, as well as more highly educated and to hold jobs that give them higher social status. They tend to live in more attractive parts of the country than people who go to state schools, and to come from more privileged and aspirational backgrounds. So should we focus any discussion about policy implications on the inequalities of income and wealth that influence people's views, rather than the fee-paying education that they make possible? The answer we have found, by controlling our data for these potential explanations, is that while they play a significant part, they are not the whole story. After taking other factors into account the divided attitudes associated with a private education are more muted, but they remain. In that sense, we can only conclude that private education does, indeed, perpetuate a form of separate development in Britain, or 'social apartheid'. The dominance in the current government of people who come from such a segregated elite can only add to concerns that it does not understand or share the views of the vast majority of the population it purports to represent.

Notes

1. The proportion of *British Social Attitudes* respondents who are privately educated is higher (at 10 to 12 per cent) than the commonly accepted seven per cent figure for the population as a whole. This reflects the fact that our question is phrased in a way that encourages people who have attended a private school even briefly to answer "yes".

2. In assembling our sample we were only able to use some, not all, of the *British Social Attitudes* data gathered since 1983 because relevant questions were only asked in certain years. This applies to the questions that supply some of our background control variables, such as father's occupational status, as well as those that frame particular issues. As data are drawn from different years, bases cannot be directly compared across tables.

3. We advised respondents that our definition of "private" primary or secondary schools included those who attended an independent school, or held a scholarship or assisted place at a fee-paying school. It excluded direct grant schools (unless fee-paying), voluntary-aided schools, grant-maintained ('opted out') schools and nursery schools.

4. People who were educated privately are also disproportionately likely to have parents who were self-employed (24 per cent compared with 11 per cent of those who attended state schools). The figures are derived from questions about father's occupation asked in 1987, 1991, 2003, 2005 and 2009.

5. For children's educational background we use *British Social Attitudes* 1985–2010 data; for spouse's educational background we are only able to use 1985–1999 data.

6. We analysed responses to a question on social class asked in the *British Social Attitudes* surveys 1983–1991 and 1996. Although not reported, we obtained similar results from an analysis of data from 2009 when a different question was asked to elicit social class. We have

further replicated our findings using the responses to another question asked in 1987, 1991 and 2009: "In our society there are groups which tend to be towards the top and groups which tend to be towards the bottom. Below is a scale that runs from top to bottom. Where would you put yourself on this scale?"

7. Table 3.1 uses data from the 1983–1991 and 1996 *British Social Attitudes* surveys.

8. Table 3.2 uses data from the 1987 and 1991 *British Social Attitudes* surveys that collected information on father's occupation as well as various measures of social status.

9. The average figures exclude views where the suggested sum is less than £3000 a year or exceeds £2 million a year. Differences between the median levels of pay suggested by privately and state-educated respondents are similar to the mean differences shown in the table.

10. Table 3.4 uses data from the 1987, 1991, 2003, 2005 and 2009 *British Social Attitudes* surveys.

11. This has changed little over time. For the "fair share" question the gap between the state and privately educated was 19 per cent in 1986 and exactly the same 24 years later in 2010. The gap does shrink somewhat over time for the other two items (for the "management" question the gap reduces from 17 per cent in 1986 to 15 per cent in 2010, and for the "one law" question the decline is from 20 per cent to 16 per cent), but these are really quite small changes.

12. The table below shows the percentage of those agreeing with questions on stiffer sentences and the death penalty, by educational background.

	State educated	Privately educated
% agreeing that...		
...people who break the law should be given stiffer sentences	81	66
Controlled for current/background factors	81	74
Base	*4112*	*567*
...for some crimes, the death penalty is the most appropriate sentence	61	47
Controlled for current/background factors	61	56
Base	*4107*	*564*

This table uses data from the 1991, 2003, 2005, and 2009 *British Social Attitudes* surveys.

13. Table 3.5 uses data from the 1987, 1991, 2003, 2005, and 2009 *British Social Attitudes* surveys.

14. Table 3.6 uses data from 1986–2010 *British Social Attitudes* surveys.

15. The interaction effect in models with all current and background controls remains in the same direction and is statistically significant for party support and the "one law for the rich" question. If the dataset is expanded by leaving out the father's class variable, which means that all surveys from 1986–2010 can be analysed giving a similar base number to that presented in Table 3.6, then the interaction effect is of a similar magnitude but is now statistically significant for all the dependent variables presented here at the 5% level. As in the raw figures, with all controls included, a university education appears to, roughly, halve the effect of private schooling.

References

Adonis, A. and Pollard, S. (1997), *A Class Act: The myth of Britain's classless society*, London: Hamish Hamilton

Boyd, D. (1973), *Elites and Their Education*, Slough: National Foundation for Educational Research (NFER)

Evans, G. (2002), 'In search of tolerance', in Park, A., Curtice, J., Thomson, K., Jarvis, L. and Bromley, C. (eds.), *British Social Attitudes: the 19th Report*, London: Sage

Hyman, H. and Wright, C. (1979), *Education's Lasting Influence on Values*, Chicago: University of Chicago Press

National Equality Panel (2010), *An Anatomy of Economic Inequality in the UK: The Report of the National Equality Panel*, London: Government Equalities Office

Norris, P. and Lovenduski, J. (1995), *Political Recruitment: Gender, race, and class in the British Parliament*, Cambridge: Cambridge University Press

Pascarella, E. and Terenzini, P. (2005), *How College Affects Students (Volume 2): A Third Decade of Research*, San Francisco: Jossey Bass

Seldon, A. (2008), Speech given at Wellington College and reported in the *Daily Mail*, available at www.dailymail.co.uk/news/article-508217/Private-schools-fuel-social-apartheid-says-headmaster-25-620-year-Wellington-College.html#ixzz1OfjwuzgK

Berwin, S.J. LLP (2005), 'Backgrounds of the Senior Judiciary in 2003', available at web. archive.org/web/20051017090402/http://www.sjberwin.com/media/pdf/publications/survey/surveyresults.pdf

Sullivan, A. and Heath, A. (2003), 'Intakes and Examination Results at State and Private Schools', in Walford, G. (ed.), *British Private Schools: research on policy and practice*, London: Woburn Press

The Sutton Trust (2010), *The Educational Backgrounds of Government Ministers in 2010*, available at www.suttontrust.com/research/the-educational-backgrounds-of-government-ministers-in-2010/

Wilson, G. and Barker, A. (2003), 'Bureaucrats and politicians in Britain', *Governance*, **16(3)**: 349–372

Appendix

The analyses we have used to control for "background and current circumstances" derive from multinomial logistic (for Tables 3.2 and 3.5), logistic (for Table 3.4) and linear (for Table 3.3) regression models. The "background controls" numbers are the predicted proportions or figures from a model that predicts the relevant variable of interest using a dummy variable for private schooling, father's occupation (measured as professional, managerial, routine non-manual, skilled manual, semi or unskilled manual, self-employed, unknown), sex, birth cohort (measured in 10 year birth cohorts) and race (white or non-white). The resulting figures represent what the population would look like if the only difference between people was educational background.

The 'background and current controls' figures are from models that include a dummy variable for private schooling, all the background controls already mentioned and controls for current circumstances. These are: household income (this is split into quintiles, with the top quintile split into the top two deciles), current occupational social class (upper service, lower service, routine non-manual, petit bourgeois, foremen and supervisors, skilled manual, semi or unskilled manual), educational qualifications (degree, some higher education such as teacher/nurse training, A-level or equivalent, O-level or equivalent, CSE or equivalent, apprenticeship, no qualification) and region (Scotland, Wales, North, Midlands and East, South West, London and the South East).

4. School choice
Parental freedom to choose and educational equality

Two considerations influence policy and thinking around school choice – the importance of parents having the freedom to choose and the potential impact of this choice on educational equality. The government recently consulted on a new Schools Admissions Code which seeks to increase parental choice by allowing the most popular schools to expand. What does the public think about secondary school choice and how much parental freedom and educational equality matter?

People generally believe parents have a right to choose their children's schools – but in practice view children attending their local schools as important.

Outright agree

63%

Agree, if schools are more equal

Disagree

22%

15%

67%

Almost seven in ten (67%) agree parents should have a **basic right** to choose their children's schools.

But an even larger proportion think parents in general should send their children to **the nearest state school**. 63% support this idea outright and a further 22%, who do not support this idea outright, would do so if schools were more equal in their quality and their mix of pupils.

There is mixed public support for the different measures some parents take to improve their child's chances of gaining places at particular schools.

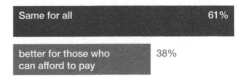

Same for all   61%

better for those who can afford to pay   38%

A majority approve of helping children to revise for tests (90%) or paying for a **private tutor** (67%), to improve their chances of gaining a place at a particular school. Far fewer – 36% – approve of moving house to be near a higher-performing school while just 6% in each case approve of renting a second address or using a relative's address.

Six in ten (61%) think the **quality of education should be the same for all children** while four in ten (38%) think parents who can afford it should be able to pay for better education.

Author: Sonia Exley*

For more than 20 years in Britain, the topic of secondary school choice has been an enduring focus of popular debate and policy making. There have been long-running debates about the extent to which parents have a 'right' to send their children to private schools or schools that select on ability, to avoid their local secondary schools and to move house to be nearer 'better' schools. Politicians such as Diane Abbott and Harriet Harman have been criticised for choosing private or selective schools for their children and pressure groups have been formed – both in defence of comprehensive education and to promote parental rights in this area. Parents' 'right to choose' schools for their children has been enshrined in government policy since the 1988 Education Reform Act in England and Wales – and the 1981 Education (Scotland) Act. This right is reflected in Article 26 of the UN Universal Declaration of Human Rights, which states that "parents have a prior right to choose the kind of education that shall be given to their children" (United Nations, 2011). However, more recent policies have sought to regulate and limit parental choice, including 'banded' school admissions systems and Brighton's 'lottery' system for allocating school places,[1] both of which have caused considerable controversy (Lipsett, 2007; Stewart, 2005). The coalition government is currently consulting on a new Schools Admissions Code, which would allow popular schools to expand – facilitating greater choice for parents, but also potentially resulting in less popular schools losing out in terms of pupil numbers and funding (Department for Education, 2011).

These debates and developments reflect a tension regarding the values which should underpin school admissions systems. Two conflicting schools of thought exist. On the one hand, it is argued that priority should be given to parental freedom. Academics supporting this view (Tooley, 1996; Hargreaves, 1996; Chubb and Moe, 1992) believe parents should be able to choose which school to send their children to, the 'best' they can achieve within the means available to them. Government involvement, in terms of managing school admissions or banning certain types of school, is regarded as an unacceptable constraint on parents' freedom and choice regarding their children's upbringing. A second school of thought, however, views a focus on freedom of choice as at odds with principles of community and equality in education. Writers supporting this view refer to the notion of 'the common school' – underlying this concept is the assumption that schools should serve a mix of children across all social backgrounds and religions, urging against extensive parental choice (Pring, 2008; Levinson, 1999). Research involving interviews with families (Gewirtz et al., 1995; Reay and Ball, 1997; Vincent, 2001; Ball, 2003) has highlighted varying experiences of school choice for parents from different social backgrounds. Middle-class families are more able to pay to send their children to exclusive private schools and more likely to secure places in high-performing selective ('grammar') schools and the best-performing non-selective state schools, relegating others to unpopular schools with the worst resources. Some feel that, with an increased emphasis on parental choice, the risks of increased polarisation between schools[2] in wealthy and disadvantaged neighbourhoods are significant. It is argued that "vilified" schools (Coldron et al., 2001) suffering from an absence of middle-class parental input will lose pupils and funding, sinking into "spirals of decline", with pupils suffering accordingly. Such polarisation between schools would be problematic,

* Sonia Exley is a Lecturer in Social Policy at the London School of Economics and Political Science.

given quality of education has been shown to strongly influence life chances, with a poor education leading to poorer jobs, lower income and lower living standards. Many therefore believe school choice should not be promoted, as it would make an unequal society (where inequalities between schools and neighbourhoods already exist) even more unequal, and that parents should simply support their local school.

Academics have attempted to reconcile these two schools of thought. Adam Swift (2003) and Harry Brighouse (2000) discuss the idea of 'legitimate parental partiality' and consider which 'partial' actions it should be legitimate for parents to take in relation to their children's education, without upsetting the balance between freedom and equality. Swift argues that, while it might be fair for parents to make some choices about their children's education, sending them to private or selective schools, which significantly improve life chances relative to others, is very problematic. Brighouse argues that although the right for parents to choose schools could be defended in a society that was relatively equal, within Britain today, where there is not a 'level playing field', extensive parental choice in education conflicts with principles of social justice to an unacceptable degree.

This chapter examines, for the first time, the attitudes of the British public to school choice and the views and concerns which inform their thinking. We start by exploring public support for the different ways of thinking about school choice described previously and seek to identify where people draw the line in balancing parents' freedom to choose schools with ideas of equality and fairness. We then consider how far the public think it is acceptable for parents to prioritise, and undertake activities to improve, their own children's educational chances relative to others, in terms of the schools they attend. We next examine how attitudes vary across the public, focusing on whether certain sections of society have distinctive views about school choice. Finally, we consider what public attitudes suggest about current government policy, popular debates and academic thinking in the area of school choice and how these should be taken on board in the future.

Support for parental choice

We begin by examining support for the right of parents to choose their children's schools. Respondents were asked whether they agreed or disagreed that:

Parents should have a basic right to choose their child's school

To further test commitment by highlighting a possible negative consequence of such an approach, respondents were also asked whether, in Britain today:

Parents have a duty to choose the best possible school for their child, even if this means schools in the local area might suffer

As shown in Table 4.1, there is considerable support for parents' right to choose their children's schools; more than two-thirds (68 per cent) agree parents should have this basic right. There is also support for the idea that parents have a duty to choose the best possible school for their child, even where other schools might suffer, with around half (50 per cent) agreeing, although a slightly higher proportion (21 per cent compared with 10 per cent) object to this than to the concept of choice, when a negative consequence is not mentioned. Slightly more than two in ten neither agree nor disagree with each statement, suggesting a degree of uncertainty or ambivalence about this issue.

Table 4.1 Support for parents' right to choose their children's school

		Agree strongly	Agree	Neither agree nor disagree	Disagree	Disagree strongly	Can't choose	Base
Parents have basic right to choose their child's school	%	20	47	21	8	1	1	1870
Parents have a duty to choose the best possible school, even if schools in the local area might suffer	%	12	38	27	18	3	2	1870

What does this majority support for parents' right to choose their children's school mean in practice? Do people believe parental choice is fundamentally important or do they support the principle because they believe a parent should be able to avoid their local school in specific circumstances – for instance when they feel it is inadequate or would not meet their child's needs? Research by Adler *et al.*, (1989, p. 113) has concluded that parents tend to "satisfice" rather than "optimise" when it comes to school choice; it is "a matter of finding a satisfactory alternative to the district school rather than making an optimum choice from a large range of possible schools". This might suggest that what is viewed as important is having a good local school, rather than a wide range of schools from which to choose. To explore public attitudes to this issue, we asked respondents if they agreed or disagreed that:

In Britain today, parents in general should send their children to their nearest state school

Those who did not agree were then asked:

What if the quality of different schools and their social mix of pupils was more equal? Would you agree that parents in general should then send their children to their nearest state school?

Responses to both questions are shown in Table 4.2. Despite broad support for the right of parents to choose schools, more than eight in ten (85 per cent) believe that parents should send their children to the nearest state school. More than six in ten support this view outright while, for more than two in ten, their agreement is tempered by a concern about unequal quality and social mixes of pupils between schools.

Fewer than one in ten disagree unconditionally with the sentiment that parents should send their children to the nearest state school.

Table 4.2 Belief that parents should send their children to the nearest state school

In Britain today, parents in general should send their children to the nearest state school	%
Agree	63
Agree, if quality and social mixes of pupils between schools was more equal	22
Neither agree nor disagree	9
Disagree	6
Base	2216

To understand which factors the public think are important in the allocation of school places, we also asked respondents:

Now please think about a school where more parents have asked for a place for their children than there are places available.

Which of these options do you think would be the best way of deciding which children should go to that school?

The options presented, and the proportions of respondents who selected each, are shown in Table 4.3. They lend further support to the idea that the public prioritises locality as a factor, when thinking about the allocation of school places. Nearly seven in ten think an oversubscribed school should prioritise those children who live closest, while around one in ten state the school should be allowed to decide which children to admit, or that places should be allocated using a ballot.

Table 4.3 Views on best way of allocating places at an oversubscribed school

	%
Give priority to those children who live closest to the school	67
Allow the school to choose which children to admit	14
Hold a ballot to select at random which children to admit	8
Base	2216

So, the public rank the location of a school as an important factor in determining which children should attend. But do they think school choice is a priority for schools? To explore this issue we asked respondents to choose from a list of priorities, presented in Table 4.4, the ones they thought it was most important for schools to achieve (although, it would be the government who would be likely to facilitate these in practice).

Parental freedom to choose does not rank highly in the public's priorities for schools. Fewer than one in twenty feel facilitating choice for parents should be schools' most important priority, compared with two-thirds who feel schools should prioritise all children, however able, doing the best they can. Four times as many as those prioritising choice for parents prioritise ensuring children from poor backgrounds do as well as children from better-off backgrounds. Thus, it is interesting to note stronger support for prioritising equality than for prioritising parental freedom. These findings show that people in Britain do support the idea of choice in relation to schools – but that this support is tempered and, in some instances, contradicted by a commitment to other ideas.

Table 4.4 Priorities which it is most important for schools to achieve

Most important priority for schools to achieve	%
Make sure all children, however able they are, do the best they can	67
Make sure that parents have a lot of choice about the kind of school their child goes to	4
Get the number of children who leave school with no qualifications down as low as possible	7
Make sure that children from poor backgrounds do as well as those from better off backgrounds	16
Base	*1870*

In practice, facilitating school choice requires measures to help parents have a choice in reality, as well as in theory. For many families, the area in which they live and their income level compromise choice – travelling to desirable schools further away is impractical and parents are unlikely to secure places in those schools because most are required to prioritise those who live closest. One measure introduced by the Labour government in England in 2006 was the payment of school travel expenses for low-income families to help their children attend schools further away. To ascertain public support for such initiatives to facilitate parental choice, respondents were asked about the following situation:

 There is stronger support for prioritising equality than for prioritising parental freedom

Say a parent on a low income wanted to send a child of theirs to a school some distance from their home, because they thought that school was better than the local school. But they cannot afford to pay the bus fare every day. What do you think should happen?

As shown in Table 4.5, when this question was first asked in 2007, respondents were evenly split over whether the child should go to a local school or the government should pay travel expenses. Since then, support for the latter option has declined, with more than six in ten now saying the child should go to his or her local school. One explanation for this change might be that, while people think facilitating choice in this way is desirable during times of economic prosperity, they see it as a luxury and do not think it should be a priority during times of economic downturn, where cuts to public services are being made elsewhere.

Table 4.5 Views on what should happen when a parent cannot afford bus fare for far-away school, 2007 and 2010

	2007	2010
	%	%
The child should go to a local school	47	63
The government should pay the bus fare	49	33
Base	*2022*	*2216*

So far, we have seen that the public does believe parents have a right to make choices about schools – but that support for parental freedom to choose is also qualified, conditional and contradicted by support for other ideals. Given these views, we now turn to examine what actions the public think are legitimate for parents to take in relation to their own children, to influence and maximise the school choices available to them. How does the public balance the freedom of parents to act partially with the inevitable effects of such an approach on educational equality? Do people believe parents should only be concerned with their own children, or the needs and interests of all children?

Should parents prioritise their children over others?
To explore the extent to which the public thinks parents should prioritise their own children over others, we asked respondents the following question:

1in3
think government should pay bus fare to far-away school, down from 1 in 2 in 2007

Some people think it is important to put your child first when choosing a secondary school whilst other people think it is also important to consider all children's needs equally, including your own child's. Which of the statements on this card comes closest to your view?

Put your child first and leave other parents to do the same

Put your child first but also consider other children's needs and interests

Consider all children's needs and interests equally, including your own child's

As shown in Table 4.6, most people (69 per cent) believe their own child should be prioritised over other children when it comes to choosing secondary schools. However, more than six in ten (61 per cent) believe the needs and interests of others should be considered to some degree, with almost three in ten believing parents should consider all children equally when choosing a secondary school. These findings suggest strong support for the idea that freedom and equality should be balanced with parental choice when parents are choosing schools – that there should be freedoms for parents to put their child first, but also that these should be kept within reasonable bounds.

Table 4.6 How children's needs should be considered when choosing a secondary school

	%
Put your child first and leave other parents to do the same	37
Put your child first but also consider other children's needs and interests	32
Consider all children's needs and interests equally, including your own child's	29
Base	*2216*

We have seen that a majority of the public thinks other children's needs and interests should be considered to some extent by a parent when choosing a secondary school for their child. Is this also the case for the various actions which parents might take to improve the school choices available for their own children? What actions are deemed acceptable and unacceptable, given their potential impact on the educational opportunities of those whose parents have not undertaken or could not undertake such actions?

There should be freedoms for parents to put their child first, but these should be kept within reasonable bounds

We asked about six different actions that parents might undertake to improve their children's chances of gaining a place at a particular school. These questions sought to test attitudes towards using different sorts of 'capital' to gain advantage for children. Helping children to revise for tests that will secure them places in selective schools can be considered an example of using 'cultural capital', while paying a private tutor is a use of 'economic capital', as is moving house to a 'better area'. Questions also tested attitudes towards less honest means of getting children into desirable schools. We explained to respondents:

When selecting pupils, schools take account of different factors such as the pupil's ability, their religion, or where they live. There are sometimes things parents can do to improve their child's chances of gaining a place at a particular school. For each one, please say how much you approve or disapprove...

> *...Helping children revise for exams or tests*
> *...Paying for a private tutor*
> *...Starting to get involved in local religious activities to help get their children into a high-performing faith school*
> *...Moving house to be nearer a higher-performing secondary school*
> *...Using a relative's address in order to be nearer a higher-performing secondary school*
> *...Renting a second home in order to be nearer a higher-performing secondary school but not generally living there*

As shown in Table 4.7, while nine in ten approve of helping children to revise for tests, a slightly lower proportion, almost seven in ten, approve of employing private tutors. Approval levels are much lower when it comes to other means by which parents might try to access schools. Less than four in ten approve of moving house to be nearer a higher-performing school and fewer than two in ten approve of becoming involved in religious activities to access faith schools. Very small proportions approve – and more than eight in ten disapprove – of parents using an address which is not their main one (or even their own) in order to access certain schools.

Table 4.7 Approval of actions by parents to improve child's chances of accessing certain schools

% approve of...	%
...helping children revise for exams or tests	90
...paying for a private tutor	67
...starting to get involved in local religious activities to help get their children into a high-performing faith school	16
...moving house to be nearer a higher-performing secondary school	36
...using a relative's address in order to be nearer a higher-performing secondary school	6
...renting a second home in order to be nearer a higher-performing secondary school but not generally living there	6
Base	2216

What do these responses tell us about the public's attitudes to the broader types of actions that parents might undertake to improve the school choices available to their children? These questions were analysed using a statistical technique called factor analysis (see Model 1 in the appendix to this chapter), which identified key underlying or latent attitudes towards different types of parental intervention. Helping children to revise for exams or tests and paying a private tutor were viewed as being similar to each other, but markedly different from other actions, which seem to be viewed collectively as manipulating the school choice system. With regard to helping children at home (the first two items), it is notable that people did not distinguish between the use of cultural and economic capital, but they did draw a distinction between one use of economic capital (paying a private tutor) and another (moving house). Moving house tended to be viewed as more in line with dishonest actions parents might undertake.

Broadly then, while some actions by parents are widely viewed as legitimate, others are not. Noden and West (2009) have highlighted a distinction between "procedural" and "substantive" fairness when it comes to school choice. While procedural fairness refers to rules ensuring no-one 'cheats the system', substantive fairness is concerned with equity. Given the extent to which inequalities may be exacerbated by parents employing private tutors to help their children access certain schools, patterns may be more influenced by procedural fairness than they are by substantive fairness. However, low approval of parents moving house to be nearer 'better' schools also suggests a concern with substantive fairness.

We asked an additional question to further explore public attitudes to parents' use of economic capital to improve the school choices available to their children. Respondents were asked:

Should the quality of education be the same for all children, or should parents who can afford it be able to pay for better education?

As demonstrated in Table 4.8, more than six in ten agree the quality of education children receive should be the same for everyone, with fewer than four in ten believing parents should be able to pay for better education for their own children.

Table 4.8 Views about whether the quality of education should be the same for all

	%
The quality of education should be the same for all children	61
Parents who can afford it should be able to pay for better education	38
Base	*2216*

We have seen so far that there is not a consensus among the public on the subject of school choice. To understand the reasons for the differences in opinion discussed previously, we now turn to consider whether attitudes to school choice vary across the population as a whole, and whether certain attitudes are more or less concentrated in particular sections of society.

Explaining attitudes to school choice

Attitudes to school choice could vary across the population in a number of ways. Given that experiences of school choice have been shown to vary substantially by social class (Gewirtz et al., 1995; Reay and Ball, 1997; Vincent, 2001; Ball, 2003), it may be that middle-class 'winners' in the school choice market are more likely than others to support choice. On the other hand, we might expect older groups to prioritise equality and fairness over choice compared to their younger counterparts, given the rise of consumerism in public services over the last three decades in Britain, replacing a post-war 'social democratic consensus'. We might also expect to see differences in attitudes between parents and non-parents. Where people are faced with school choice decisions personally, as parents, might they think more individualistically about choice? Research has highlighted the way in which mothers tend to undertake the greatest degree of "emotional labour" when it comes to school choice (David et al., 1994), so we might expect to see more pro-choice attitudes among women. Anxiety about choice might also arise among families seeking religious schools. Most such families are unlikely to have an ideal faith-based institution as their nearest school, so might be more likely to support choice. We might also expect to see greater support for parental choice in urban areas like London, where competition for school places is at its most intense. Experiences of education might also matter. Where parents hold specific views about an education they themselves have received, they may pass these views on to their children. Decisions made about schooling could also influence attitudes; if people have decided to send their children to private schools, it could mean they subsequently hold more individualist views. Finally, attitudes to choice could be explained by wider political attitudes. Showing concern for educational equality might be a proxy for left-wing values, so we might expect to see left-wing views among those rejecting school choice. Policies for choice are historically the realm of the Conservative Party, so, conversely, there may be greater support for these among Conservative supporters.

Identifying the characteristics which influence attitudes to school choice is a complex process. While people in London might be pro-choice, this may simply be because they share the characteristics of those who live in big cities. Similarly, while political identity might appear to explain attitudes, differences could result from the tendency for supporters of different parties to have certain socio-economic backgrounds. Multivariate analysis in the form of multiple and logistic regression was carried out; the results are presented in the appendix to this chapter (Tables A.1–A.6). Multivariate analysis allows us to account simultaneously for many possible factors that might explain attitudes to school choice, identifying which predict attitudes when their relationships with other factors are controlled for.

38%

believe parents should be able to pay for better education for their own children

Analysis was undertaken for support for the basic right of a parent to choose their children's school (Model 2), belief in putting one's child first (Model 3), agreement with choosing the best possible school even if this means others in the area might suffer (Model 4) and the view that parents in general should send children to the nearest state school (Model 5). We also explore attitudes towards parents 'working the school choice system' (Model 6), building on earlier factor analysis.[3] Levels of agreement with the idea that parents have a basic right to choose their children's school, by the characteristics found to independently predict attitudes to school choice, are presented in Tables 4.9–4.12 below.

Parents and their values
Parents are significantly more likely than those without children to support a 'right to choose' (Model 2). As shown in Table 4.9, this is the case for around seven in ten parents and six in ten of those who do not have children. Parents with children under 16 – those who are arguably closest to school choice – are more likely to support this notion even where other schools might suffer (Model 4). In a similar vein, it is notable that women are confirmed as being more likely to support school choice (Model 2), and less likely to agree parents should stay local (Model 5). Models 2–6 all confirm a strong link between sending one's child to private school and holding more individualist views about choice, with stronger support for parental freedoms and extensive parental partiality among those who have 'gone private'; in Model 2, this is also the case for parents who have sent children to a selective school. As shown below, almost eight in ten of those who have sent a child to a private school agree that a parent has a right to choose their child's school, compared with less than seven in ten overall. These findings are unsurprising; parents may hold certain views as part of justifying decisions they have made or may have made these decisions because they hold such views.

Models 2–6 all indicate significant effects of age on attitudes towards school choice, irrespective of whether or not someone is a parent. Older respondents are more likely, across a range of questions, to take a more collectivist and less consumerist or individualist stance, providing some evidence to suggest that living through an earlier social democratic period for public services in Britain may contribute to explaining attitudes. However, beyond this, there also remain the effects on respondents of their parents' educational experiences. Those whose parents attended grammar schools and private schools are more likely than others to reject school choice, parental partiality or the notion that one's own child should come first. As discussed above, findings here may reflect 'middle-class guilt' among families regarding their own educational privilege. People who benefited most within a divisive educational system of grammar schools and secondary moderns in England and Wales (or senior and junior secondaries in Scotland) may also be those with the strongest sense among their cohort of the importance of educational equality, passing these values onto their children.

Parents are significantly more likely than those without children to support a 'right to choose'

Table 4.9 Agreement parents should have a basic right to choose their child's school, by demographic characteristics and educational experience

Demographic characteristic or educational experience	% agree parents have a basic right to choose their child's school	Base
All	68	1870
Sex		
Men	65	811
Women	70	1059
Age		
18–24	72	129
25–34	75	243
35–44	70	356
45–54	63	333
55–64	61	347
65+	68	460
Parental status		
Children under 16 living at home	72	663
Children over 16	68	716
No children	62	491
Educational experience of respondent and family		
Respondent went to private school	73	161
Sibling went to private school	76	115
Sent child to private school	78	133
Respondent went to selective school	66	309
Sibling went to selective school	62	197
Sent child to selective school	78	105
Parent went to selective/private school	60	275

A question of ideology?

Given earlier discussion about differing social class experiences of school choice, we might expect class to contribute heavily in explaining attitudes. While class does feature to some degree (see for example Model 6), attitudes towards choice are much more obviously driven by politics. Analysis using two scales included on the *British Social Attitudes* survey to measure 'left–right' and 'libertarian–authoritarian' attitudes shows that those who are more 'left-wing' disapprove more of 'working the school choice system' or of considering one's own child to the exclusion of others. Support for a right to choose and for manipulating the school choice system is higher among those with authoritarian views – with their emphasis on respect for family values and tough law and order. Associations here might be explained by a focus on family values among respondents, fitting with an idea of individual families making their own decisions.

Beyond this, Labour supporters are significantly less likely than Conservatives to support parental choice, when other factors are controlled for. Seven in ten Conservative supporters support the right of parents to choose their child's school, compared with slightly more than six in ten Labour supporters. This makes sense given that markets in public services are traditionally the realm of the Conservative Party. Still, moves towards choice under Labour governments from 1997 onwards make this a noteworthy finding. Labour supporters and Liberal Democrats are also less likely than others to say one should put their own child first without considering the needs of others.

Table 4.10 Agreement that parents should have a basic right to choose their child's school, by party identification

	% agree parents have a basic right to choose their child's school	Base
All	68	1870
Party identification		
Conservative	70	569
Labour	64	583
Liberal Democrat	68	241
Other	58	100
None	73	263

Geographical effects
As shown in Table 4.11, people who live in cities or the suburbs of cities do tend more than others towards supporting parental choice and rejecting a duty to send children to the nearest school. Patterns here are likely to relate to the fact that within cities there are larger numbers of schools in close proximity, so competition between schools and between parents for school places is more intense. However, regional differences also prevail, with those in London holding the most pro-choice and pro-partiality views (see Models 4, 5 and 6). This may be indicative of particularly intense competition for school places and high social inequalities between areas in London. Respondents in Scotland are significantly less likely than those in England or Wales to support a parental right to choose. This reflects the work of academics such as Paterson (2003) and Humes and Bryce (2003), who have drawn attention to a distinctive left-wing commitment to local comprehensive education in Scotland.

7 in 10

Conservative supporters support the right of parents to choose their child's school, compared with 6 in 10 Labour supporters

Table 4.11 Agreement parents should have a basic right to choose their child's school, by geographic characteristics

	% agree parents have a basic right to choose their child's school	Base
All	68	1870
Type of area		
A big city	74	139
The suburbs/outskirts of a big city	72	474
A small city or town	65	850
Rural	64	405
Region		
North East	68	91
North West	76	230
Yorkshire and Humber	66	157
East Midlands	70	154
West Midlands	66	160
South West	73	176
Eastern	63	184
London	82	183
South East	64	252
Wales	58	94
Scotland	49	189

Religion

Finally, regression analyses confirm the effects of religion on attitudes. Catholic respondents are less likely to agree children should go to their nearest school, and people with non-Christian religious beliefs are more likely to support 'working the school choice system' and a parental right to choose as shown in Table 4.12 below, although the small sample size available means we should treat this finding with caution. Nevertheless, they may reflect a preference among religious groups for faith-based educational provision, not necessarily provided by the nearest schools. Non-Christian faith schools are few in number across Britain – and parents may feel compelled to exercise extra parental assertiveness – which could explain stronger support for 'working the system'.

 Catholic respondents are less likely to agree children should go to their nearest school

Table 4.12 Agreement that parents should have a basic right to choose their child's school, by religion

	% agree parents have a basic right to choose their child's school	Base
All	68	1870
Religion		
Church of England	70	407
Roman Catholic	75	166
Other Christian	68	278
Other non-Christian	88	76
No religion	64	939

Clearly public attitudes to school choice are not developed in a theoretical vacuum but vary substantially – not only in response to individuals' own and their families' experiences of school choice, but in relation to a range of wider systems of beliefs and values.

Conclusions
Government education policy since the 1980s in Britain has involved a growing focus on parents' right to choose schools for their children, tempered by qualifying concerns about community and equality. In 2010 a majority of the public shows support for the notion of school choice. However, this support is conditional and problematic when examined in depth. Large proportions support the idea that parents should send their children to the nearest state school – and when they do not support this idea, it is largely because they feel the quality and social mixes of pupils between schools are too uneven, not because they have a fundamental conviction that people should always be able to choose from a range of schools. Choice is not viewed as a priority and in some instances there is ambivalence towards it.

Attitudes to the interventions parents might undertake to improve the choices available to their own children are often contradictory. While some parental uses of resources are viewed as fair, support does not extend as far as moving house to an area with 'better' schools or paying for private education. Complex patterns explaining differences in attitudes can be seen, ranging from parents justifying decisions to 'go private', through political attitudes or their local area, to the possible effects of living

Choice is not viewed as a priority and in some instances there is ambivalence towards it

through a more social democratic age in Britain. Overall, while most believe parents should put their own children first when choosing schools, most also believe parents should consider the impact their actions may have on others.

The fact that majorities in Britain support both a parental right to choose and greater educational equality sit in obvious contrast with the literature on school choice discussed at the beginning of this chapter. Such literature presents parental choice in the current British context as being in clear tension with educational equality, but this tension appears to go unrecognised by many, and there seems to be some disconnect in the public mind between inequality in the school system overall and an exercising of extensive parental partiality. Perhaps a greater role for academics, then, in drawing attention to the contradictions between school choice and social justice, is needed.

The public prioritises supporting local schools and attaches value to considering the needs and interests of all children. This should serve as an important caution to the coalition government in England as it moves towards ever more extensive policies for school choice, allowing popular schools to flourish while others "feel the squeeze" (Vasagar, 2011). If such policies lead to a situation where more parents feel unable to send their children to their nearest state school, or some become stuck in schools which have been pushed into "spirals of decline", then these policies could be highly unpopular. Overall, they may ultimately damage public confidence in the likelihood that government will deliver on "giving all children the chance of world-class schools" (Department for Education, 2011).

Notes

1. Banding is a system for allocating school places, which ensures that schools take in proportionate spreads of pupils across the whole ability range. Lottery allocations of school places ensure that, where a school is oversubscribed, places are allocated randomly, rather than giving priority to those who, for example, live closest (see West *et al.*, 2011, for more information on both banding and lotteries).

2. There are empirical debates about whether this has already happened. Gorard and Fitz (2000) argue it has not, but Goldstein and Noden (2003) argue that it has.

3. A scale has been created combining attitudes towards: getting involved in religious activities to access high-performing faith schools; moving house to be nearer higher-performing schools; using relatives' addresses; and renting second homes to be nearer higher-performing schools. Low scores on the scale signify approval of these actions, whereas high scores signify disapproval. Cronbach's Alpha for this scale is 0.70.

References

Adler, M., Petch, A. and Tweedie, J. (1989), *Parental Choice and Educational Policy*, Edinburgh: Edinburgh University Press

Ball, S.J. (2003), *Class Strategies and the Education Market: The Middle Classes and Social Advantage*, London: RoutledgeFalmer

Brighouse, H. (2000), *School Choice and Social Justice*, Oxford: Oxford University Press

Chubb, J.E. and Moe, T.M. (1992), *A Lesson in School Reform from Great Britain*, Washington DC: Brookings

Coldron, J., Williams, J., Fearon, J., Stephenson, K., Logie, A. and Smith, N. (2001), *Admissions Policies and Practices of Selective and Partially Selective Schools in England* Paper presented at the British Educational Research Association Annual Conference, University of Leeds, 13–15 September

David, M., West, A. and Ribbens, J. (1994), *Mother's Intuition? Choosing Secondary Schools*, London: Falmer

Department for Education (2011), *New admissions code: more places in good schools, a fairer and simpler system*, Press notice, 27 May

Gewirtz, S., Ball, S.J. and Bowe, R. (1995), *Markets, Choice and Equity in Education*, Buckingham: Open University Press

Goldstein, H. and Noden, P. (2003), 'Modelling Social Segregation', *Oxford Review of Education*, **29(2)**: 225–237

Gorard, S. and Fitz, J. (2000), 'Markets and Stratification: A View from England and Wales', *Journal of Educational Policy*, **14**: 405–428

Hargreaves, D.H. (1996), 'Diversity and Choice in School Education: A Modified Libertarian Approach', *Oxford Review of Education*, **22(2)**, 131–141

Humes, W. and Bryce, T. (2003), (eds.), *Scottish Education – 2nd Edition, Post-Devolution*, Edinburgh: Edinburgh University Press

Levinson, M. (1999), *The Demands of Liberal Education*, Oxford: Oxford University Press

Lipsett, A. (2007), 'Brighton's School Lottery Backed in Ruling', *The Guardian*, 13 July

Noden, P. and West, A. (2009), *Secondary school admissions in England: admission forums, local authorities and schools*, London: RISE Trust

Paterson, L. (2003), *Scottish Education in the Twentieth Century*, Edinburgh: Edinburgh University Press

Pring, R. (2008), *The Common School and the Comprehensive Ideal: A Defence*, Oxford: Wiley-Blackwell

Reay, D. and Ball, S.J. (1997), 'Spoilt for Choice: The Working Classes and Educational Markets', *Oxford Review of Education*, **23(1)**: 89–101

Smith, G., Exley, S., Smith, T. and Jaquette, O. (2005), *Mapping the Flow of DfES Funding To Disadvantaged Areas: A Feasibility Study and Research Review*, London: Office of the Deputy Prime Minister

Stewart, W. (2005), 'Banding by ability may spark 'riots in the streets'', *Times Educational Supplement*, 25 November

Swift, A. (2003), *How Not to be a Hypocrite*, London: Routledge

Tooley, J. (1996), *Education Without the State*, London: Institute of Economic Affairs

United Nations Universal Declaration of Human Rights, available at www.un.org/en/documents/udhr/inde4.shtml#a26 (accessed 4 October 2011)

Vasagar, J. (2011), 'Michael Gove says new admissions code will aid popular schools', *The Guardian*, 22 May

Vincent, C. (2001), 'Social Class and Parental Agency', *Journal of Education Policy*, **16(4)**: 347–364

West, A., Barham, E. and Hind, A. (2011) 'Secondary school admissions in England 2001 to 2008: changing legislation, policy and practice', *Oxford Review of Education*, **37(1)**: 1–20

Acknowledgements

Thanks to the Economic and Social Research Council for Research Grant RES-000-22-3989 which funded all questions seen in this chapter. Thanks also to Dr Judith Suissa, co-applicant on the grant, for her comments on a draft of this chapter.

Appendix

Table A.1: Factor analysis of views about parent 'partiality' towards their own children: scores for principal axis factoring with varimax factor rotation

	'Working the school choice system'	'Helping children at home'
Helping children revise for exams or tests		0.48
Paying for a private tutor		0.75
Starting to get involved in local religious activities to help get their children into a high-performing faith school	0.40	
Moving house to be nearer a higher-performing secondary school	0.41	
Using a relative's address in order to be nearer a higher-performing secondary school	0.74	
Renting a second home in order to be nearer a higher-performing secondary school but not generally living there	0.80	

Base: 1717

Model 2: Agreement "parents should have a basic right to choose their child's school"
The multivariate analysis technique used is logistic regression, about which more details can be found in Appendix I of the report. The dependent variable is agreement that "parents should have a basic right to choose their child's school". A positive coefficient indicates that the group is more likely than the reference group (shown in brackets) to support this idea while a negative coefficient indicates the group is less likely to support it. Independent variables: age, household income, highest educational qualification, party identification, sex, marital status, children under 16 living in household, region, type of area, newspaper readership, respondent/family members at private/selective school, social class, religion, left–right attitudes, libertarian–authoritarian attitudes, welfarist attitudes.

Table A.2: Agreement "parents should have a basic right to choose their child's school"

Category	Coefficient	Standard error	Odds ratio	p value
Baseline odds	-0.33	0.60	0.72	0.579
Age	-0.02**	0.01	0.98	0.001
Sex (men)				
Women	0.27*	0.12	1.31	0.024
Political party (no party)				
Conservative	-0.08	0.17	0.92	0.922
Labour	-0.33*	0.16	0.72	0.722
Liberal Democrat	-0.09	0.20	0.91	0.914
Other party	-0.21	0.26	0.81	0.809
Parents went to private school	-0.54*	0.27	0.58	0.041
Parents went to selective school	-0.62**	0.17	0.54	0.000
Sibling went to private school	0.74*	0.30	2.10	0.012
Sent child to private school	0.62*	0.26	1.87	0.016
Sent child to selective school	0.73*	0.29	2.07	0.012
Children (no children)				
Children under 16 living at home	0.46**	0.17	1.59	0.005
Children over 16	0.50**	0.19	1.65	0.008
Region (North East)				
North West	0.43	0.32	1.53	0.176
Yorkshire and Humber	-0.23	0.32	0.80	0.479
East Midlands	0.18	0.34	1.20	0.591
West Midlands	-0.13	0.32	0.88	0.681
South West	0.16	0.33	1.17	0.634
Eastern	-0.42	0.31	0.66	0.179
Inner London	0.69	0.45	2.00	0.128
Outer London	0.28	0.35	1.32	0.432
South East	-0.16	0.30	0.58	0.583
Wales	-0.40	0.37	0.28	0.277
Scotland	-0.91**	0.32	0.40	0.004
Religion (no religion)				
Church of England	0.18	0.16	1.19	0.257
Roman Catholic	0.39	0.23	1.48	0.083
Other Christian	0.23	0.17	1.26	0.172
Other non-Christian	1.05**	0.36	2.85	0.003
Type of area (rural)				
A big city	0.23	0.28	1.26	0.415
The suburbs/outskirts of a big city	0.35*	0.17	1.42	0.043
A small city or town	0.04	0.15	1.04	0.777
Libertarian–authoritarian attitudes	0.50**	0.10	1.65	0.000

Base: 1717

* significant at 95% level ** significant at 99% level

Model 3: Belief in "putting your child first and leaving others to do the same"

Logistic regression (see Model 2 for details) with independent variables: age, household income, highest educational qualification, party identification, sex, marital status, children under 16 living in household, region, newspaper readership, respondent/family members at private/selective school, social class, religion, left–right attitudes, libertarian–authoritarian attitudes, welfarist attitudes.

Table A.3: Belief in "putting your child first and leaving others to do the same"

Category	Coefficient	Standard error	Odds ratio	p value
Baseline odds	-1.71**	0.54	0.18	0.002
Age	-0.01*	0.01	0.99	0.032
Political party (no party)				
Conservative	-0.09	0.16	0.91	0.560
Labour	-0.35*	0.15	0.70	0.021
Liberal Democrat	-0.40*	0.19	0.67	0.036
Other party	0.60*	0.25	1.82	0.015
Parents went to private school	-0.54*	0.27	0.58	0.041
Sent child to selective school	0.73*	0.29	2.07	0.012
Left–right attitudes	0.19*	0.08	1.21	0.013

Base: 1770

---

* significant at 95% level ** significant at 99% level

Model 4: Agreement that "parents have a duty to choose the best possible school for their child, even if this means schools in the local area might suffer"

Logistic regression (see Model 2 for details) with independent variables: age, household income, highest educational qualification, party identification, sex, marital status, children under 16 living in household, region, newspaper readership, respondent/family members at private/selective school, social class, religion, left–right attitudes, libertarian–authoritarian attitudes, welfarist attitudes.

Table A.4: Agreement that "parents have a duty to choose the best possible school for their child, even if this means schools in the local area might suffer"

Category	Coefficient	Standard error	Odds ratio	p value
Baseline odds	-1.11*	0.56	0.33	0.046
Age	-0.01*	0.01	0.99	0.012
Parents went to selective school	-0.41*	0.17	0.66	0.013
Respondent went to selective school	0.35*	0.16	1.41	0.027
Sibling went to selective school	-0.44*	0.18	0.64	0.012
Sent child to selective school	0.65**	0.23	1.91	0.004
Children (no children)				
Children under 16 living at home	0.42**	0.16	1.52	0.007
Children over 16	0.28	0.18	1.33	0.115
Region (North East)				
North West	0.61*	0.28	1.84	0.031
Yorkshire and Humber	-0.03	0.30	0.98	0.932
East Midlands	0.37	0.30	1.45	0.223
West Midlands	0.40	0.30	1.49	0.178
South West	0.41	0.30	1.51	0.166
Eastern	-0.19	0.29	0.83	0.519
Inner London	1.41**	0.41	4.11	0.001
Outer London	0.50	0.31	1.65	0.110
South East	-0.01	0.28	1.00	0.986
Wales	0.16	0.35	1.17	0.643
Scotland	-0.29	0.30	0.75	0.346
Religion (no religion)				
Church of England	0.13	0.14	1.14	0.366
Roman Catholic	0.08	0.19	1.09	0.668
Other Christian	0.15	0.16	1.17	0.328
Other non-Christian	0.53*	0.26	1.71	0.041
Income (less than £1,000 per month)				
£1,001–£2,200 per month	-0.39**	0.14	0.67	0.004
£2,201–£3,700 per month	-0.11	0.15	0.90	0.488
£3,701 or more per month	0.07	0.16	0.94	0.674
Libertarian–authoritarian attitudes	0.36**	0.09	1.43	0.000

Base: 1775

* significant at 95% level ** significant at 99% level

Model 5: Agreement that "parents in general should send their children to their nearest state school"

Logistic regression (see Model 2 for details) with independent variables: age, household income, highest educational qualification, party identification, sex, marital status, children under 16 living in household, region, newspaper readership, respondent/family members at private/selective school, social class, religion, left–right attitudes, libertarian–authoritarian attitudes, welfarist attitudes.

Table A.5: Agreement that "parents in general should send their children to their nearest state school"

Category	Coefficient	Standard error	Odds ratio	p value
Baseline odds	0.71	0.59	2.03	0.230
Age	0.02**	0.01	1.02	0.000
Sex (men)				
Women	-0.28*	0.11	0.75	0.013
Highest educational qualification (lower than GCSE level)				
Degree or other higher education	-0.41*	0.18	0.66	0.021
A level or equivalent	-0.23	0.19	0.79	0.219
GCSE level or equivalent	-0.11	0.18	0.90	0.551
Parents went to selective school	0.37*	0.17	1.45	0.031
Sibling went to selective school	-0.60*	0.26	0.55	0.019
Sent child to selective school	-0.51*	0.22	0.60	0.019
Region (North East)				
North West	-0.88**	0.32	0.41	0.006
Yorkshire and Humber	-0.39	0.34	0.68	0.249
East Midlands	-0.83*	0.34	0.44	0.015
West Midlands	-0.60	0.34	0.55	0.076
South West	-0.69*	0.34	0.50	0.039
Eastern	-0.96**	0.33	0.38	0.003
Inner London	-0.53	0.41	0.59	0.198
Outer London	-0.79*	0.35	0.45	0.022
South East	-0.99**	0.31	0.37	0.002
Wales	-0.38	0.40	0.69	0.343
Scotland	0.50	0.36	1.65	0.162
Religion (no religion)				
Church of England	0.05	0.15	1.05	0.745
Roman Catholic	-0.39*	0.20	0.67	0.046
Other Christian	-0.04	0.17	0.97	0.827
Other non-Christian	-0.07	0.24	0.93	0.773
Type of area (rural)				
A big city	-0.73**	0.27	0.48	0.006
The suburbs/outskirts of a big city	0.00	0.17	1.00	0.981
A small city or town	-0.02	0.15	0.98	0.872

Base: 1788

* significant at 95% level ** significant at 99% level

Model 6: Correlates for 'working the school choice system' scale

The multivariate analysis technique used is OLS regression, about which more details can be found in Appendix I of the report. The dependent variable is an attitude scale combining answers to several questions, as indicated in the main chapter text. A positive coefficient indicates stronger disapproval of 'working the system' and a negative coefficient means stronger approval.

For categorical variables, the reference category is shown in brackets after the category heading. Independent variables included in the model: age, household income, highest educational qualification, party identification, sex, marital status, children under 16 living in household, region, newspaper readership, respondent/family members at private/selective school, social class, religion, left–right attitudes, libertarian–authoritarian attitudes, welfarist attitudes.

Table A.6: Correlates for 'working the school choice system' scale

Individual characteristics (comparison group in brackets)	Coefficient	Standard error	Odds ratio
Age	0.24**	0.00	0.000
Region (North East)			
North West	-0.07	0.09	0.100
Yorkshire and Humber	-0.05	0.09	0.175
East Midlands	-0.07	0.09	0.055
West Midlands	-0.04	0.09	0.269
South West	-0.03	0.09	0.479
Eastern	-0.07	0.10	0.083
Inner London	-0.20**	0.09	0.000
Outer London	-0.13**	0.08	0.001
South East	-0.06	0.10	0.203
Wales	-0.05	0.09	0.123
Scotland	-0.03	0.09	0.511
Religion (no religion)			
Church of England	-0.03	0.04	0.311
Roman Catholic	-0.01	0.06	0.790
Other Christian	-0.02	0.05	0.330
Other non-Christian	-0.07**	0.07	0.005
Social class (Semi-routine/Routine)			
Managerial/Professional	-0.05	0.04	0.121
Intermediate	-0.05*	0.06	0.040
Small employer/Own account worker	-0.04	0.06	0.159
Lower supervisory/Technical	-0.03	0.06	0.234
Child went to private school	-0.08**	0.06	0.001
Parent went to selective school	0.05*	0.05	0.049
Left–right attitudes	-0.08**	0.02	0.001
Libertarian–authoritarian attitudes	-0.09**	0.03	0.002

Base: 1791

* significant at 95% level ** significant at 99% level

5. Higher education
A limit to expansion? Attitudes to university funding, fees and opportunities

The coalition government's approval for a large-scale increase in university tuition fees in England has prompted street protests and contributed to a drop in support for the Liberal Democrats. But the public's wider views on the expansion and funding of higher education may not be as clear-cut as the political debate implies.

Support for the continued expansion of higher education has fallen in England as the number of university places has increased. Opposition to students paying for tuition and taking out loans to cover their living costs has decreased (though the survey preceded the latest fee increase).

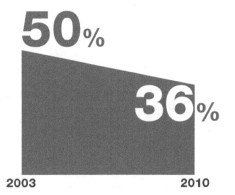

2003   **2010**

Public support for **expanding higher education** opportunities for young people peaked at 50% in 2003 and has since fallen to 36%.

Most (70%) think that some students or their families should pay university **tuition fees**, and the proportion wholly opposed to them has fallen from 25% in 2007 to 16%. Despite the political uproar following the Liberal Democrat's post-election change of position on tuition fees, only a small minority of Liberal Democrat supporters are wholly opposed to fees (13%).

70% some students should pay

16% no students should pay

Those who are most privileged educationally and economically are less likely to support university expansion, and more likely to support fees.

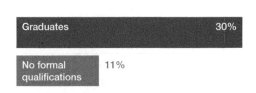

Graduates   30%

No formal qualifications   11%

Graduates (30%) are much more likely to support a reduction in the number of university places, than those without formal qualifications (11%).

42%

Those who are opposed to tuition fees are more likely to support the expansion of higher education than those who want tuition fees for all (42% compared with 19%).

Authors: Anna Zimdars, Alice Sullivan & Anthony Heath*

Higher education funding and the cost of obtaining a university degree has proved to be one of the most contentious political issues since the 2010 General Election. The coalition government's decision to increase the top rate of fees that universities in England can charge from £3,290 to £9,000 (Department for Business, Innovation and Skills, 2010) prompted large-scale public demonstrations during 2011. Opposition within Parliament and on the streets has been fuelled by criticism of the coalition government's junior partner, the Liberal Democrats, who had actively campaigned during the election to phase out university tuition fees for first degrees. Indignation has focused on this political *volte-face* as well as the jump in fees that will take place from the autumn of 2012, and the much larger loans that most students will need to meet them.

Fieldwork for the 2010 *British Social Attitudes* survey took place after the election, but before the government had announced its intention to raise tuition fees (based on recommendations from a review of university funding by the industrialist Lord Browne (2010)). But the response to our questions seeking people's views about access to higher education and how to pay for it sheds new light on a debate whose intensity increased dramatically a few months later. We wanted to know how far the public supports the 40-year trend that has seen higher education expand from the preserve of an elite group in society to something experienced by nearly half the young people in Britain. The last time views were obtained about the number of young people going to university was in 2007 when there were signs that support for a continued increase was starting to fall. We were keen to find out whether that apparent shift in public opinion has been sustained.

In the same way, we wanted to know whether attitudes to tuition fees, government maintenance grants and student loans have altered over time. Tuition fees were introduced by Labour in 1998, with variable rate fees (top-up fees) added in 2004. As the cost of funding higher education has been transferred from the state to individual students and their families, we wonder if the public has become more accepting of the loan system. Alternatively, has opposition to the new system intensified – at least in England where students are required to pay full tuition fees?

The situation for students whose family homes are in England differs, of course, from those of students normally resident in Scotland, for whom the devolved government has abolished tuition fees (Scottish Government, 2010). More recently the Welsh Assembly Government, in response to the latest rise in tuition fees, has decided to 'cap' the fees paid by Welsh students at UK universities at their current level, using public money to fund the difference (Welsh Government, 2010). Given these different approaches now being taken to the funding of higher education in Scotland and Wales, we have decided to confine our analysis of public attitudes in this chapter to responses from people in England. It is their views that can be expected to carry the greatest resonance for the current political debate about fees.

....

* Anna Zimdars is a Lecturer in Higher Education at King's College London, Alice Sullivan is Director of BCS70 and Senior Lecturer at the Institute of Education, Anthony Heath holds professorial appointments in the Department of Sociology, Oxford University and the Institute for Social Change, Manchester University.

But while concentrating on public opinion in England, we must also take account of the possibility that any overall trends we identify disguise a more subtle interplay of attitudes between different social and political groups. Recognising this, we not only look at trends over time, but also how the views expressed in 2010 vary according to social status. We also examine how far people's views on the expansion of higher education are linked or consistent with their attitudes concerning university fees. Might some people welcome fees as a means of restricting access to universities? Do others, by contrast, accept the argument made by some politicians that higher fees and loans are necessary to enable universities to continue to expand to meet the higher education aspirations of many? We go on to compare people's views with their political affiliations and consider how far they accord with the stated policies of the parties they support.

Trends in attitudes towards participation, fees and loans

Policies for increasing the number of young people reaching higher education have been pursued by both Labour and the Conservatives, with the last Labour government setting a target – still unmet – of 50 per cent of young people attending university with the current Higher Education participation rate being 47 per cent (Department for Business, Innovation and Skills, 2011). While the Liberal Democrat manifesto at the 2010 election pledged to scrap this target, but restore free tuition for first degrees (Liberal Democrats, 2010), the Conservative manifesto promised 10,000 extra university places (Conservative Party, 2010). Posing a question about participation in higher education that has been consistently used in the *British Social Attitudes* series, we asked people:

*Do you feel that opportunities for young people in Britain to go on to **higher education** – to a university or college – should be increased or reduced, or are they at about the right level now?*

Figure 5.1 describes the trends recorded since this question was first asked. It shows that – as in 1983 – there are more people in England who think the level of higher education opportunities is "about right" than believe they should be increased or reduced. But the similarities end there because in 2010 the proportion favouring further expansion has fallen over recent years (35 per cent), while the percentage recommending reduced rates of university participation has reached its highest level to date (16 per cent). So, as the proportion of young people in higher education has continued to increase in recent years, so support for further increasing participation has gone into decline.

Policies for increasing the number of young people reaching higher education have been pursued by both Labour and the Conservatives

Figure 5.1 Trends in views on the level of higher education participation, 1983–2010

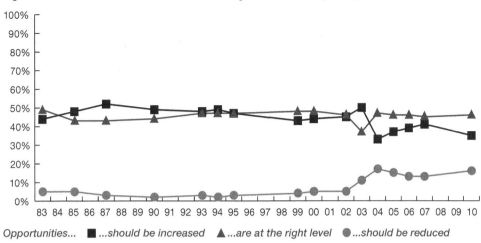

Opportunities...   ■ ...should be increased   ▲ ...are at the right level   ● ...should be reduced

Base: England only
The data on which Figure 5.1 is based can be found in the appendix to this chapter

A high point in public support for the expansion of higher education was reached in 2003 when 50 per cent of those interviewed wanted more opportunities in higher education – and the proportion content with existing provision fell below 40 per cent. Support for expansion fell in 2004 to 33 per cent, perhaps as a result of debates surrounding the proposal in January 2004 to introduce £3,000 tuition fees. Following a gradual increase to 2007 (41 per cent), support decreased again in 2010 to 35 per cent. Meanwhile, the proportion of respondents saying that opportunities for participation should be reduced increased from five per cent in 2000 to 16 per cent in 2010.

Nevertheless, those wanting more university opportunities for young people still outnumber those calling for a reduction by more than two to one. Of course, this trend reflects the increasing proportion of young people participating in higher education. The downward trend in support for expansion could therefore partly reflect consistent views about the optimum level of participation. But we can still see that a significant minority of the population – one in six – now think it is time to reverse the process. It will be interesting, later in this chapter, to see how far this group is distinct in terms of social status and party politics from people who favour continued expansion.

For now, we continue to focus on trends, by examining people's opinions about university tuition fees and student loans. Since 2004, *British Social Attitudes* has asked the public what it thinks "about university or college students or their families paying towards the costs of their tuition, either while they are studying or after they have finished". The question asks respondents which of three views they think is closest to their own:

***All** students or their families should pay towards the costs of their tuition*

***Some** students or their families should pay towards the costs of their tuition, depending on their circumstances*

***No** students or their families should pay towards the costs of their tuition*

Table 5.1 shows a fairly stable picture between 2004 and 2007, with two in three people accepting that some students or their families should pay tuition fees, and up to one in four maintaining they should not. However, by 2010 this minority has shrunk from 25 per cent in 2007 to 16 per cent, while the proportion thinking that some should pay, depending on their circumstances, has increased somewhat from 66 per cent to 70 per cent. There has also been an increase in the minority of people who suggest that all students or families should pay tuition fees, from eight per cent to 13 per cent.

Table 5.1 Attitudes towards tuition fees, 2004–2010

	2004	2005	2007	2010
Who should pay towards tuition costs?	%	%	%	%
All students/families should pay	11	9	8	13
Some students/families should pay	66	67	66	70
No students/families should pay	22	22	25	16
Base	2684	1796	2617	913

Base: England only

An increasing body of opinion that students or their families should pay may, in part, reflect increasing acceptance of tuition fees as the *status quo*. Although people were interviewed before the government decided to raise maximum fees to £9,000 a year, we can also expect opinions to have been influenced by the recession and widely-debated concerns about public spending.

Seeking views on the complementary issue of student living expenses, we asked two further questions. The first advised respondents that currently "some full-time British university students get grants to help cover their living costs" with grants depending "upon the student's circumstances and those of their family". Respondents were invited to say whether:

all students should get grants to help cover their living costs,

some students should get grants to help cover their living costs

or, that no grants should be given to help cover students' living costs?

70%

say some students should pay tuition fees, depending on their circumstances

On student loans, people were advised that many full-time university students "are now taking out government loans to help cover their living costs" and that "they have to start repaying these loans when they begin working". The question asked, generally speaking, if they thought that:

students should be expected to take out loans to help cover their living costs

or

students should not be expected to take out loans to help cover living costs

Table 5.2 displays the responses to the question about loans since it was first asked in 1995, and to the grants question since 2000. Replies to the latter show a modest decline in support for universal maintenance grants from 27 per cent 10 years ago to 21 per cent, while support for grants being awarded to some students has remained relatively stable (67 per cent in 2000, and 70 per cent in 2010). Opposition to any grants being given at all is very low, although it stands at four per cent compared with one per cent in 2000.

Table 5.2 Views on higher education loans and grants, 1995–2010

	1995	2000	2010
Should students get grants to help cover their living costs?	%	%	%
All students	n/a	27	21
Some students	n/a	67	70
No grants	n/a	1	4
It depends	n/a	4	4
Base	*n/a*	*959*	*913*
Should students be expected to take out loans?	%	%	%
Should be expected	27	28	43
Should not be expected	64	58	42
It depends	8	12	14
Base	*1041*	*959*	*913*

Base: England only

Opinion about student loans shows more movement over time. In 1995, four years after government-sponsored loans were first introduced, two out of three (64 per cent) people thought students should not be expected to borrow money to cover their living costs. Little more than one in four (27 per cent) took an opposite view. By 2000, this was still the balance of opinion, although the majority opposing loans was smaller (58 per cent). Ten years later, we find opinion is evenly divided with 42 per cent saying students should not be expected to take out a loan, and 43 per cent insisting that they should. This increased acceptance may simply be due to the long standing of the policy, and the political reality of support for loans from both major parties.

But while loans have become the norm in higher education, they continue to attract widespread criticism – not least through concerns that the level of debt needed to complete a university course will deter some applicants. The government argues that poorer young people should not be deterred by debt because loan repayments are only sought after the graduate borrower has passed a minimum income threshold. Against those who insist that state-funded higher education would be fairer, it is typically argued that funding from general taxation is far from equitable because the students who benefit still come disproportionately from affluent backgrounds. But are members of the public who support tuition fee charges and maintenance loans really more 'egalitarian' in their outlook? Or are their views linked to a more 'elitist' view of higher education that considers higher education is expanding too far? We explore these possibilities in the remainder of the chapter.

Attitudes held by different social groups

Having reported on how the public's views about participation, fees and loans have changed over time, we consider how their responses in the most recent survey vary according to occupational status and educational background. We categorise occupational background into three groups: (1) professional and managerial occupations, (2) intermediate occupations, that is those in non-manual employment outside the professional and managerial sector and (3) those in either skilled, semi-skilled or unskilled manual employment, that is traditional working-class employment. In Table 5.3 we can see that those in traditional working-class jobs are rather more likely (50 per cent) to think the current level of opportunities "about right" than those from professional and managerial (39 per cent) backgrounds. A more striking difference emerges among the minority who favour a contraction of existing opportunities; 10 per cent of those in traditional working-class jobs think opportunities should be reduced, compared with 26 per cent of those from professional and managerial backgrounds.

Our analysis based on educational attainment reveals an even stronger series of contrasts. People with qualifications below degree level are very much more likely to favour an expansion of university opportunities (40 per cent) and those who have been to university are least positive. Conversely, 30 per cent of graduates think that higher education opportunities should be reduced; far exceeding the proportion among those with lower qualifications (14 per cent) or no qualifications at all (11 per cent). From this, we can see that the minority who believe that there should be fewer places in higher education consists disproportionately of people who have been to university themselves.

When we apply the same social background analysis to people's views about tuition fees, distinctions by social class and educational attainment are discernable,

30%

of graduates think that higher education opportunities should be reduced

but much less marked. A larger minority of professional and managerial respondents think that all students should pay (16 per cent) than those from intermediate (11 per cent) or working-class (12 per cent) backgrounds. Graduates (18 per cent) are also more likely to take this view than people with qualifications below degree level (10 per cent) or no qualifications at all (14 per cent). Conversely, those without qualifications are rather more likely to insist that no students should have to pay tuition fees (21 per cent) than those with degrees (16 per cent) or lower qualifications (14 per cent). We must, however, recognise that – as in the population as a whole – most people in most of these demographic groups accept that some students should pay something. Knowing that the 2010 survey took place before the government's decision to institute a dramatic rise in tuition fees, we might speculate that this general acceptance of student fees is linked to the relatively low amounts being demanded at the time. But only time will tell.

Table 5.3 Attitudes towards higher education opportunities, by demographic characteristics

		Higher education opportunities...			
		...should be increased	...are about right	...should be reduced	Base
Occupational class					
Professional/managerial	%	34	39	26	163
Intermediate	%	33	45	18	361
Working class	%	38	50	10	351
Educational attainment					
Degree or higher	%	28	40	30	182
Below degree level	%	40	45	14	426
No qualifications	%	31	54	11	211
Whether the respondent has a child living in household					
Child in household	%	41	56	12	365
No child in household	%	32	46	19	563
All	%	35	46	16	913

Base: England only

When we turn to views on maintenance grants and student loans, the differences by occupational status and educational background become more pronounced. Most people in most groups think that *some* students should receive grants, but support for *all* students receiving grants is highest among working-class respondents (24 per cent) and those with no qualifications (23 per cent). This compares with

15 per cent of people from professional and managerial backgrounds and 16 per cent of graduates. These latter groups provide the strongest support for students being expected to take out loans: 56 per cent of managerial and professional respondents and 51 per cent of graduates, compared with 36 per cent of working-class respondents and 31 per cent of those without qualifications. Conversely, 46 per cent of people from working-class backgrounds and 45 per cent without qualifications say students should not be expected to take out loans; falling to 34 per cent among professionals and managers and 37 per cent among graduates. So, the even balance between views about loans that we find across the public as a whole does not exist for these particular social groups.

These findings provide some support for the suggestion that an 'elitist' strand of opinion might exist among graduates and the managerial and professional classes that wants to reduce access to higher education and make those who do reach university pay for it themselves. They also suggest that people who have not been to university tend to be more broadly 'egalitarian' in their thinking, believing that access to higher education should continue to grow and that students should receive state funding.

Another possible explanation for these differences of view might be that they reflect people's self-interest. As a way of testing the extent of people's self-interest or altruism, we compared the responses from people with children in the household, with those who did not have children living with them. Support for increasing higher education opportunities is higher among those who have a child living in the household (41 per cent) compared with those without a child in the household (33 per cent). This suggests that self-interest does play a role in determining the views of parents of a child who could go on to university.[1]

Links between attitudes
The coalition government – like the previous Labour government – has argued that the nation cannot afford current or future levels of participation in higher education unless students themselves carry more of the costs. But does the wider public make this connection? To find out, we analysed our data to see which strands of opinion on university expansion are linked to particular views about tuition fees.

Table 5.4 suggests that people do not generally see any connection between increasing fees and the continued expansion in higher education. Instead, those who think students should not pay tuition fees are the most likely to want participation in higher education to increase (42 per cent), while those who believe that all students should pay fees are the least likely to favour expansion (19 per cent). While acknowledging that nearly half the population in England think that current levels of university access are "about right", we can still interpret these findings in terms of the distinction between a minority of 'elitists' who oppose expansion and support fees, and another of 'egalitarians' who favour expansion but oppose fees being charged to students.

 The minority who believe that there should be fewer places in higher education consists disproportionately of people who have been to university themselves

Having investigated these links – and the way that they diverge from the defence of policy mounted by both the current government and its predecessor – we turn, finally, to people's views in relation to their support for political parties.

Table 5.4 Attitudes towards higher education opportunities, by attitudes towards university fees

	Who should pay towards tuition costs?			
	All students/ families should pay	Some students/ families should pay	No students/ families should pay	All
Higher education opportunities...	%	%	%	%
...should be increased	19	37	42	35
...are about right	54	45	44	46
...should be reduced	22	16	13	16
Base	113	638	146	913

Base: England only

Attitudes and support for political parties

Do Conservative voters align themselves with the party's election commitment to expand university entrance? Do Labour supporters share the outgoing government's support for tuition fees and for a higher proportion of young people attending university? Most interesting of all, are the views of Liberal Democrat supporters closer to the party's opposition to charging students' tuition fees during the election, or to its support for fees once in government?

As with the general public in England, we find that people who think the level of higher education opportunities is "about right" are the largest single group among supporters of each of the main parties (Conservative and Labour 46 per cent, Liberal Democrat 45 per cent). Nevertheless, a noticeably higher proportion of Conservative supporters (25 per cent) favour a reduction in opportunities, than those aligned with the Liberal Democrats (15 per cent), or Labour (12 per cent), or those stating no party affiliation (eight per cent). Similarly, although 27 per cent of those who identify with the Conservatives want increased university opportunities for young people, the proportion of Labour (40 per cent) and Liberal Democrat (38 per cent) supporters saying the same is higher. So, about a quarter of Conservative supporters appear to agree with the party's manifesto policy of creating 10,000 extra places in higher education, but another quarter endorse a policy of reducing access.

The most remarkable feature of the responses on tuition fees is not the differences of view between supporters of different parties, but the similarities. Prior to the 2010 UK general elections, the Liberal Democrats took a distinctive position against tuition fees, and they are perceived to have been damaged among the electorate by their *volte-face* on this issue once they joined the coalition government. We might therefore have expected to see strong anti-fees attitudes among Lib Dem supporters in 2010, but, as Table 5.5 shows, this is not the case.

Instead, views of the three major parties are remarkably similar. Comparable proportions of Liberal Democrat supporters (76 per cent), Labour supporters (70 per cent) and Conservatives (74 per cent) think that some students or their families should pay fees. Only a small minority of 13 per cent of Liberal Democrat supporters believe no students or their families should pay, while the largest minority opposed to students paying their own tuition fees is among those who do not identify with any party at all (23 per cent).

Table 5.5 Attitudes towards university fees, by party identification

| | Party identification | | | | |
	Conser-vative	Labour	Liberal Demo-crat	None	All
Who should pay towards tuition costs?	%	%	%	%	%
All students/families should pay	15	14	11	11	13
Some students/families should pay	74	70	76	67	71
No students/families should pay	11	16	13	23	16
Base	270	249	125	162	913

Base: England only

Table 5.6 shows that when it comes to living costs, Labour supporters and the unaffiliated appear to be the most likely to support universal grants (24 per cent in each case) compared with 18 per cent of Conservative and 17 per cent of Liberal Democrat supporters. However these are not significant differences, and overall the three major parties are similar in their views on grants. A majority of all groups supported the view that some but not all students should receive grants.

On the issue of student loans, however, the differences of opinion between party supporters are not only more marked, but also reveal a striking change of alignment. While rather more than half of Conservative supporters (53 per cent) say students should be expected to take out loans, a similar proportion of Liberal Democrat supporters (52 per cent) maintain the opposite view. The views of Labour supporters lie in-between, but considerably closer to Liberal Democrat supporters. Thus, intriguingly, Liberal Democrat supporters are closest to Conservative supporters on the issue of tuition fees and grants, but closer to Labour supporters on loans. Whether this remains the case following the coalition government's decision to raise tuition fees is, for the time being, a matter for conjecture. It is certainly surprising that people who identify with the Liberal Democrats are less exercised about university tuition fees than about the somewhat different issue of loans.

Table 5.6 Attitudes towards grants and loans, by party identification

	Conservative	Labour	Liberal Democrat	None	All
			Party identification		
Who should receive grants?	%	%	%	%	%
All students should get grants	18	24	17	24	21
Some students should get grants	73	68	76	66	70
No grants should be given	5	3	3	2	4
It depends	4	3	3	4	4
Base	*270*	*249*	*125*	*162*	*913*
Should students be expected to take out loans?	%	%	%	%	%
Students should be expected to take out loans	53	40	37	40	43
Students should not be expected to take out loans	34	46	52	39	42
It depends	13	13	11	16	13
Base	*270*	*249*	*125*	*162*	*913*

Base: England only

Conclusions

There has been a clear change in attitudes towards higher education funding over time towards greater support for tuition fees and a decline in opposition towards loans. In the case of tuition costs, we can see that the change is not so much a consequence of opinions altering slowly over time as a fall in public opposition to fees between 2007 and 2010. This suggests that hardening support for students paying their own way through university may be linked to the financial crisis in the late-2000s. Nevertheless, support for student grants has not declined in the same way. Of course, the actual level of the fee increases to up to £9,000 that has emerged has surprised many, and we will need to wait for the next survey to see how this has affected attitudes.

The Liberal Democrats pledged to abolish tuition fees for students taking their first degree if they were elected in 2010, a policy which clearly differentiated them from the other main parties in England, and they appear to have been damaged politically by their decision to drop this policy when they entered into coalition with the Conservatives. So, it is surprising that only a fraction of Liberal Democrat supporters are entirely opposed to fees. This indicates that support for the Liberal Democrats manifesto position was low even among Liberal Democrat supporters, although this may not apply in constituencies with large student populations, where the Liberal Democrats campaigned particularly strongly on an anti-fees platform. We also need to bear in mind that party affiliation is not the same thing as voting behaviour, as people may vote for a party that they do not identify with for tactical reasons – and around 17% of respondents had no party affiliation. However, it may be that it is the appearance of untrustworthiness in breaking a pledge that has damaged the Liberal Democrats as much as the substance of the policy itself.

The Liberal Democrats are, meanwhile, not the only party whose higher education policies appear somewhat out of tune with those of their declared supporters. More Labour supporters oppose the policy of expecting students to take out loans to cover their living costs than support it. Conservative supporters are the most likely to think that students should be expected to take out loans, but also the most strongly in favour of reducing access to university – a view that contrasts with the expansion pledge in the party's 2010 manifesto.

Party politics aside, we have seen that the public does not seem wholly convinced by the proposition that young people's access to university should continue to expand and that tuition fees and student loans are the way to make this affordable. Most people think that levels of participation in higher education are either 'about right' or already too high. And while a majority agree that some students should pay tuition fees, opinion is evenly divided on the question of whether they should be expected to take out loans. Some have argued that free higher education is a subsidy to the middle classes, as they are the most likely to benefit from higher education. This argument would suggest the hypothesis that respondents from manual occupations should be most likely to support tuition fees. However, our analysis shows that the opposite is the case. Opposition to fees and loans and support for grants is highest among the manual groups and those without degree level qualifications. However, overall, class differences in attitudes towards higher education fees are perhaps surprisingly small.

We can conclude from this that support for further expanding higher education enjoys broadly the same demographic base as opposition to tuition fees and loans, coupled with support for maintenance grants. Our analysis also demonstrates that people who support charging tuition fees to students and who expect them to take out maintenance loans are more likely than others to call for a reduction in the number of university places. There is little evidence that people's opinions are driven by a calculation of their immediate self-interest. Significant and consistently opposed minorities do, however, appear to hold views that reflect something approaching a class-based interest or ideology. The middle classes and existing graduates are more likely to seek to protect the value of their investment in higher education by restricting access to it, while those in manual occupations and without a university degree are more likely to wish to reduce barriers to participation.

Notes

1. As a further test of self-interest we compared the responses from parents who told us it was fairly or very likely that their children would go on to higher education, with those who said it was not likely. Since the latter group constituted a very small proportion of our overall sample (36 respondents) we do not place much weight on the analysis. However it is interesting to note that support for reducing university opportunities is at a similar level among those who think it likely their children will attend university, and the few parents who think their child is unlikely to go on to higher education (45 per cent compared with 47 per cent).

References

Conservative Party (2010), *Invitation to join the Government of Britain: The Conservative Manifesto*, available at www.conservatives.com/Policy/Manifesto.aspx (accessed 18/8/11)

Department for Business, Innovation and Skills (2010), *Draft Higher Education (Higher Amount) (England) Regulations 2010*, CM 7986, London: The Stationery Office, available at www.official-documents.gov.uk/document/cm79/7986/7986.pdf (accessed 18/8/11)

Department for Business, Innovation and Skills (2011), *Participation rates in Higher Education: Academic Years 2006/2007–2009/2010 (provisional)*, available at stats.bis.gov.uk/he/ Participation_Rates_in_HE_2009-10.pdf (accessed 18/8/11)

Browne, J. (2010), *Securing a Sustainable Future for Higher Education, An Independent Review of Higher Education Funding and Student Finance*, available at www.bis.gov.uk/assets/biscore/ corporate/docs/s/10-1208-securing-sustainable-higher-education-browne-report.pdf (accessed 18/8/11)

Liberal Democrats (2010), *Manifesto 2010. Change that works for you: Building a fairer Britain*, available at www.libdems.org.uk/our_manifesto.aspx (accessed 18/8/11)

Scottish Government (2010), *Scotland says no to tuition fees*, available at www.scotland.gov.uk/ News/Releases/2010/06/04093741 (accessed 18/8/11)

Welsh Government (2010), *Wales unveils future of fees*, available at wales.gov.uk/newsroom/ educationandskills/2010/101130fees/?lang=en (accessed 18/8/11)

Acknowledgements
The *National Centre for Social Research* is grateful to the Department for Business, Innovation and Skills (BIS) for their financial support which enabled us to ask the questions reported in this chapter. The views expressed are those of the authors alone.

Appendix
The data for Figure 5.1 are shown below.

Table A.1 Trends in views on the level of higher education participation, 1983–2010

	1983	1985	1987	1990	1993	1994	1995	1999
Opportunities for young people to go on to higher education...	%	%	%	%	%	%	%	%
...should be increased	44	48	52	49	48	49	47	43
...are at the right level	49	43	43	44	47	47	47	48
...should be reduced	5	5	3	2	3	2	3	4
Base	*1495*	*1538*	*2402*	*1205*	*1260*	*996*	*1090*	*920*
	2000	**2002**	**2003**	**2004**	**2005**	**2006**	**2007**	**2010**
Opportunities for young people to go on to higher education...	%	%	%	%	%	%	%	%
...should be increased	44	45	50	33	37	39	41	35
...are at the right level	48	46	37	47	46	46	45	46
...should be reduced	5	5	11	17	15	13	13	16
Base	*959*	*2897*	*2767*	*2684*	*1796*	*2775*	*2617*	*913*

Base: England only

6. Environment
Concern about climate change: a paler shade of green?

Environmental disasters around the world have provided recent reminders of the challenges facing our planet. How has public concern and behaviour in this area evolved in recent years? Have they been affected by events such as the 'climategate' row over scientific evidence and the onset of recession?

Public concern about the threat posed by different types of environmental pollution declined over the past decade, and scepticism concerning the seriousness of such threats increased.

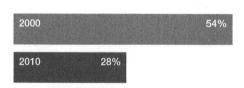

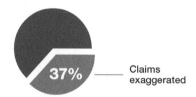

28% regard **air pollution from cars** as "very" or "extremely" dangerous to the environment, down from 54% in 2000.

37% think many claims about **environmental threats are exaggerated**, up from 24% in 2000. The proportion who think it is "definitely true" that fossil fuels contribute to climate change has fallen from 35% to 20%.

Some green behaviours are much more common than others, and, aside from recycling, are most likely to be practised by those who are concerned about the environment.

39%
Reduce energy
use at home

Recycling is now very common, but other forms of **environmentally-friendly behaviour** are far less common. Four in ten (39%) reduce energy use in the home and just two in ten (19%) cut back on driving the car.

Higher rates are found among those who think the rise in the world's temperature caused by climate change is dangerous, half (52%) of whom reduce their energy use in the home.

Author: Eleanor Taylor*

On the face of it, there should be few political or social issues more epic or pressing than those concerning the environment and the future of our planet. To quote Sir Nicholas Stern's report to the British government on the economics of climate change (2006):

> The scientific evidence is now overwhelming: climate change is a serious global threat, and it demands an urgent global response

A decade ago, there was strong evidence from *British Social Attitudes* that the public agreed. The 2000 survey showed that a large majority of people were concerned about the threat of rising temperatures and air pollution from cars and industry, and that this concern was increasing (Christie and Jarvis, 2001). The following decade has seen a succession of international catastrophes, from drought, flooding and deforestation to major oil leaks that have – irrespective of any specific link to climate change – kept issues of environmental pollution to the fore. In addition to well-publicised international incidents like Hurricane Katrina and the disaster at BP's Deepwater Horizon oil rig in the Gulf of Mexico, Britain itself experienced destructive flooding in Cornwall in 2004, in Cumbria the following year and across the country during the summer of 2007. These are all reasons why we might anticipate that concern about risks to the environment, not least carbon emissions linked to climate change, might have increased over the past 10 years. Politically, we can also observe how all the main parties have sought to emphasise their climate-friendly credentials; not least the Conservatives who gave environmental issues a central role in their re-branding under David Cameron and campaigned in the 2008 local elections under the slogan: "Vote blue – go green". Indeed, within days of forming his coalition administration with the Liberal Democrats in 2010, Mr Cameron told civil servants that he wanted it to be "the greenest government ever".

However, as we start to examine whether opinion in Britain has kept pace with the nation's policy makers, we may also note other reasons why the public might be less concerned about environmental issues. For example, in 2004 a public opinion survey found that terrorism, in the wake of the 9/11 attack in New York three years earlier, had displaced climate change as the most serious perceived threat to the world (Norton and Leaman, 2004). More recently, political and media commentators who reject the science of climate change have made much of a sequence of leaked emails between researchers at the University of East Anglia (UEA). These were alleged to show that data had been manipulated or withheld to strengthen the case for climate change. The international furore over 'climategate' was widely reported in 2009; not least in the United States where the Republican Vice-Presidential candidate, Sarah Palin, claimed that man-made climate change had been disproved. Although independent investigations subsequently cleared the UEA scientists of any tampering with research data, the negative publicity at the time may have shaken some people's trust in the science concerning man-made climate change. We might also anticipate that recession and other negative economic circumstances have influenced people's views. Unemployment increased in the two years preceding the 2010 *British Social*

* Eleanor Taylor is a Researcher at the *National Centre for Social Research* and a Co-Director of the *British Social Attitudes* survey series.

Attitudes survey and the financial 'pinch' was felt especially by people on lower incomes, as food, fuel and other prices rose through 2009 and 2010. We know from existing studies that issues such as the economy and unemployment are seen as higher priorities for the government than dealing with pollution and the environment (Thornton, 2009), and that people are reluctant to take action to help the environment if personal cost is involved (Lynn and Longhi, 2011). So it follows people may no longergive environmental issues such priority in their own lives – particularly if they feel there is a price that they are no longer willing to pay themselves for reducing levels of pollution.

British Social Attitudes sought people's views on the environment in 1993, 2000 and most recently in 2010. This chapter uses data from those three years to examine trends in the public's level of concern about dangers posed by pollution, climate change and other environmental hazards. To gain a more detailed impression of the way opinion has shifted, we also draw on annual data collected between 2005 and 2010 monitoring views on the impact of transport on climate change. We look at changing levels of activism and environmentally-friendly behaviour before launching an exploration of possible reasons for the trends that are highlighted by our analysis.

Dangers to the environment

We first consider whether public concern about environmental issues has increased or diminished in the last 10 years. To do this, we compare the responses in 1993, 2000 and 2010 to questions that measure the perceived danger of five specific threats to the environment. These are: "air pollution caused by cars", "air pollution caused by industry", "pesticides and chemicals used in farming", "pollution of Britain's rivers, lakes and streams" and "a rise in the world's temperature caused by climate change".[1] For each of these we asked respondents whether they think it is:

extremely dangerous for the environment

very dangerous

somewhat dangerous

not very dangerous, or

not dangerous at all for the environment

Table 6.1 shows the percentage of people in each of the three years who consider each pollutant or threat to be "very dangerous" or "extremely dangerous" to the environment. From this we can see that less than half the population (43 per cent) currently consider climate change to be dangerous for the environment. If anything,

43%

consider climate change to be dangerous for the environment

people are rather more concerned by air pollution from industry (48 per cent) and water-borne pollution (46 per cent). Just 28 per cent think that air pollution caused by cars is dangerous for the environment.

We can also see a clear decline since 2000 in the perceived threat posed by different pollutants to the environment. On all but one of the measures (pesticides and chemicals in farming), the level of concern has dipped below that first recorded in 1993. The most dramatic fall is in perceptions of the risk posed by air pollution from cars, which has declined by 26 per cent since 2000 when 54 per cent considered it dangerous to the environment. There have also been decreases over the past decade in the perceived danger of air pollution from industry (15 percentage points), water pollution (16 points), and pesticides and chemicals used in farming (12 points). This decline in concern about dangers to the environment echoes the findings of other recent studies, for example, a study funded by the Department for Transport found that concern about climate change has fallen significantly since the mid-2000s (Department for Transport, 2011).

The decline in concern contrasts with the increases that occurred between 1993 and 2000 in relation to all the listed threats, apart from climate change. It could be that these changes in outlook reflect a view that specific pollution threats, widely publicised in the 1980s and 1990s, have since been tackled effectively. The fitting of pollution-filtering catalytic converters on new cars and the phasing out of leaded petrol may have convinced many motorists that their cars – despite continued concern about carbon emissions – are no longer such a threat to the environment. Action to clean up the Thames, the Mersey and other rivers once notorious for the extent of industrial pollution has produced positive news stories about the increasing diversity of fish and other wildlife now found in their waters. A widening choice of organic and pesticide-free produce in shops and supermarkets may further explain why people have become less concerned by the use of chemicals in farming. Even so, it is a striking discovery that people tend to be less alarmed by environmental hazards than 10 years ago. Remarkably, this decline in concern about climate change has occurred after repeated warnings from the UN Intergovernmental Panel on Climate Change (IPCC, 2007), the Stern report (2006) and others that the issues must be tackled faster and more effectively to avoid catastrophic long-term consequences around the world.

Table 6.1 Perceived danger of threats to the environment, 1993–2010

	1993	2000	2010
% who consider these "very" or "extremely dangerous" to the environment			
Air pollution from industry	54	63	48
Air pollution caused by cars	48	54	28
A rise in the world's temperature caused by climate change[1]	51	50	43
Pollution of Britain's rivers, lakes and streams	61	62	46
Pesticides and chemicals used in farming	37	49	37
Base	*1261*	*972*	*928*

To gain further insight into people's thinking, we asked two further questions inviting people to agree or disagree with statements about the way that society in general treats environmental issues:

We worry too much about the future of the environment and not enough about prices and jobs today

People worry too much about human progress harming the environment

Knowing that concern about pollution and climate change has decreased in the past decade; we might expect to find an accompanying increase in support for these statements, suggesting that concern for the environment has been overplayed. The results, presented in Table 6.2, confirm this. The percentage agreeing that too much emphasis is placed on the environment and not enough on prices and jobs is eight points higher than in 2000 (43 per cent compared with 35 per cent) and the proportion agreeing that people worry too much about human progress harming the environment is up by seven points (35 per cent compared with 28 per cent). Meanwhile disagreement with both statements has fallen considerably since 2000. Notably, for the first time in 2010 more people agreed than disagreed that we worry too much about the environment and not enough about prices and jobs (43 per cent compared with 34 per cent).

Table 6.2 Views on public concern about the environment, 1993–2010

	1993	2000	2010
We worry too much about the future of the environment and not enough about prices and jobs today	%	%	%
Agree	36	35	43
Neither	13	13	20
Disagree	48	50	34
People worry too much about human progress harming the environment	%	%	%
Agree	30	28	35
Neither	18	22	25
Disagree	47	46	36
Base	*1261*	*972*	*928*

This suggests that the public has not only become less concerned about the threat posed by different types of pollution, but is also rather more sceptical that a problem really exists.

'Green' activism and environmentally-friendly behaviour

Before considering the reasons for this loss of concern in more detail, we will briefly look at trends in people's participation in activities related to environmental protection and 'green' activism. While the key focus of the chapter is environmental attitudes, it is also important that we consider behaviour, and the relationship this has with concern about environmental issues. We asked respondents whether they had taken part in any of the following activities in the last five years:

...signed a petition about an environmental issue?
...given money to an environmental group?
...taken part in a protest or demonstration about an environmental issue?

We also asked:

Are you a member of any group whose main aim is to preserve or protect the environment?

The questions are designed to identify different levels of commitment. So it comes as little surprise to discover in Table 6.3 that more people take part in 'non-committal' activism, such as signing a petition (22 per cent) or giving money (16 per cent), than in environment-related protests or demonstrations (three per cent). But we also see there has been a marked decrease in the levels of participation compared with 20 years ago – although this only applies to non-committal activism. For example, the proportion who say they have given money to an environmental group is 13 points lower than in 1993. Involvement in committed environmental activism has stayed at a low, but stable level. Six per cent say they are members of an environmentalist group, and three per cent have taken part in a demonstration about an environmental issue.

Table 6.3 Taking part in environmental activism, 1993–2010

	1993	2000	2010
% who...			
...have signed a petition about an environmental issue	36	30	22
...have given money to an environmental group	29	23	16
...have taken part in a protest or demonstration about an environmental issue	3	3	3
...are a member of a group to protect the environment	6	6	6
Base	*1261*	*972*	*928*

35%

agree people worry too much about human progress harming the environment

We also asked respondents how often they engaged in a number of environmentally-friendly behaviours, by making "a special effort" to:

...sort glass or tins or plastic or newspapers and so on for recycling
...buy fruit or vegetables grown without pesticides or chemicals

They were also asked how often they:

...cut back on driving the car for environmental reasons
...reduce the energy or fuel you use at home for environmental reasons
...choose to save or re-use water for environmental reasons
...avoid buying certain products for environmental reasons

Table 6.4 shows that the vast majority of people (86 per cent) say they "always" or "often" make an effort to recycle. This is followed by 39 per cent who reduce their energy use at home, 37 per cent who make an effort to buy organic fruit and vegetables and 32 per cent who practise water conservation. Twenty-eight per cent avoid buying certain products for environmental reasons. A rather lower proportion of one in five (19 per cent) say they cut back on driving, but the response when the question was previously asked shows that this is on an upward trend (from 14 per cent in 2000 and nine per cent in 1993). As we see in our chapter on transport, there is widespread recognition among the public that individuals should reduce their car use for the sake of the environment – though many have not done so, even while recognising it would be as easy to make particular journeys by alternative modes of transport. Although trend data does not exist for all the behaviours, we can also see a much more striking increase in the proportion of the population who make efforts to recycle. Ten years ago it was 35 points lower at 51 per cent, and in 1993 it stood at just 42 per cent. We can reasonably expect that the driving force behind this major change in behaviour has been the legislation introduced in 2003 which required all English local authorities to provide doorstep recycling collections.[2]

Table 6.4 'Environmentally-friendly' behaviours, 1993–2010

	1993	2000	2010
% Always/often...			
...make an effort to recycle	42	51	86
...reduce energy use in the home	n/a	n/a	39
...make an effort to buy fruit and vegetables grown without pesticides/chemicals	20	n/a	37
...choose to save/re-use water	n/a	n/a	32
...avoid buying certain products	n/a	n/a	28
...cut back on driving the car	9	14	19
Base	*1261*	*972*	*928*

n/a = not asked

There is, however, a clear disparity between the rates of recycling identified and people's involvement in other environmentally-motivated behaviours. A possible explanation is a contrast between the ease with which people can nowadays put out their recycling for collection and the inconvenience that many people might experience from making less use of their cars. Meanwhile, fruit and vegetables grown without pesticides and chemicals are generally more expensive than non-organic food, suggesting cost may be another reason why people may choose not to behave in a more environmentally-friendly manner.

It seems, generally, that people may be less likely to change their behaviour for the sake of the environment if this will cost them money, time or effort. If they are also feeling less worried about climate change they may feel there is even less reason to alter their behaviour, but is there evidence supporting a link between environmentally-friendly behaviours and concern about the environment?

In Table 6.5 we see that rates of recycling do not differ according to level of concern about the danger of climate change; in fact even among those who believe climate change is not dangerous to the environment, 85 per cent say they always or often recycle. However behaviours that require more radical lifestyle change, such as reducing energy use and driving less, are clearly associated with concern about climate change. For example, around half (52 per cent) of those who believe climate change is dangerous say they regularly reduce energy use in the home, compared with only a fifth (21 per cent) of those who believe it is not dangerous. A similar pattern is evident for cutting back on driving, with 28 per cent of those showing concern about climate change doing this regularly compared with 16 per cent of those who are not concerned.

Table 6.5 'Environmentally-friendly' behaviours, by perceived danger of climate change

| | Rise in world's temperature caused by climate change is... | | | |
	...dangerous	...somewhat dangerous	...not dangerous	All
% Always/often...				
...make an effort to recycle	89	86	85	86
...reduce energy use in the home	52	35	21	39
...cut back on driving the car	28	13	16	19
Base	*392*	*335*	*120*	*928*

The nature of the associations between concern and actions seen in Table 6.5 highlight the ascension of recycling to a national social norm. Furthermore we see the importance of the role of public concern about perceived dangers to the environment in engaging people in environmentally-motivated behaviours. We now return to the search for reasons why people in Britain are significantly less concerned about the environment than they were 10 years ago.

Understanding changes in levels of concern

The measures of concern for the environment we have described so far do not allow us to consider trends in people's views at points in time between 2000 and 2010. This makes it difficult to ascertain whether there was a sudden downturn, or whether the downward trend occurred more slowly over time. Fortunately we are able to examine the responses to three further questions about travel in the context of climate change. Every year since 2005 we have asked:

...how concerned are you about the effect of transport on climate change?

We have also asked respondents to say how much they agree or disagree with the following statements:

The current level of car use has a serious effect on climate change

The current level of air travel has a serious effect on climate change

Table 6.6 shows that there has been a decline in public concern about the effect of transport on climate change since 2006, and that a particularly sharp fall occurred between 2009 and 2010. In 2009, 75 per cent of people said that they were concerned about the effect of transport on climate change, but this fell to 68 per cent a year later. A similar pattern can be seen for the questions about car use and air travel. While 73 per cent said that car use has a serious effect on climate change in 2009, this dropped to 64 per cent in 2010. Similarly 71 per cent in 2009 said that air travel has a serious effect on climate change, falling to 66 per cent in 2010. We also see in our chapter on transport, which focuses on the environmental dangers of car use in more detail, that concern about exhaust fumes specifically is in decline; 81 per cent were concerned about this in 2005, compared to 70 per cent now.

Table 6.6 Views on the effect of transport on climate change, 2005–2010

	05	06	07	08	09	10
% concerned about the effect of travel on climate change	80	81	76	74	75	68
% agree that car use has a serious effect on climate change	77	80	72	73	73	64
% agree that air travel has a serious effect on climate change	64	74	70	72	71	66
Base	*1101*	*3220*	*3094*	*3364*	*3421*	*3297*

Explaining changing attitudes

Earlier we described the possible effect that the changing economic climate might have on levels of environmental concern. The banking and financial crisis of recent years first hit in 2008, a year or so before the downturn in concern between 2009 and 2010 illustrated in Table 6.6. So there is no conclusive proof here of a link between Britain's economic woes and declining environmental concern. However, this does not rule out a relationship between the two; there could have been some delay before the financial crisis was felt by individuals to the point where it altered the priority they placed on environmental issues.

Another potential explanation for the changing attitudes we have observed is the influence of climate change sceptics in the media and the extensive coverage given to the 'climategate' affair of 2009–2010. To examine this possibility we can consider how people respond to a question inviting them to agree or disagree that:

Many of the claims about environmental threats are exaggerated

They are also invited to say whether the following statement is "definitely true", "probably true", "probably not true" or "definitely not true":

Every time we use coal or oil or gas, we contribute to climate change[3]

Although it is the consensus view among scientists that the burning of carbon-based fuels is a major cause of climate change, Table 6.7 suggests there has been significant increase in public scepticism that this is so since 2000. A decade ago, a quarter (24 per cent) of respondents agreed that many claims about environmental threats are exaggerated; but in 2010 this has risen to 37 per cent. Fewer people, meanwhile, fully accept that fossil fuels contribute to climate change. For example, where 35 per cent in 2000 believed it was 'definitely' true that personal use of fossil fuels contributes to climate change, only 20 per cent are nowadays so certain. Around half say it is probably true (51 per cent), while 17 per cent think it is probably or definitely untrue.

Table 6.7 Scepticism about climate change, 2000, 2010

	2000	2010
Many claims about environmental threats are exaggerated	%	%
Agree	24	37
Neither agree nor disagree	25	26
Disagree	45	32
Every time we use coal or gas or oil we contribute to climate change[3]	%	%
Definitely true	35	20
Probably true	46	51
Definitely/Probably not true	12	17
Base	*972*	*928*

Can we be quite sure that the rise in scepticism about environmental threats is related to declining levels of concern about climate change and other issues? Table 6.8 compares people's replies to our question about the degree of danger posed by the world's rising temperature with their views on whether claims about environmental threats have been exaggerated, and whether use of fossil fuels contributes to climate change. We can think of those who agree with the statement "many claims about environmental threats are exaggerated" as climate change 'sceptics' and those who disagree as 'believers' in climate change. In 2000, 34 per cent of the sceptics described a rise in the world's temperature as "very" or "extremely" dangerous, compared with 60 per cent of believers. But this distinction appears even stronger in 2010, when just 24 per cent of sceptics show concern about the world's rising temperatures, compared with 73 per cent of believers.

Table 6.8 Agreement that a rise in the world's temperature is dangerous to the environment, by climate change scepticism, 2000, 2010

	% Agree that a rise in world's temperature is very/extremely dangerous			
	2000	*Base*	**2010**	*Base*
Many claims about environmental threats are exaggerated				
Agree (sceptics)	34	235	24	345
Neither agree nor disagree	37	236	36	225
Disagree (believers)	60	343	73	233
Every time we use coal or gas or oil we contribute to climate change[3]				
Definitely true (believers)	75	329	76	164
Probably true	43	442	48	470
Definitely/Probably not true (sceptics)	29	123	10	162
All	50	972	43	928

We see a similar pattern when comparing views about whether use of fossil fuels contributes to climate change. In 2000, 75 per cent of those who said it definitely contributes to what was then widely referred to as the 'greenhouse' effect agreed that rising temperatures are particularly dangerous, while 29 per cent of 'sceptics' (despite doubting the contribution made by burning fossil fuels) said the same. Again in 2010 this effect was more pronounced, with just 10 per cent of 'sceptics' agreeing that a rise in temperatures is dangerous.

We can, therefore, see that climate change scepticism has not only grown since 2000, but is also directly linked to a decline in concern about the effects of climate change. This, coupled with the notable fall in concern about the effect of transport on climate change between 2009 and 2010, means we may reasonably suspect that the drop in public concern about the environment is to some extent connected with the media furore surrounding the 2009 'climategate' affair.

Changing views among social groups

By examining the views of different social groups, we will now try to find out which sections of society are most concerned about the threat from climate change, which are the most sceptical and which – over a 10 year period – have demonstrated the greatest tendency to change. Table 6.9 shows changes in the perceived danger of air pollution from cars, and a rise in world temperature caused by climate change by age, educational attainment, level of income and identification with a political party.

The expression of strong concern about climate change has declined markedly among three particular groups: older people, those with the lowest educational qualifications, and those in the lowest income groups. Thus in 2000, people over 65 were less likely than other age groups to regard a rise in world temperature as alarming (47 per cent). But in 2010, little more than a quarter (28 per cent) view it as particularly dangerous. Meanwhile people aged 55–64, who were the most likely to show strong concern (56 per cent) in 2000, have become rather less worried (43 per cent) than younger people; the age groups whose view have changed least since 2000. In terms of educational background, we see that the biggest decline in serious concern about climate change has been among people without qualifications (from 47 per cent to 28 per cent), while the proportion of graduates considering it particularly dangerous to the environment is around the same level as a decade earlier. A comparable pattern emerges in relation to income where views among people in the lowest income quartile are the most likely to have changed (from 54 per cent to 37 per cent), and the proportion of those in the highest income quartile is around a half, and has not altered.

Data on party political sympathies, meanwhile, reveals some distinct differences. Conservative supporters (38 per cent) are markedly less likely to show strong concern about the environmental consequences of global warming than those who lean towards Labour (49 per cent) or the Liberal Democrats (55 per cent). However, while the level of concern among Conservative and Liberal Democrat sympathisers is much the same as in 2000, concern among Labour supporters shows a modest five point decline.

While concern about climate change has only decreased among certain demographic groups, all groups saw a considerable drop in concern about the danger of pollution from cars. This holds true even among groups that have remained stable in their level of concern about climate change. For example, concern about car pollution among younger people aged 18–34 has declined by 18 points since 2000, from 51 per cent to 34 per cent. Likewise, concern about car pollution among those with degree level education has fallen by almost a quarter, from 62 per cent to 39 per cent.

37%

agree that many claims about environmental threats are exaggerated

Table 6.9 Concern about the dangers to the environment, by demographic group, 2000 and 2010[4]

	% "Extremely dangerous" or "very dangerous" to the environment					
	Air pollution from cars			Rise in world's temperature caused by climate change		
	2000	2010	% change	2000	2010	% change
Age						
18–34	51	34	-18	52	48	-3
35–54	54	27	-27	49	48	-1
55–64	58	29	-29	56	43	-13
65+	56	21	-35	47	28	-19
Educational attainment						
Degree or higher	62	39	-23	61	63	1
Below degree level	53	26	-27	49	42	-7
No qualifications	51	25	-26	47	28	-19
Household income (quartiles)[5]						
Lowest quartile	59	27	-32	52	37	-15
2nd lowest quartile	53	28	-26	48	36	-11
2nd highest quartile	57	31	-26	55	50	-5
Highest quartile	47	27	-20	49	52	3
Party identification						
Conservative	45	21	-24	40	38	-2
Labour	60	32	-28	54	49	-5
Liberal Democrat	61	36	-25	56	55	-1
All	54	28	-26	50	43	-7

Since age, educational background, income and political inclination are interrelated; our next step is to apply statistical controls to discover whether any one of these factors is particularly influential in predicting concern about climate change. (A more detailed account of our regression analysis can be found in the appendix at the end of this chapter.) From this, we find that educational qualifications and party identification are strongly related to the level of concern that people express. However, after taking account of education and age, income ceases to be a significant predictor of people's views. Overall, educational attainment and political party identification explain much of the variation in levels of concern about pollution from cars, while only educational attainment was found to account for the variation in concern about climate change.

Financial sacrifices

Notwithstanding our finding that income does not predict people's concerns about climate change independently of their age and educational background, we can strongly suspect that it influences their willingness to pay for environmental protection out of their own pockets. The *British Social Attitudes* survey asks:

How willing would you be to pay much higher prices in order to protect the environment?

And how willing would you be to pay much higher taxes in order to protect the environment?

And how willing would you be to accept cuts in your standard of living in order to protect the environment?

Given the deterioration in Britain's economic fortunes during recent years, we would expect people's willingness to pay higher prices and taxes to have decreased since last measured in 2000. Table 6.10 shows that this is not only the case among people living on low incomes, but across the income distribution. Whereas, 43 per cent a decade ago said they would be willing to pay higher prices to protect the environment, this is nowadays only true of 26 per cent. There has been a similar fall in the proportion prepared to pay higher taxes (31 to 22 per cent), but a smaller decline in relation to cuts in the standard of living (26 per cent to 20 per cent). We can see equivalent increases in the proportion of respondents who say they would be unwilling to do these three things for the sake of the environment.

People in the lowest income quartile are rather less willing than others to accept cuts in their living standards to protect the environment (54 per cent), but the proportion among the highest income quartile saying the same is not hugely different, having risen from 40 per cent in 2000 to 48 per cent. There is little difference in the levels of opposition to higher taxes across all four groups, but willingness to pay more to help the environment (while lower than in 2000) is greater among those with higher incomes. People in the highest income quartile are more willing than others to accept higher prices (36 per cent), but this is well below the proportion 10 years earlier (52 per cent). Although we do not have any data for the intervening years, we can continue to suspect that the recession and its aftermath are implicated in the way that people's views have changed. However, we may also be witnessing a two-way process where reduced willingness to make sacrifices for the sake of the environment is linked to rising levels of scepticism, and *vice versa*.

26%

say they would be willing to pay higher prices to protect the environment, down from 43% a decade ago

Table 6.10 Willingness to make sacrifices for the sake of the environment, 2000 and 2010, by income band (quartiles)

	2000					2010				
	Household income (quartiles)[5]				All	Household income (quartiles)[5]				All
	Lowest quartile	2nd lowest quartile	2nd highest quartile	Highest quartile		Lowest quartile	2nd lowest quartile	2nd highest quartile	Highest quartile	
Pay much higher prices	%	%	%	%	%	%	%	%	%	%
Willing	43	37	42	52	43	23	24	27	36	26
Unwilling	27	25	26	21	24	40	39	41	30	38
Pay much higher taxes	%	%	%	%	%	%	%	%	%	%
Willing	29	24	35	41	31	17	17	28	27	22
Unwilling	38	43	42	33	40	49	49	51	47	50
Accept cuts in your standard of living	%	%	%	%	%	%	%	%	%	%
Willing	21	25	28	32	26	19	16	19	29	20
Unwilling	51	50	48	41	48	54	51	51	48	53
Base	*295*	*221*	*212*	*174*	*972*	*233*	*173*	*184*	*205*	*928*

Conclusions

Having established in this chapter that public concern about climate change and a range of other environmental issues has declined in Britain over the past decade, we have explored some of the potential reasons for this. These principally relate to the way people have been affected by the recession and economic hardship and to the fact that there is greater public scepticism about the science of climate change than 10 years ago.

The rise in public scepticism may be connected with a sense of environment 'fatigue'

We have seen that income, although correlated with serious concerns (or a lack of them) about climate change, is not directly implicated after taking account of people's age and educational background. But we have also observed a large decline among people on the lowest incomes in assessments of the danger level created by global warming and in their personal willingness to pay higher prices in order to protect the environment. Since we have also seen a significant dip between 2009 and 2010 in concerns about the effect that car use and air travel have on climate change, there is a case for thinking that economic uncertainties have, indeed, played a part in making people less concerned about pollution and the consequences of climate change. Economic recovery, if and when it comes, may serve to restore flagging public interest in tackling environmental challenges – especially if it restores people's willingness to accept more of the personal cost implications.

The evidence also suggests, not surprisingly, that greater scepticism about climate change has influenced the extent to which people view climate change as dangerous. The timing of the fall in concerns about car and air travel points the finger more specifically in the direction of the 'climategate' row that erupted towards the end of 2009. Notwithstanding the way that the charges levelled at climate change science, and scientists, have since been nullified, it seems the initial publicity may have exerted a disproportionate influence on British public opinion. From this we conclude that media coverage may make a difference – not least 'new' media and the internet 'blogosphere' where unfounded opinion can sometimes be favoured over scientific fact.

Another possibility we must consider in the light of these findings is that the rise in public scepticism may be connected with a sense of environment 'fatigue'. People, despite their exposure to mounting evidence concerning the negative future consequences of climate change, may have come to feel over time that climate change has little to do with them personally or their lives. We know from existing research that people who feel distant geographically or chronologically from the impact of environmental threats, tend to think of them as a problem affecting 'other people' (see, for example, Lorenzoni *et al.*, 2005). They may also consider that the problems that come closest to their daily experiences, such as car emissions and river pollution are being tackled and that there is less to worry about than 10 or 20 years ago.

As we have seen, there is a link between people's concern about climate change and their engagement in environmental behaviours. However it is those behaviours that involve a higher personal cost, both financially and in terms of lifestyle change, that are most strongly linked with environmental concern. If the government is to increase the prevalence of such behaviours among the general public, addressing levels of concern and scepticism about the causes of climate change may be a logical place to start.

Notes

1. The wording of this question differed in 2010 to that used in 2000 and 1993. In the two earlier surveys we asked: *"In general, do you think that a rise in the world's temperature caused by the 'greenhouse effect' is…"* The 2010 survey replaced the term 'the greenhouse effect' with 'climate change' to reflect the changing terminology being used between 2000 and 2010 in discourse surrounding the greenhouse effect and its consequences in terms of climate change and global warming.

2. The Household Waste Recycling Act of 2003 required that English local authorities introduce kerbside collections for at least two types of recyclable waste by the year 2010. The act in full is available at www.legislation.gov.uk/ukpga/2003/29/pdfs/ukpga_20030029_en.pdf

3. The wording of this question differed in 2010 to that used in 2000 and 1993. In these earlier surveys we asked: *"Every time we use coal, oil or gas, we contribute to the greenhouse effect"*. The 2010 survey replaced the term 'the greenhouse effect' with 'climate change'. The reason for this is discussed in Note 1.

4. Bases for Table 6.9 are as follows:

| | % "Extremely dangerous" or "very dangerous" to the environment | | | |
| | Air pollution from cars | | Rise in world's temperature caused by climate change | |
	2000	2010	2000	2010
Age				
18–34	257	187	257	187
35–54	382	347	382	347
55–64	125	175	125	175
65+	207	218	207	218
Education				
Degree or higher	130	202	130	202
Qualification below degree	552	428	552	428
No qualifications	269	207	269	207
Household income (quartiles)				
Lowest quartile	295	233	295	233
2nd lowest quartile	221	173	221	173
2nd highest quartile	212	184	212	184
Highest quartile	174	205	174	205
Party identification				
Conservative	274	280	274	280
Labour	409	279	409	279
Liberal Democrat	89	129	89	129
All	972	928	972	928

5. Household income quartiles in Tables 6.9 and 6.10 are as follows: for 2000, the lowest quartile is £10,000 or less per year, the second lowest quartile is £10,001 to £20,000 per year, the second highest quartile is £20,001 to £34,999 per year, the highest quartile is £35,000 or more per year; for 2010 the lowest quartile is £12,000 or less per year, the second lowest is £12,001 to £26,400 per year, the second highest is £26,401 to £44,400 per year, and the highest quartile is £44,401 or more per year.

References

Christie, I. and Jarvis, L. (2001), 'How green are our values?' in Park, A., Curtice, J., Thomson, K., Jarvis, L. and Bromley, C. (eds.), *British Social Attitudes: the 18th Report – Public policy, Social ties*, London: Sage

Department for Transport (2011), *Attitudes to climate change and its impact on transport,* available at www.dft.gov.uk/statistics/releases/attitudes-to-climate-change-and-its-impact-on-transport-august-2010

Intergovernmental Panel on Climate Change (2007), *Climate Change 2007 – Synthesis Report.* Geneva: United Nations Intergovernmental Panel on Climate Change

Lynn, P. and Longhi, S. (2011), 'Environmental attitudes and behaviour: who cares about climate change?' *Understanding society: early findings from the first wave of the UK's household longitudinal study*, Colchester: Institute for Social and Economic Research, University of Essex

Norton, A. and Leaman, J. (2004), *The day after tomorrow: Public opinion on climate change,* London: MORI Social Research Institute

Poortinga, W. and Pidgeon, N. F. (2003), *Public perceptions of risk, science and governance – Main findings of a British survey on five risk cases*, Technical Report, Centre for Environmental Risk, Norwich: University of East Anglia

Stern, N. (2007), *The Stern Review: the Economics of Climate Change*, Cambridge: Cambridge Press

Thornton, A. (2009), *Public attitudes and behaviours towards the environment – tracker survey: A report to the Department for Environment, Food and Rural Affairs*, available at www.defra.gov.uk/statistics/files/report-attitudes-behaviours2009.pdf

Acknowledgements

The *National Centre for Social Research* would like to thank the Economic and Social Research Council (grant number RES-501-25-5002) and the Department for Transport for their financial support which enabled us to ask the questions reported in this chapter. The views expressed are the author's alone.

Appendix

The multivariate analysis technique used is logistic regression – more details can be found in Appendix I of the report. The dependent variable for Table A.1 is whether the respondent thinks that air pollution from cars is "extremely" or "very dangerous", rather than "somewhat", "not very" or "not dangerous at all". A positive coefficient indicates that the group is more likely than the reference group (shown in brackets) to think air pollution from cars is dangerous while a negative coefficient indicates the group is less likely than the reference group to think it is dangerous.

Table A.1 Logistic regression on whether people think that air pollution from cars is dangerous to the environment

	Coefficient	Standard error	p value
Sex (male)			
Female	0.192	0.156	0.218
Age (18–34)			0.515
35–54	-0.123	0.208	0.553
55–64	0.059	0.250	0.814
65+	-0.289	0.269	0.283
Household income quartiles			
(lowest quartile)			0.479
Second lowest quartile	-0.129	0.242	0.593
Second highest quartile	-0.264	0.247	0.286
Highest quartile	-0.451	0.266	0.090
Education (Degree)			0.002
Higher education below degree	-0.318	0.269	0.237
A level or equivalent	-0.540	0.265	0.042
O level or equivalent	**-0.948	0.250	0.000
No qualifications	**-0.817	0.277	0.003
Party identification (Conservative)			0.034
Labour	**0.605	0.207	0.003
Liberal Democrat	0.398	0.250	0.111
Other party	0.334	0.222	0.133
Constant	-0.476	0.344	0.166

Base: 883

* significant at 95% level
** significant at 99% level

The dependent variable for Table A.2 is whether the respondent thinks that a rise in the world's temperature caused by climate change is "extremely dangerous" or "very dangerous", rather than "somewhat", "not very" or "not dangerous at all". A positive coefficient indicates that the group are more likely than the reference group (shown in brackets) to think climate change is dangerous to the environment while a negative coefficient indicates the group are less likely than the reference group to think it is dangerous.

Table A.2 Logistic regression on whether people think that a rise in the world's temperature caused by climate change is dangerous to the environment

	Coefficient	Standard error	p value
Sex (male)			
Female	0.103	0.146	0.483
Age (18–34)			0.090
35–54	0.153	0.198	0.442
55–64	0.064	0.240	0.789
65+	-0.474	0.257	0.065
Household income quartiles			
(lowest quartile)			0.975
Second lowest quartile	-0.141	0.230	0.540
Second highest quartile	-0.085	0.232	0.715
Highest quartile	0.021	0.247	0.933
Education (Degree)			0.000
Higher education below degree	-0.146	0.263	0.579
A level or equivalent	-0.440	0.250	0.079
O level or equivalent	**-1.021	0.232	0.000
No qualifications	**-0.956	0.268	0.000
Party identification (Conservative)			0.131
Labour	0.358	0.192	0.062
Liberal Democrat	0.359	0.233	0.123
Other party	0.015	0.204	0.941
Constant	0.257	0.329	0.435

Base: 847

* *significant at 95% level*
** *significant at 99% level*

7. Transport
Congested Britain?
Public attitudes to car use

The coalition government's transport strategy aims to tackle traffic congestion and the environmental damage caused by car use by improving public transport, promoting the use of low emission vehicles and changing public behaviour in relation to short journeys. Understanding public attitudes is vital, to determine how these strategies will work in practice.

Concern about the negative impacts of car use is widespread, particularly in relation to environmental damage, but it has declined.

43% view **congestion** in towns and cities as a serious problem (down from 52% in 2001).

A clear majority are concerned about **exhaust fumes** from traffic (70%) and the effect of transport on climate change (68% – but this has fallen by 12 percentage points since 2005).

There is little public appetite for strategies to reduce car use, though a majority recognise people should do this for the sake of the environment. But there is clear capacity for changing public behaviour in relation to short car journeys.

57%

There is little support for **charging for road use**; just one in five think people who drive on busy roads (19%) or at the busiest times (18%) should pay more. But more than half (57%) agree that those who drive cars that are better for the environment should pay less to use the roads than others.

43%

63% of people make a **journey of less than two miles** by car at least once a week. Around four in ten say they make journeys by car that could easily be completed by walking (41%), by cycling (43%) or on the bus (35%).

Author: Eleanor Taylor*

Car and van travel currently accounts for 64 per cent of all trips made, and 78 per cent of all distance travelled in Britain (Department for Transport, 2011c).[1] The public's reliance on cars as their main mode of transport poses a problem for government as current levels of car use cause congestion on the roads and have a range of negative environmental impacts. This chapter examines what the public thinks about the negative impacts of car use, and explores views on various policy options to reduce these effects.

Recent governments have discussed and introduced a range of strategies to tackle congestion and the environmental impacts of car use. The 10 Year Plan, published by the Labour government in 2000, included a key aim of reducing congestion by 2010 (Labour, 2000). However, transport policy experienced a lack of continuity in leadership – by 2004 there had been eight transport ministers – and commentators viewed the aims of the 10 Year Plan as effectively abandoned (e.g. *The Independent*, 19 January 2004). The current coalition government aims to tackle the problem of the environmental impacts of driving, primarily by promoting and facilitating the adoption of low emission vehicles. In tackling congestion on the roads, the coalition government policy focuses on improving the flow of traffic on the existing road network rather than increasing road capacity (Department for Transport, 2011a).

In *The 24th Report*, Stradling *et al.* (2008) noted a high level of public concern about the effects of car travel on the environment and found popular support for a reduction in car use. Here, we use data from the 2010 *British Social Attitudes* survey to present an up-to-date picture of public attitudes to the negative impacts of car use and potential policies to reduce it. We begin by examining attitudes to congestion and the environmental impacts of car use and how these have changed over time. Next, we consider reactions to and support for various strategies for reducing car use that have been implemented or considered – including increasing road capacity and a range of initiatives to change public behaviour. Drawing the findings together, we consider what our findings mean for the coalition government. Is the government's aim to reduce the negative effects of car use widely supported by the public? And how might the public react to various strategies for achieving this?

Negative impacts of car use

We first consider whether the public regards current levels of car use as problematic, in terms of causing congestion and damage to the environment. We asked respondents the following question about congestion:

Now thinking about traffic and transport problems, how serious a problem ***for you*** *is...*

> *...congestion on motorways?*
> *...traffic congestion in towns and cities?*

....

* Eleanor Taylor is a Researcher at the *National Centre for Social Research* and a Co-Director of the *British Social Attitudes* survey series.

Figure 7.1 shows responses to these items since they were first asked in 1997. Traffic congestion in towns and cities is more widely viewed as problematic; 43 per cent state congestion in towns and cities is a serious problem, compared to 26 per cent who think this about motorways. Unsurprisingly drivers are more likely than non-drivers to view urban congestion (46 per cent compared with 35 per cent), and congestion on motorways (29 per cent compared with 19 per cent) as problematic. Nevertheless, more than one in three non-drivers view congestion in towns and cities as a serious problem, presumably because of journeys they have taken as passengers in cars or taxis, or on buses.

In *The 20th Report* Exley and Christie (2003) concluded that congestion in towns and cities was perceived to be less of a problem than in previous years. It was considered that, while this could result from improvements such as traffic diversions, it could also be that people had become more used to, and accepting of, congestion as part of their day-to-day lives. With more recent strategies to reduce congestion such as the introduction of the London congestion charge in 2003, and with a slow but steady decrease in car use since the early 2000s (Department for Transport, 2011b) we might logically expect agreement with the view that congestion is a problem to have declined further.

While the proportion who view congestion as a serious problem in towns and cities has reduced considerably since 2000, when 72 per cent thought this, the bulk of this reduction took place between 2000 and 2001, when this proportion fell by 20 percentage points. As noted in *The 20th Report* this change is likely to be the result, at least in part, of a change in the questionnaire. The question had been asked immediately after a question about rural congestion until 2000, after which the rural congestion question was dropped from the questionnaire (Exley and Christie, 2003). Since then, the proportion considering urban congestion to be a problem has fluctuated around the 50 per cent mark, though a further, less marked, decline of seven percentage points occurred between 2009 and 2010. The proportion viewing congestion on motorways as a problem has remained relatively stable since the question was first asked in 1997. However, the current proportion of 26 per cent is the lowest recorded for this question.

43%

think congestion in towns and cities is a serious problem, 26% think congestion on motorways is a serious problem

Figure 7.1 Views on congestion on motorways and in towns and cities, 1997–2010
% saying congestion is a serious problem

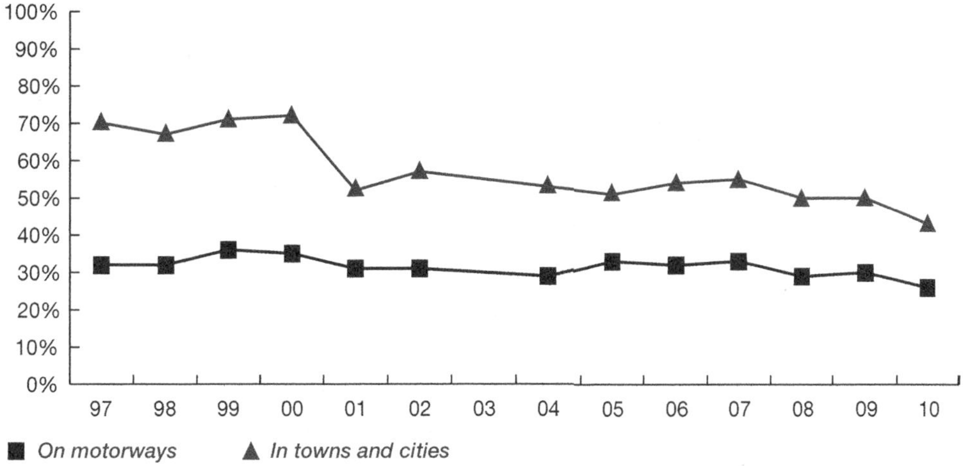

■ On motorways   ▲ In towns and cities

The data on which Figure 7.1 is based can be found in the appendix to this chapter

We have seen that congestion in towns and cities is viewed as less of a problem than it used to be. But what about the environmental impacts of car use? We asked respondents the following questions to gauge their level of concern about this issue:

How concerned are you about exhaust fumes from traffic?

How concerned are you about the effect of transport on climate change?[2]
[Very concerned, fairly concerned, not very concerned, not at all concerned]

Comparing the results from Figure 7.1 with Table 7.1, we see that the environmental effects of transport are of greater public concern than traffic congestion. Seven in ten in each case say they are very or fairly concerned about the effect of transport on climate change and about exhaust fumes from traffic. Nevertheless, levels of concern have fallen since 2009, by seven percentage points in both instances. Indeed, concern about both issues appears to have been in a period of gradual decline since 2006. There are a number of possible reasons for this, discussed in greater detail in our chapter on the environment, which highlights a general decline in concern and a rise in scepticism about environmental dangers. It points to a dramatic fall in the perception of the risk posed by air pollution from cars, (in 2000, 54 per cent considered this to be dangerous to the environment, a proportion which has now declined by 26 percentage points). Given this context, we might expect a reduction in public concern about the environmental impact of road transport.

The environmental effects of transport are of greater public concern than traffic congestion

Table 7.1 Concern about the environmental impacts of transport, 2005–2010

	05	06	07	08	09	10
% concerned about exhaust fumes	81	82	79	74	76	70
% concerned about the effect of transport on climate change	80	81	76	74	75	68
Base	1101	3220	3094	3364	3421	3297

Despite the overall decline in concern, around seven in ten express concern about exhaust fumes and the effect of transport on climate change, while four in ten still view urban congestion as a problem. Given such widespread concern about the effects of car use, we now turn to examine public attitudes to the strategies that would ultimately address these issues.

Ways of reducing car use and congestion
A number of strategies for reducing car use and traffic congestion have been proposed or implemented in recent years. We now assess how palatable these would be to the public.

Increasing road capacity
One way to reduce traffic congestion is to increase road capacity. However, this approach would not negate the environmental impacts of car use – and could potentially increase them, by encouraging further car use, or by causing damage to the countryside. To explore attitudes to this approach, we asked a range of questions about the effects of increasing road capacity. Respondents were also asked whether they agreed or disagreed that:

The government should build more motorways to reduce traffic congestion[3]

Building more roads just encourages more traffic

We also asked the following question:

How concerned are you about damage to the countryside from building roads? [Very concerned, fairly concerned, not very concerned, not at all concerned]

The responses, presented in Table 7.2, show higher opposition than support for the building of more motorways to reduce congestion. While three in ten agree the government should do this, almost four in ten disagree. The fact that around three in ten neither agree nor disagree suggests some indecision or ambivalence – perhaps not surprising, as we saw earlier that only a minority view congestion on motorways as a problem in the first place. There is also a widespread awareness of the potentially negative effects of increasing road capacity on both congestion and the environment; more than six in ten express concern about the damage to the countryside from building roads while around four in ten agree building more roads just encourages more traffic.

Table 7.2 Attitudes to road-building

	All
Government should build more motorways to reduce congestion	%
Agree	30
Neither agree nor disagree	28
Disagree	38
Base	*928*
Agreement that building roads just encourages more traffic	%
Agree	44
Neither agree nor disagree	21
Disagree	31
Base	*928*
Concern about damage to the countryside from building roads	%
Concerned	64
Not concerned	36
Base	*3297*

Overall, the public do not tend to favour building more roads as a strategy for reducing congestion. What, then, are public attitudes towards reducing car use within the existing road infrastructure through changing public behaviour?

Changing public behaviour
We begin by exploring perceptions of the responsibility of individual motorists to reduce their car use for the sake of the environment – as it was envisaged that attitudes to this issue would influence individual willingness to reduce car use. We asked respondents whether they agreed or disagreed with the following statements:

People should be allowed to use their cars as much as they like, even if it causes damage to the environment

For the sake of the environment everyone should reduce how much they use their cars

6 in 10

agree that everyone should reduce how much they use their cars for the sake of the environment

Their responses, presented in Table 7.3, demonstrate majority support for the idea that everyone should reduce how much they use their cars for the sake of the environment; almost six in ten agree with this sentiment. However, support is far from unanimous – and nearly three in ten agree people should be allowed to use their cars as much as they like, regardless of environmental damage. We might expect the latter view to be more popular among drivers, as non-drivers might have stopped using, or chosen not to own a car, because of environmental concerns. The results are not so straightforward. In fact a similar proportion of drivers and non-drivers agree that people should be allowed to use their cars as much as they like (28 per cent compared with 23 per cent), however drivers are less likely to disagree with the statement (29 per cent compared with 41 per cent).

Table 7.3 Views on car use and the environment

	All
For the sake of the environment everyone should reduce how much they use their cars	%
Agree	58
Neither agree nor disagree	23
Disagree	15
Base	*3,297*
People should be allowed to use their cars as much as they like, even if it causes damage to the environment	%
Agree	27
Neither agree nor disagree	36
Disagree	33
Base	*3,297*

While a majority think motorists should reduce their car use for the sake of the environment, this could only happen in practice if viable alternatives for completing individual journeys were available. The coalition government has a specific target to increase the number of short journeys (defined as being five miles or less) made by walking, cycling or public transport (Department for Transport, 2011a). In the 2010 *British Social Attitudes* survey, we explored the potential for such a strategy to reduce car use, focusing on the shortest of these journeys – those of two miles or less. When we asked respondents how many such journeys they made by car in a typical week, around two in three (63 per cent) reported making at least one such

63%

make a journey of two miles or less by car at least once a week

journey, indicating a strategy to reduce car use, targeting short journeys, could have considerable impact. To explore the viability of such a strategy, we asked respondents whether they agreed or disagreed with the following statements:

Many of the journeys of less than two miles that I now make by car I could just as easily...

> *...walk*
> *...go by bus*
> *...cycle, if I had a bike*

As shown in Table 7.4, around four in ten feel that they make short car journeys that they could just as easily make by walking (41 per cent), by bus (35 per cent) or cycling (43 per cent), as by car. Many therefore feel they could just as easily complete their journeys by another mode of transport – yet have not done so. This is despite the fact that majorities of each group feel people should reduce their car use for the sake of their environment – 66 per cent, in each case, of those who could just as easily complete their short journeys by walking, by bus, or by cycling. There appears to be a barrier in translating the sentiment that motorists should reduce their car use for the sake of the environment into individual practice. In fact, as shown in our chapter on the environment, just 19 per cent of drivers say that they have cut back on driving the car for environmental reasons – indicating a sizeable proportion think individuals should be doing this, but have not done so yet themselves.

Table 7.4 Views on making short car journeys less often by walking, taking the bus or cycling

	All
% agree many car journeys of less than two miles could be made as easily...	%
...walking	41
...by bus	35
...cycling, if I had a bike	43
Base	*2,791*

It may therefore be the case that more coercive measures are needed to reduce car use, by making the car a less attractive option for completing particular journeys. We focus our attention on this range of strategies next.

Many feel they could just as easily make their short journeys without their car – yet have not done so

Charging for road use

An alternative way of tackling car use is through discouraging travel by car, by making it less attractive. One way of doing this that has been discussed, and implemented in certain areas, is to charge drivers who drive on busy roads or at the busiest times, providing a disincentive to adding to congestion. The current government has chosen not to use this approach in tackling congestion, but what are the public's views on this type of policy? We asked people how much they agreed or disagreed with the following statements:

People who drive on busy roads should pay more to use the roads than people who drive on quiet roads

People who drive at the busiest times should pay more to use the roads than people who drive at other times

People who drive at busy times only do so because they have no other alternative

People who drive cars that are better for the environment should pay less to use the roads than people whose cars are more harmful to the environment

It is too complicated to charge drivers different amounts depending on when and where they drive

We analysed the views of those living in London separately, as this city has had direct experience of a congestion scheme since the London Congestion Charge was introduced in 2003.

As shown in Table 7.5, there is little support for charging people who drive on busy roads or at busy times; just one in five support each of these strategies. The low support for such schemes is likely to reflect their inherent flaw; in many areas of the country, people have no alternative to using their cars to travel to work, for example. This argument is upheld by the fact that more than six in ten feel people who drive at busy times only do so because they have no other alternative. Another flaw is the complication of implementing such an approach, with almost seven in ten agreeing it is too complicated to charge drivers different amounts depending on when and where they drive. Interestingly though, we do find majority support for the idea that those who drive cars which cause less damage to the environment should be charged less than those who do not – almost six in ten agree with such a strategy.

Those living in London exhibit higher support for congestion charging schemes, compared with those living elsewhere. For example, those living in London are more likely to show support for charging those who drive on busy roads (27 per cent

1in5

support charging people who drive on busy roads or at busy times

compared with 17 per cent) and charging those who drive at busy times (27 per cent compared with 16 per cent).[4] It could be that such schemes are unpopular in theory, but are viewed more positively once the public has seen them operate in practice. Perhaps people have become aware of the benefits of the London scheme, and have changed their opinions as a result. However, perhaps a more significant reason for the higher level of support in London is the high standard of alternative methods of transport available.

Clearly, across Britain as a whole, there is little support for charging motorists for use of the roads as a way of reducing congestion. However there is majority support for lower charges for cars that are environmentally friendly.

Table 7.5 Views on charging drivers different amounts, by area

	Inner and outer London	Outside of London	All
% agree people who...			
...drive on busy roads should pay more	27	17	19
...drive at the busiest times should pay more	27	16	18
...drive at busy times only do so because they have no other alternative	61	65	65
...drive cars that are better for the environment should pay less to use the roads than people whose cars are more harmful to the environment	50	58	57
% agreeing			
It is too complicated to charge drivers different amounts depending on when and where they drive	63	68	67
Base	*267*	*2,524*	*2,791*

Conclusions

Public concern about both traffic congestion and the environmental damage caused by car use has declined, nevertheless, the majority of the public remains concerned about the impact of transport on the environment, and urban congestion is still a serious problem for many. A key challenge for the coalition government will be translating this sentiment into practice and achieving changes in public behaviour.

A key challenge for the coalition government will be translating this sentiment into practice and achieving changes in public behaviour

In tackling the problem of congestion, the government's current strategy focuses on improving traffic flow on existing roads, an approach which is likely to be well-received given that the public has little appetite for building new roads. The avoidance of schemes that penalise those using busy roads may also be a popular decision among the general public, not least because, if such schemes were to be put in place, it is felt that many drivers would have no alternative ways of making their journeys. However, with considerable public support for a reduction in car use for the sake of the environment, how can the government attempt to reduce the number of cars on the road? Perhaps the most promising avenue would be to focus on short journeys – as a sizeable proportion of the public agree that many of these could be made just as easily by an alternative mode of transport. Yet, the fact that many continue to use cars for such journeys, suggests that translating attitudes that are supportive of reducing car use into actual behaviour change, is likely to be a particular challenge.

Notes

1. It should be noted that this follows a slight decrease in car use since the mid-1990s. Figures from the National Travel Survey (NTS) show that the number of car trips taken as a driver has fallen by five per cent since 1995–97, while the number of car trips taken as a passenger has fallen by 11 per cent since 1995–97 (Department for Transport, 2011b).

2. The question about climate change asks about all forms of transport, rather than just road transport, meaning respondents may have also considered air travel when responding to it. However, due to the location of the question in a set of questions about road transport, this can be seen to provide a good indication of concern about the effect of road transport on the environment.

3. This question refers to building more motorways specifically; it is possible that respondents' attitudes to motorway building differ from their attitudes to road building in general.

4. Support for charges for drivers at busy times and on busy roads is highest among people living in inner London, however due to the small base size of those living in inner London, this analysis groups together inner and outer London residents.

References

Department for Transport (2011a), Business Plan 2011–2015, available at http://assets. dft.gov.uk/publications/business-plan-2011-2015/DFT-Business-Plan.pdf

Department for Transport (2011b), National Travel Survey 2010: How people travel, available at http://assets.dft.gov.uk/statistics/releases/national-travel-survey-2010/nts2010-03.pdf

Department for Transport (2011c), National Travel Survey 2010 Statistical Release, available at http://assets.dft.gov.uk/statistics/releases/national-travel-survey-2010/nts2010-01.pdf

Exley, S. and Christie, I. (2003), 'Stuck in our cars? Mapping transport preferences', in Park, A., Curtice, J., Thomson, K., Jarvis, L. and Bromley, C. (eds), British Social Attitudes: the 20th Report – Continuity and change over two decades, London: Sage

Grice, A. and Clement, B. (2004), 'Prescott's ten-year plan for integrated transport is dead', The Independent, available at www.independent.co.uk/news/uk/politics/prescotts-tenyear-plan-for-integrated-transport-is-dead-573674.html

Labour (2000), Transport Ten Year Plan 2000, available at http://webarchive.nationalarchives.gov.uk/+/http:/www.dft.gov.uk/about/strategy/whitepapers/previous/transporttenyearplan2000

Stradling, S., Anable, J., Anderson, T. and Cronberg, A. (2008), 'Car use and climate change: do we practise what we preach?', in Park, A., Curtice, J., Thomson, K., Phillips, M., Johnson, M. and Clery, E. (eds.), *British Social Attitudes: the 24th Report,* London: Sage

Appendix
The data for Figure 7.1 are shown below.

Table A.1 Views on congestion on motorways and in towns and cities, 1997–2010													
	97	98	99	00	01	02	04	05	06	07	08	09	10
% saying congestion is a serious problem...													
...on motorways	32	32	36	35	31	31	29	33	32	33	29	30	26
...in towns and cities	70	67	71	72	52	57	53	51	54	55	50	50	43
Base	*1355*	*1075*	*1031*	*1133*	*1099*	*1148*	*1053*	*1101*	*3220*	*3094*	*3364*	*3421*	*3297*

8. Housing
Homes, planning and changing policies

Public opinion affects the direction and consequences of housing policies and may become even more influential following the government's decision to allow greater local control over planning decisions. At a time of regional housing shortages, people's views could prove critical in deciding whether and what type of new development goes ahead.

Opposition to new homes is strongest in the south of England, where housing shortages are most severe. However, most people accept that some new homes are needed and those who initially say they would not support development can be swayed if plans include new amenities for their community.

45%
Oppose new homes

Across Britain people who oppose more **homes being built** in their area outnumber supporters by 45% to 30%. In the south of England, opposition is higher (50%) – and support lower (27%).

Developments that include side benefits like new employment, parks, schools and transport links would achieve a more even division of opinion in towns and suburbs of the south of England – although opponents would still outnumber supporters in rural areas.

While rising house prices and restricted access to mortgages have seen falling levels of home ownership in recent years, it remains the tenure of choice for the vast majority.

86%
Would buy
SOLD

32%
Say high rents a disadvantage

Given a free choice, 86 per cent would **buy their own home**, rather than rent. One in five (19%) say the main disadvantage of home ownership is the expense.

The perceived **disadvantages of renting** depend on the landlord. High rents are the most commonly cited disadvantage of renting from a private landlord, mentioned by 32%, while 39% say the main disadvantage of renting from a local authority or housing association is anti-social behaviour on estates.

Author: Glen Bramley*

Public attitudes play an important part in the formation of housing policies and in determining their consequences. People's views about the desirability of building new houses and the places where they are prepared to accept development can strongly influence their elected MPs and councillors. Widespread controversy about the possible consequences of the Draft National Planning Policy Framework (Department for Communities and Local Government, 2011b) illustrates the strength of opinion and emotion over this. However, the key feature of planning in Britain, reinforced by the government's decentralisation measures, is that the decisions about new development are predominantly in the hands of local elected representatives.

Known preferences between the three main types of tenure – home ownership (usually achieved through mortgage borrowing), 'social' renting from a local authority or housing association, and renting from a private landlord – are also influential. The electoral dividend that Margaret Thatcher's government enjoyed after giving social housing tenants the 'Right to Buy' their properties at discounts remains an outstanding example of this.

The social and economic context in which this chapter examines attitudes related to housing policy issues is, however, very different to 30 years ago. The housing market has experienced growing instability and uncertainties in recent years. Since housing questions were last included in the *British Social Attitudes* survey in 2005 a property boom has given way to a banking crisis and credit crunch characterised by mortgage rationing. A decline in the proportion and number of owner-occupied homes that started in 2003 has accelerated.

Recession and its aftermath have, meanwhile, exacerbated a decline in house building and sales from which recovery remains uncertain. The number of new homes completed in 201011 in England was the lowest since the 1920s (Oxford Economics, 2011). There are housing shortages across the South, both for 'affordable' social renting and to buy. House prices, despite a recessionary dip, remain at historically high levels. The counter-cyclical boost to public spending by the outgoing Labour government has, meanwhile, been replaced by the coalition government's focus on deficit reduction. Post-election budgets have seen cutbacks in the grants available for new social house building, while Housing Benefit paid to low-income tenants (in private as well as social housing) is being reduced.

In England, at least, the coalition government has signalled changes in the nature and function of social housing by questioning its current security of tenure and rights of access for homeless families. It argued that social housing should provide homes for those who need them most, but only for as long as they need them (Department for Communities and Local Government, 2010b, p.5). They also want to see greater use made of private rented housing for homeless households and other groups in need.

Against this background, we explore how public opinion may help or hinder efforts to increase the housing supply by asking people whether they support or oppose

....

* Glen Bramley is Professor of Urban Studies at Heriot-Watt University, Edinburgh.

new housing being built in their local area. To discover how far their opinions might be swayed we also find out whether those who are negative or non-committal about development are prepared to support new house building if it includes extra amenities or economic opportunities for the community. Recognising that the acceptability of new housing may also depend on the kind of property being proposed, we also investigate whether people perceive a greater need for some types of home and tenure than others.

The chapter then looks at attitudes concerning tenure itself. While the continued popularity of home ownership can be easily predicted, we know that policy makers and housing providers are having to take increasing account of households who would like to set foot on the ownership ladder, but are prevented by high local prices or restricted access to mortgages. We, therefore, report on people's views about the advantages and disadvantages of social and private renting and consider how these accord with the government's current efforts to reshape state support for tenants.

Attitudes to new house building

The outgoing Labour government sought to promote new housing and more affordable homes through targets determined by a regional planning system (Barker, 2004; Bramley, 2007). The Conservative-Liberal Democrat coalition government has swept away those 'top down' mechanisms as part of a cross-cutting 'localist' approach, where policies are made a matter of local choice. Despite some new financial incentives that the government has introduced for authorities that support new development (Conservatives, 2010; Department for Communities and Local Government, 2010a), local planning authorities have greater autonomy to decide how much housing to allow in their area. However, they must set that decision in an adopted plan backed by appropriate evidence if they are to be confident it will prevail over the broader planning principle of 'the presumption in favour of sustainable development' (Department for Communities and Local Government, 2011b).

Even under Labour, many local authorities proved reluctant to increase their planned levels of new homes; especially in the south of England where the pressures on the existing housing stock are greatest. While making it questionable whether the government's new financial incentives will succeed (Bramley, 2010), this suggests that residents holding NIMBY ("Not In My Back Yard") views may be in an even stronger position to sway local planning decisions under the new arrangements. But how far is that hypothesis supported by the latest evidence concerning public opinion?

A new survey question in 2010 asked people:

Would you support or oppose more homes being built in your local area?
[Strongly support, support, neither support nor oppose, oppose, oppose strongly]

45%

oppose more homes being built in their area

Table 8.1 shows that across Britain as a whole those opposed to more homes outnumber supporters by three to two (45 per cent versus 30 per cent).[1] While not quite forming a majority among all respondents, the opponents of local house building are in the majority among those who express a definite opinion, and especially among those who hold strong views (15 per cent strongly oppose local house building, while five per cent strongly support it).

Table 8.1 Support and opposition for more homes being built in local area, by tenure

| | Housing tenure | | | |
	Owners	Social Renters	Private Renters	All
	%	%	%	%
Support	24	48	36	30
Neither support nor oppose	23	18	25	22
Oppose	51	32	35	45
Base	*2220*	*599*	*443*	*3297*

Not unexpectedly, opposition to local house building is strongest among existing homeowners, (51 per cent compared with 24 per cent) who account for more than two-thirds of all households. By contrast, those who rent in the private sector are almost equally likely to support new homes as oppose them (36 per cent compared with 35 per cent), while those renting from a local authority or housing association are substantially in favour (48 per cent compared with 32 per cent). Given the public's general preference for home ownership (see below), support among tenants for development is likely to be driven by frustrated aspirations to buy, as well as a desire to see more homes being built for rent.

Regional differences

To better understand the implications of the opinions expressed nationally we next examine the findings by region.[2] This is because the availability of housing and its affordability in relation to local incomes varies widely by area, with the greatest need for new properties occurring in the south of England (Bramley and Karley, 2005; National Housing and Planning Advice Unit (NHPAU), 2009). The broad regional analysis in Table 8.2 shows that opposition to development is notably strongest in the South (excluding London) (50 per cent) and outer London (58 per cent). Within London, the equivalent figures reveal a striking contrast between the capital's outer areas and the more deprived boroughs of inner London, where the concentrations of rented housing are higher. In the former, opposition to new housing is particularly strong at 58 per cent, whereas in the latter the supporters of local development are in a clear majority (49 per cent compared with 31 per cent).

Across the rest of England – the Midlands and the North – positive support for development stands at 29 per cent, but the level of opposition is lower than in the South at 43 per cent.

Table 8.2 Support and opposition to more homes being built in local area, by region

	England				Wales	Scotland	All
	North & Midlands	South	Inner London	Outer London			
	%	%	%	%	%	%	%
Support	29	27	49	25	31	43	30
Neither support nor oppose	25	21	19	16	21	21	22
Oppose	43	50	31	58	47	34	45
Base	1432	1057	117	189	189	313	3297

Scotland stands out for showing overall positive support for new local house building (43 per cent compared with 34 per cent), while in Wales the levels of opposition (47 per cent) and support (31 per cent) are much the same as for Britain as a whole. This suggests that the devolved government in Scotland will tend to face less pressure from public opinion when determining housing policy than its Welsh counterpart.

In outer London and the south of England, where high house prices offer continuing testimony to an excess of demand over supply, it is apparent that residents do not generally favour new house building in their locality despite the evidence of need. Inner London appears a notable exception, but in this case there is little spare land to build on.

On the evidence of people's immediate responses to the possibility of new homes in their locality, the prospects for new building to address housing shortages in the south of England appear bleak. This, however, assumes that people who oppose development – alongside the one in five who say they neither support nor oppose it – cannot be persuaded to change their minds.

Incentives for supporting development
To find out how far incentives might serve to reduce opposition to local house building, we invited those who were uncommitted or actively opposed to development to consider some "advantages to local residents" that can occur when new homes are built. Shown a list of improvements to local amenities or economic opportunities, they were asked to say which, if any, would be "the main thing to make you support new homes".

 Scotland stands out for showing overall positive support for new local house building

Table 8.3 suggests that side benefits – known as 'planning gain' – do have the potential to secure greater support for housing developments, provided the incentives are realistically promised and delivered. While less than half those who were strongly opposed to development responded positively to the listed incentives, two-thirds of those less strongly opposed and nearly four-fifths of those without a clear initial view showed they could potentially be swayed.

The most persuasive single advantage identified is more employment opportunities, which 17 per cent of all those originally opposed to development or uncommitted give as a main reason to support new homes. However, new employment opportunities may prove more difficult for developers and local authorities to deliver than improved amenities such as green space and parks, which is the next most attractive incentive selected (11 per cent). The same proportion gives priority to new or improved transport links, followed by schools (eight per cent), leisure facilities (six per cent) and shops (five per cent). Relatively few people say they would support development on the basis of "financial incentives to existing residents" (two per cent).

Table 8.3 Incentives that could persuade those initially opposed to local house building (or uncommitted) to support it, by level of opposition

	Initial view on house building			
Main reason would support new homes	Neither support nor oppose	Oppose	Oppose strongly	All
	%	%	%	%
Employment opportunities	21	18	9	17
Green spaces and parks	15	9	9	11
Transport links	11	12	7	11
Schools	9	9	7	8
Leisure facilities	7	7	5	6
Shops or supermarkets	6	5	3	5
Medical facilities	4	5	4	4
Financial incentives to existing residents	2	2	2	2
None of these	22	31	54	23
Base	732	1000	498	2230

Question only put to those initially opposed to new homes in their area or uncommitted
Response options with less than two per cent of response were not included in this table

Given the range of views expressed, it seems that developers and local authorities should negotiate to assemble packages that consist of several side benefits. But this still begs the question of whether those packages would sway enough potential objectors and create a climate of local opinion where planning permission was more likely to be given. To find out some indication of the impact such planning gain incentives could achieve in different regions, we have used the opinion data to calculate potential levels of support for two different 'planning gain' packages.

One is focused on additional public services and facilities and the other on employment, transport and commercial facilities.[3] Our analysis[4] shows that either package is capable of securing majorities for new housing in most areas of the North and inner London. Both also seem likely to have a significant impact in the South and outer London. Even so, it seems probable that the opponents of development would continue to outnumber the supporters, albeit narrowly. For example, in the South and outer London, numbers supporting or opposing development would be equal in suburban and town locations, while in rural areas people were still more likely to oppose development than support it by between three and 14 per cent (depending on the package). Employment and transport improvements would sway more residents to support development in rural locations than public service improvements. In other words, 'planning gain' incentives may be crucial to securing public support for new housing in many localities where it is objectively needed, but they are probably not sufficient to overcome local objections in the most sensitive areas of the South.

Perceptions of housing need

Public perceptions of the types of new housing that are most needed are another important source of information for planners and for those seeking to influence planning decisions in favour of development. We showed people a list of property types and asked them:

If new homes were to be built in your local area, which, if any, of these types of homes do you think are most needed?

We then showed respondents a list of different types of tenure and asked them the same question.

Despite the levels of opposition to local development so far identified, Table 8.4 shows that only one in five respondents maintain that no new housing is needed in their area. However, at a time when the proportion of flats built in England has risen rapidly (Bramley *et al.*, 2010a) it is interesting that relatively few respondents (14 per cent) believe that more flats or maisonettes are what is needed most in their area. There is more support (35 per cent) for building new one and two-bedroom houses – typical 'starter' homes – and this may reflect a rising proportion of one and two-person households nationally, although there is similar support for family-sized three and four-bedroom homes. There is contrastingly little support (three per cent) for building large houses with five or more bedrooms, even though it is a market that some developers currently favour.

35%

would choose new houses in the area to be one and two-bedroom houses

Table 8.4 Type and tenure of new housing needed locally

	All
Types of new homes needed	%
No new homes needed	20
Flats/maisonettes	14
1–2 bedroom houses	35
3–4 bedroom houses	37
5+ bedroom houses	3
Bungalows	12
Base	*3297*
Tenures of new homes needed	%
No new homes needed	20
Homes to buy	27
Homes to rent from private landlords	8
Homes to rent from local authorities or housing associations	39
Homes to part-own and part-rent	25
Base	*3297*

Asked about tenures, more than a quarter of the public think the type of housing most needed locally is homes to buy, with a similar level of support for part-own/part-rent homes. But they are outnumbered by nearly four in ten (39 per cent) who consider that social housing for rent is the priority. Private renting is seen as the prime need by fewer than one in ten. Further analysis, not included in the table, shows that while social housing tenants are most likely to prioritise more of the same (66 per cent), a similar proportion of home owners give priority to homes for social renting (32 per cent) rather than to more housing for sale (31 per cent).

These findings suggest opportunities to garner support for new development by ensuring the proposed mix of tenure and housing types is matched to local needs and preferences. Doing this would require an emphasis on providing new council or housing association homes for rent. It also seems to imply a more interventionist approach at national or regional level than the deregulatory approach advocated by part of government (HM Treasury, 2011a).

Policies for affordable housing
Given the large minority who see subsidised social housing as a priority for their area, it is interesting to know whether people hold complementary views about the government's role in making housing more affordable. Respondents were asked:

If the government were going to do something to make homes more affordable, what do you think the most useful action would be?

Giving "some sort of financial assistance to first-time buyers" is the most popular choice (30 per cent) from a list of actions that government might take, although general across-the-board subsidy would be costly and could just push up prices. Shared ownership is a more targeted form of subsidy and this attracts moderate support at 11 per cent. Another 22 per cent say government should "get banks to increase access to mortgages", quite rightly highlighting the most critical current difficulty in the market. We can, therefore, see that the public's priorities are focused mainly on getting government help to would-be home owners.

In contrast with the previously-expressed views about a priority need for more social housing, only 19 per cent think government could most usefully "give more money to housing associations and local authorities to build social homes for those on low incomes". It is also worth highlighting how relatively few respondents (five per cent) think government should simply "allow developers to build more homes". This poses a challenge to the current consensus among many economists that increasing the supply of housing is important in the long term to make it more affordable (Barker, 2004; Office of the Deputy Prime Minister, 2005; National Housing and Planning Advice Unit, 2009).

Views about tenure

We now turn from the supply of new housing to the existing stock; and people's attitudes towards different forms of tenure. Policy makers, planners and housing providers have a self-evident interest in knowing whether the existing range of homes and tenures meets public expectations and aspirations. In recent years, for example, they have needed to take account of a growing number of people who would like to embark on home ownership but cannot afford it. Beyond this, the government's plans to reform social housing tenancies and Housing Benefit, referred to at the start of this chapter, add resonance and policy relevance to our findings about the perceived advantages and disadvantages of home ownership, private renting and tenancies in social housing.

Home ownership

For a quarter of a century, *British Social Attitudes* has charted the public's strong preference for living in homes that they own themselves. Yet, as previously noted, the actual level of home ownership has gone into decline. Since 2003 the proportion of owner-occupied homes has fallen from 71 per cent to 68 per cent in England, while an accelerating trend has seen an absolute decline of 280,000 owner-occupier households between 2007 and 2010 (Department for Communities and Local Government, 2011c). The suggested reasons include high prices, mortgage rationing and high deposit requirements for first-time buyers, as well as negative price expectations and perceptions of risk. But how far do results from the 2010 survey support this interpretation?

 The British public have a continued strong preference for living in homes that they own themselves

One question that has been repeatedly asked over time is whether people, given a free choice would "choose to rent their accommodation or buy". Comparing the response in 2010 with previous surveys in the 1990s, we find remarkable stability with 86 per cent expressing a theoretical preference for home ownership, compared with 87 per cent in 1999 and 84 per cent in 1996. However, the answers to a different question provide what is arguably a more sensitive barometer of people's pragmatic assessment of the housing market. This asks people:

Suppose a newly-married young couple, both with steady jobs, asked your advice about whether to buy or rent a home. If they had the choice, what would you advise them to do?

Figure 8.1 shows how proportions advising the young couple to "buy a home as soon as possible" or, more cautiously, to "wait a bit then try to buy a home" have fluctuated since 1986. It demonstrates how a peak of confidence in making an early purchase in the mid-1980s gave way to greater caution following the house-price slump of the early 1990s. Advice then became more positive up to 2004, when more than seven in ten respondents (71 per cent) recommended an early purchase and fewer than a quarter (24 per cent) thought it better to wait a bit. In 2008, amid the credit crisis and market downturn, there was a dramatic fall among those suggesting the couple should buy as soon as they could to a minority 45 per cent. The proportion urging delay rose to 40 per cent.

Figure 8.1 Advice for a young married couple (both working) about housing, 1986–2010

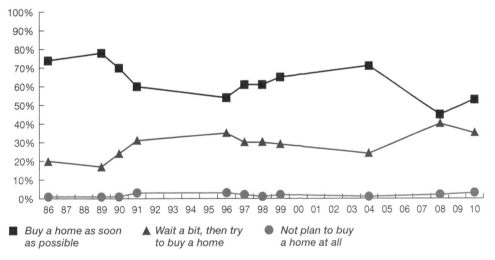

The data on which Figure 8.1 is based can be found in the appendix to this chapter

The 2010 survey shows a slight recovery in public confidence, with 53 per cent advising early entry into the housing market. But with 35 per cent encouraging the young couple to wait, there is still considerable caution.

Advantages and disadvantages of ownership
Another notable feature of the response to the 'advice' question is that even when market conditions have been at their most difficult, those guiding the newly-weds "not to plan to buy a home at all" have never exceeded three per cent.

This raises further questions about the reasons why people so determinedly choose ownership over other tenures. Launching a sequence of similar questions about different tenures, we began by asking people to identify:

...the main advantage of owning a home rather than renting it

followed by:

...the main disadvantage of owning a home rather than renting it

The answers based on choices presented on a card indicate that the most often perceived advantage of home ownership, cited by 26 per cent, is that it represents a good investment. Current home owners are rather more likely than those who rent to share this opinion. The next most popular choice is that home ownership "is more secure in the long term than renting" (23 per cent) and that it gives people "the freedom to do what you want" with a property (21 per cent). The suggestions that ownership "works out less expensive than paying the rent" (15 per cent) and that a property "is something to leave to your family" (12 per cent) are less frequently cited.

No front-runner emerges from people's perceptions of the main disadvantage of home ownership, but 19 per cent say "it is expensive" and the same proportion refer to the "need to have a steady job". Another 18 per cent mention the "need to make repairs yourself". Difficulties "keeping up with mortgage payments" are mentioned by eight per cent overall as is the view that ownership is restrictive and makes it "hard to move". Another five per cent cite difficulties buying "in a nice area". While scarcely surprising, it is also worth noting that one in four private tenants (25 per cent) and more than one in five social housing tenants (22 per cent), view expense as the major drawback to ownership.

Perhaps the biggest change in the perceived advantages of owning since the 1980s is the big drop in the proportion who cite "easier to move", probably reflecting difficulties experienced in the recessions of the early 1990s and late 2000s. This also points up a key comparative advantage of the resurgent private rented sector.

Advantages and affordability of renting
To explore people's views about tenancy, we reversed the previous question to ask about "the main advantage of renting a home rather than owning it". Notwithstanding the fact that most people are owner-occupiers, the vast majority are prepared to acknowledge that renting can carry practical advantages. As seen in Table 8.5, only one in nine current owners and less than one in ten respondents overall insist there is no advantage in renting.

Perhaps the biggest change in the perceived advantages of owning since the 1980s is the big drop in the proportion who say it is "easier to move"

Table 8.5 Main advantages of renting over owning, by tenure

	Housing tenure			
	Owners	Social Renters	Private Renters	All
Advantages of renting over owning	%	%	%	%
Flexibility to move at short notice	28	14	28	25
Someone else is responsible for repairs and maintenance	23	37	22	25
Greater choice over where to live	9	9	12	10
Don't have to worry about taking on a mortgage	8	13	11	10
Less risky than owning a home	7	11	9	8
Less responsibility than owning a home	9	6	6	8
Less upfront costs	3	4	4	4
No advantage	11	4	7	9
Base	*2231*	*548*	*485*	*3297*

Response options with less than two per cent of response were not included in this table

By contrast, one in four see flexibility to move home at short notice as the main advantage, while another quarter say it is the lack of personal responsibility for repairs and maintenance. One in ten refer to having greater choice over where to live, with private renters the most enthusiastic. Another 10 per cent mention a lack of worry about taking on a mortgage. Social renters are prominent among those insisting it is less risky than owning a home, while owners are more likely to suggest that renting carries a lower level of responsibility (both cited by eight per cent overall). A much smaller proportion (four per cent) think the main advantage of renting is having fewer upfront costs.

On the issue of costs we also asked current tenants:

How easy or difficult is it for your household to afford the rent?

This revealed that while two-thirds find their payments relatively easy to meet, there are 24 per cent who say it is "fairly difficult" and another seven per cent who find it "very difficult". Private sector tenants (35 per cent) are more likely to report difficulties than those in social housing (29 per cent).

35% of private sector tenants find it difficult to afford their rent

Advantages and disadvantages of private renting

Written off a quarter of a century ago as a shrinking, residual sector, private renting has undergone a revival in England, expanding rapidly by 80 per cent between 1988 and 2008–2009. The transformation was triggered by rent deregulation policies and has been fuelled by the popularity of 'Buy-to-Let' property investment. Rising house prices and growth in the number of students and single person households have simultaneously boosted demand for private rented accommodation.

These market changes, though dramatic, tell us little about the public's perceptions and preferences concerning the private rental sector. The responses to questions about the major 'pros' and 'cons' of private renting help to fill that gap. We asked people "from what you know or have heard" to identify from a list of possible answers:

...the main advantage of renting a home privately as opposed to renting it from a local authority or housing association

Opinion proves to be split with people pointing to several different benefits. A "wider choice of location" is specified by 21 per cent making it the most popular choice. This is followed by a "better choice of types of properties available" (16 per cent) and by a view that privately rented properties "are in better condition" than those in social housing (10 per cent). However, private renters (14 per cent) are more likely to take this latter view than those who live in council (11 per cent) or housing association (six per cent) properties. Another 10 per cent refer to properties being "more easily available" followed by nine per cent who cite "getting repairs done" and "less responsibility for upkeep". Others see the main advantage as "no social stigma" (eight per cent) or "more flexible tenancy arrangements".

Views about the major disadvantage are less mixed, with almost one third (32 per cent) in all tenures responding that "rents are too high". This appears consistent with the responses we received about finding the rent difficult to afford (see above) as well as other evidence that affordability problems are becoming more prevalent in the private rented sector (Bramley *et al.*, 2010b; Bramley, 2011). However, while private tenants (34 per cent) select this answer more often than home owners (29 per cent), an even higher proportion of social housing tenants (43 per cent) view cost as the major drawback to becoming a private tenant.

The next most commonly stated drawbacks are "problems with landlords or letting agents" (21 per cent, including 17 per cent of private tenants) followed – at a distance – by "little choice over what happens to the property" (12 per cent). Another 12 per cent cite "restrictions around the length of time you can stay living in the property". Interestingly, social housing tenants are considerably more likely (16 per cent) to choose this as the main disadvantage than their private sector counterparts (nine per cent). Most private tenancies are short term (six months to one year), but concern about this lack of security is not very common in the sector itself, while being a greater concern for those currently in social tenure.

Rising house prices and growth in the number of students and single person households have simultaneously boosted demand for private rented accommodation

The balance of attitudes suggests that while tenants may be attracted to private renting by the choice of locations and properties, a large minority are unhappy with the level of rents. Social housing tenants – who include a higher concentration of lower income households – are even more worried by rent levels in the private sector and by the limitations on security of tenure. So, at a time when government is challenging the need for social tenancies to last a lifetime, it appears that many who rent from councils and housing associations regard private renting a housing alternative which is both unaffordable and insecure.

Advantages and disadvantages of social renting

To gain a direct perspective on the way the public views social housing, we reversed the direction of the previous questions by asking people to say what they thought were the main advantage and disadvantage of:

...renting from a local authority or housing association as opposed to renting a home privately

The answers reveal that the most popular main advantage is "the option to purchase property through a scheme such as the Right to Buy". That it is cited by 29 per cent is a rather surprising finding given that higher prices and restrictions on discounts have made Right to Buy arrangements less affordable in recent years and sales have fallen to a low level. However, we note that social housing tenants are considerably less likely to cite the Right to Buy (18 per cent) than private tenants or owner-occupiers, suggesting that people outside the sector are less aware than insiders that this option has been curtailed in recent years. The next most frequently cited advantages are having "more secure tenancy arrangements" and "low/affordable rents" (18 per cent each). Existing social tenants particularly value tenure security (24 per cent).

Strikingly, when it comes to specifying the main disadvantage of social housing compared with private renting, much the most common reply is "anti-social behaviour problems on estates". This is cited by 39 per cent of all respondents, including 31 per cent of social renters themselves. Another seven per cent across all tenures select "anti-social neighbours". Taken together, these replies suggest that approaching half the population, and a large minority of social housing tenants, see anti-social behaviour and neighbour nuisance as the main drawback to renting from a local authority or housing association. This is despite the evidence from researchers in the late-2000s that the quality of social housing had improved and that heavy concentrations of social disadvantage had begun to recede (Fitzpatrick and Stephens, 2008), albeit with continuing difficulties in some areas (Hill, 2007). However, the continued prominence of anti-social behaviour issues in political debate about social housing is, given the strength of public opinion in our survey, unsurprising.

39%
say the main disadvantage of social housing is anti-social behaviour problems on estates

Next in importance, though a much less commonly mentioned disadvantage, is having "little choice over location" (12 per cent). This is followed by it being "difficult to move to other types of property when needs change" (eight per cent). These reflect acknowledged difficulties within the sector, where mobility and choice is constrained by a limited stock of properties.

Who is social renting for?

Subsidised social housing has for most of the past half-century been the principal provider of longer-term decent quality housing for people who cannot afford to buy on the open market. However, given the re-evaluation of its purpose under the coalition government, we posed a further question inviting people to say which of four possible factors on a list:

...should be treated as a priority in deciding who should be allocated housing rented from a local authority or housing association

This found that the strongest support (30 per cent) is for people "living in overcrowded accommodation", which may reflect objective evidence that overcrowding has increased in recent years (Bramley *et al.*, 2010b). Close behind comes "being on a very low income" (28 per cent) with an implied suggestion that social housing should primarily provide a 'safety net' for the poor. However, nearly as many respondents (26 per cent) select "not being able to afford to buy or rent independently", suggesting a much wider range of eligibility for social housing. The fourth factor, "being a key worker such as a nurse or a teacher", is supported by fewer people (14 per cent).

These views offer some support for the government's emphasis on targeting social housing on the most 'needy' groups, including those on very low incomes; notwithstanding the fact that one in four show support for social housing as a broader provider of affordable housing.

Conclusions

Past experience and recent studies both suggest that a 'localist' planning system will tend to further restrict new housing supply (Bramley 2010, 2011a, 2011b; National Housing Federation, 2010). This is particularly true in southern England where the need for extra housing is greatest. People's opinions, presented here, reinforce existing evidence by showing that a substantially greater number of people in England and Wales (but not Scotland) are minded to oppose new housing in their locality than support it, especially in the South.

There is, nevertheless, some evidence that indirect 'planning gain' benefits from permitting new housing – whether in terms of improved public facilities or local economic opportunities – would persuade more people to support development. This is an important message for policy makers, planners and would-be developers.

30%

think those living in overcrowded accommodation should be given priority in allocating social housing

Yet even assuming that these different types of side-benefit could be offered on a wide enough scale, our findings suggest that the opponents of development could still be expected to prevail in sensitive areas. Those seeking to counter local NIMBYism can, however, take some encouragement from the priority need that people see for new social housing and helping first-time buyers, and perhaps from seeing more local control over the type of housing built.

In the private rented sector, planned restrictions on Housing Benefit can be expected to increase difficulties that a significant minority of tenants already report in affording their rent. Looking at government intentions, it also seems likely that two major perceived advantages of social renting – relative low cost and secure tenure – will also be eroded by higher rents for many new tenants and less long-term security.

Since the Right to Buy – although the most frequently perceived advantage of social housing – has been much curtailed in recent years, it seems that social renting may come to be seen less as a 'tenure of choice' and more a 'tenure of necessity'. Increasingly, it will become a transitional option rather than one that the tenant can expect to last a lifetime. Restricting social housing to a more transient population of those considered 'needy' may, in turn, make it harder to tackle the problems of anti-social behaviour that are already viewed as the major drawback to social renting.

Notes

1. Note that the fieldwork for the 2010 *British Social Attitudes* survey was conducted during the summer months of 2010. As this was prior to the full scope of planning reforms being announced by the new government, respondents may have answered these questions with the current system in mind.

2. Most references to policy changes in this chapter refer specifically to England, although some 'reserved matters' including benefits policies apply throughout the United Kingdom. However, the *British Social Attitudes* survey data cover Britain and we report on some of the differences found in the devolved nations where policies and market conditions may differ, particularly in Scotland.

3. Package 1 consists of new or improved green space, schools, medical facilities, library and leisure facilities; package 2 involves improved transport links, more employment opportunities and more and better shops or supermarkets.

4. The level of support versus opposition with different packages was calculated by adding those who said they would change their view and support housing development to those who generally supported development, and (if the respondent had previously been opposed) subtracting them from the opposition. The regions singled out for comparison are those with the strongest differences in attitudes to new house building, for example the South and outer London are the most negative.

References

Barker, K. (2004), *Review of Housing Supply: Delivering Stability: Securing our Future Housing Needs, Final Report & Recommendations*, London: TSO/HM Treasury

Bramley, G. (2007), 'The sudden rediscovery of housing supply as a key policy issue', *Housing Studies*, **22:2**, 221–241

Bramley, G. (2010), 'Housing Supply and Planning', paper presented at Cambridge Centre for Housing and Planning Research Conference: *Housing: the next 20 years. Learning from the evidence*, Cambridge, 17 September 2010

Bramley, G. (2011a), 'Localised planning, sub-regional housing markets and affordability outcomes: early views of a large scale policy experiment'. Workshop WS04 (Metropolitan Dynamics: Urban Change, Market and Governance). Paper presented at European Network for Housing Research Conference, Toulouse, July 2011

Bramley, G. (2011b), 'Localised planning, sub-regional housing markets and affordability outcomes: what is likely to happen?' Paper presented at Martin Centre Seminar, Cambridge University, October 2011

Bramley, G. and Karley, N.K. (2005), 'How much extra affordable housing is needed in England?' *Housing Studies*, **20:5**, 685–715

Bramley, G., Dunmore, K., Dunse, N., Gilbert, C., Thanos, S. and Watkins, D. (2010a), *The Implications of Housing Type/Size Mix and Density for the Affordability and Viability of New Housing Supply*, Titchfield: National Housing and Planning Advice Unit

Bramley, G., Pawson, H., White, M., Watkins, D. and Pleace, N. (2010b), *Estimating Housing Need*, Housing Research Report, Department for Communities and Local Government, available at www.communities.gov.uk/publications/housing/estimatinghousingneed

Conservatives (2010), *Open Source Planning*, Policy Green Paper No. 14

Department for Communities and Local Government, (2010a), *Localism Bill*, available at www.publications.parliament.uk/pa/bills/lbill/2010-2012/0071/2012071pt1.pdf

Department for Communities and Local Government, (2010b), *Local Decisions: a fairer future for social housing*, Consultation Paper, available at www.communities.gov.uk/publications/housing/socialhousingreform

Department for Communities and Local Government, (2011a), *Positive planning: a new focus on driving sustainable development,* Press Notice, available at www.communities.gov.uk/news/planningandbuilding/newsettlement

Department for Communities and Local Government, (2011b), *Draft National Planning Policy Framework*, available at www.communities.gov.uk/publications/planningandbuilding/draftframework

Department for Communities and Local Government (2011c), *Housing Statistics Live Tables 104*, available at www.communities.gov.uk/housing/housingresearch/housingstatistics/housingstatisticsby/stockincludingvacants/livetables

Fitzpatrick, S. and Stephens, M. (2008), *The Future of Social Housing*, London: Shelter

HM Treasury with Department for Business, Innovation and Skills (2011), *The Plan for Growth*, London: HM Treasury, available at www.hm-treasury.gov.uk/ukecon_growth_index.htm

Hills, J. (2007), *Means and Ends: The Future Roles of Social Housing in England*, CASE Report 34. ISSN 1465–3001. Centre for Analysis of Social Exclusion, London School of Economics

Humphrey, A. and Bromley, C. (2005), 'Home Sweet Home', in Park, A., Curtice, J., Thompson, K., Bromley, C., Phillips, M. and Johnson, M. (eds.), *British Social Attitudes: the 22nd Report – Two terms of New Labour: The public's reaction*, London: Sage

National Housing Federation (2011), *The Abolition of Regional Spatial Strategies, Submission to the Communities and Local Government Committee*, available at www.housing.org.uk/publications/find_a_publication/development_and_regeneration/abolition_of_rss.aspx

National Housing and Planning Advice Unit (2009), *More Homes for More People: building the right homes in the right places,* Titchfield: National Housing and Planning Advice Unit

Office of the Deputy Prime Minister (2005), *Affordability Targets: Implications for Housing Supply.* London: Office of the Deputy Prime Minister

Oxford Economics (2011), Housing Market analysis, July 2011. A report for the National Housing Federation, available at www.housing.org.uk/news/housing_market_crisis_as_home.aspx

Acknowledgements
The *National Centre for Social Research* is grateful to the Department for Communities and Local Government (DCLG) for their financial support which enabled us to ask the questions reported in this chapter. The views expressed are those of the authors alone.

Appendix
The data for Figure 8.1 are shown below.

Table A.1 Advice for a young married couple (both working) about housing, 1986–2010

	86	89	90	91	96	97	98	99	04	08	10
	%	%	%	%	%	%	%	%	%	%	%
Buy a home as soon as possible	74	78	70	60	54	61	61	65	71	45	53
Wait a bit, then try to buy a home	20	17	24	31	35	30	30	29	24	40	35
Not plan to buy a home at all	1	1	3	2	3	2	1	2	1	2	3
Base	*1416*	*1297*	*1233*	*1224*	*3085*	*1080*	*2531*	*2450*	*2609*	*1012*	*1870*

9. NHS
Taking the pulse: attitudes to the health service

We know that the spending increases and improvements in service delivery that took place under Labour were reflected in increased public satisfaction with the NHS. Here we examine the state of public attitudes towards the start of the Coalition government's term in office, a period during which they have proposed a number of radical reforms in relation to the NHS.

Satisfaction with the NHS overall is at its highest ever level, though the picture in relation to specific services is more mixed.

Seven out of ten people (70%) are satisfied with the NHS overall, the highest level ever recorded by the survey; the figure is up from 34% in 1997, when it was at its lowest point.

Conservative and Liberal Democrat supporters' satisfaction increased by eight and nine percentage points respectively between 2009 and 2010, while Labour supporters' satisfaction levels remained stable.

61%

Satisfied with A and E departments

Satisfaction with most NHS services has not changed substantially since 2009. However, satisfaction with emergency services has increased in the last two years. For example, satisfaction with hospital accident and emergency departments now stands at 61%, up from 53% in 2008 and 43% in 2001.

Expectations about waiting times have improved dramatically over the last decade. Positive views on waiting times are linked to satisfaction with the NHS overall, so this presents a challenge to the Coalition: how to maintain these high levels of satisfaction now that certain targets on waiting times have been dropped.

The proportion who think they would get an outpatient appointment for a bad back within three months stands at 73%, up from 50% just four years earlier in 2006.

50%
2006

73%
2010

Author: Elizabeth Clery*

In *The 27th Report*, we found unprecedented levels of satisfaction with the National Health Service (NHS) in the final year of the Labour administration (Appleby and Robertson, 2010). Since that time, the political landscape in relation to healthcare in Britain has changed dramatically. The election of the Conservative–Liberal Democrat coalition government in May 2010 heralded wide-ranging discussions around how the NHS is structured, managed and monitored, within a broader context of proposed substantial reductions to government spending. While the new administration has guaranteed increases in real terms to government spending on health, which currently accounts for around 18 per cent of government spending, it has proposed and implemented a range of initiatives to make the NHS more cost-efficient and effective. These include the abolition and revision of a number of patient waiting time targets introduced by Labour, as well as extensive discussions around giving control of commissioning decisions to clinicians including GPs.

It therefore seems timely, one year on, to revisit public attitudes to the NHS in the period immediately after the Coalition took power. Our 2010 fieldwork took place shortly after the general election, meaning it is too soon to expect to see any clear impact of the new government and its policies on public attitudes. However, throughout the chapter we look for any clues about whether the trends seen under Labour are set to continue or not; in particular, it may be that in a general election year people are more likely to take stock and think about public services, and different parties' policies towards them. Our analysis will also give us baseline measures against which, in future reports, we can monitor attitude change over the course of the current administration.

We start by examining satisfaction with the NHS and its component services. We then focus on expectations and perceptions about waiting times – an issue on which the Labour administration devoted considerable attention and resources and where the coalition government have already adopted and implemented a very different approach. On the basis of developments in both areas, the chapter concludes by considering likely public reactions to planned coalition government reforms. Although policy-making powers in relation to many aspects of healthcare are devolved, our analysis, as in previous years, covers attitudes across Britain as a whole.[1]

Satisfaction with the NHS
Since the *British Social Attitudes* survey series began in 1983, we have regularly asked about satisfaction with the NHS:

All in all, how satisfied or dissatisfied would you say you are with the way in which the National Health Service is run nowadays?

In 2009, the public expressed unprecedented levels of satisfaction with the NHS, with 65 per cent saying they were "very" or "quite" satisfied, a proportion which had increased from 36 per cent in 1996 (the year before Labour came to power). When our fieldwork took place in the summer of 2010, the newly-elected coalition government

....

* Elizabeth Clery is a Research Director at the *National Centre for Social Research* and a Co-Director of the *British Social Attitudes* survey series.

had not yet implemented any substantial changes to the management or funding of the NHS, meaning we would not expect our trend data to reflect public perceptions of coalition initiatives and their impact at this stage. In fact, as demonstrated in Figure 9.1, satisfaction levels rose even further – with 70 per cent reporting satisfaction, an increase of five percentage points since 2009 and representing the highest reported level of satisfaction since the survey began.

Is this just a continuation of the upwards trend of the last five years? It is not simply the case that the proportion who are dissatisfied with the NHS has declined as the proportion who are satisfied has risen, though that has been the case in the past. Dissatisfaction levels were similar in 2009 and 2010 (19 and 18 per cent respectively). Conversely, it is the proportion saying "neither satisfied nor dissatisfied" that has reduced – from 16 per cent in 2009 to 12 per cent in 2010. With the election of a new government in May 2010 it may be that people have been weighing up the standpoints of the different parties in relation to healthcare, and therefore are more inclined to express an opinion – although there is no evidence of such an effect occurring in relation to previous general elections.

Given the change in government from Labour to a Conservative-Liberal Democrat coalition, a pertinent question is whether the satisfaction levels of supporters of particular parties have changed and, if they have, whether these shifts are driving overall satisfaction. We already know that party supporters are more satisfied with the NHS when 'their' party is in power; in the first two years of the Labour administration, elected in 1997, there was a surge in satisfaction among Labour supporters, while the satisfaction levels of Conservative supporters declined slightly (Appleby and Alvarez-Rosette, 2003). We see a similar effect in 2010, with the satisfaction levels of those supporting the incumbent coalition government increasing markedly (by nine percentage points for Conservative identifiers and eight percentage points for their Liberal Democrat counterparts). However, rather than declining (as in 1997), the satisfaction levels of the supporters of the losing party have remained stable. Perhaps Labour identifiers view the improvements in the NHS as a reflection of the ongoing legacy of their party's term in office. If so, this may be a 'cusp' year, in which supporters of all the main parties had a reason to be satisfied. That suggests that the increase in satisfaction between 2009 and 2010 could be a temporary effect, rather than simply a continuation of the upward trend of the last few years.

70%

reported satisfaction with the NHS, an increase of five percentage points since 2009

Figure 9.1 Satisfaction with the NHS, 1983–2010

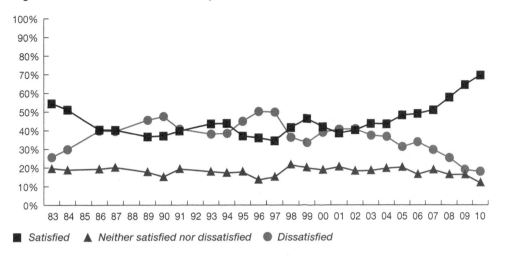

The data on which Figure 9.1 is based can be found in the appendix to this chapter

Satisfaction with the NHS as a whole is a powerful overarching measure, but in order to get a more nuanced understanding of satisfaction with health services, we also ask about satisfaction with a range of individual services including GPs, dentists, hospital inpatient and outpatient services, ambulance services, hospital accident and emergency departments and diagnostic services (such as X-rays, scans or hearing tests).

The picture over time is mixed. As we saw in *The 27th Report*, satisfaction with GPs initially fell under Labour, only starting to recover in 2005. Satisfaction with dentists was in long-term decline until 2004 where it flattened out, beginning to rise again in 2009. And, while satisfaction with outpatient departments rose in the last years of the Labour regime to their highest level to date, satisfaction with inpatient services were in decline for much of the period, only beginning to recover in 2007 (Appleby and Robertson, 2010).

Between 2009 and 2010 satisfaction with GPs, NHS dentists, inpatient and outpatient services, diagnostic services and NHS Direct has remained reasonably steady, with minor, though not significant, fluctuations occurring in both directions. The satisfaction levels for these services presented in Table 9.1 are very similar to those which we reported on in 2009. In particular, it is notable that satisfaction with GPs has not changed significantly since 2009, despite government plans for their role to expand to include the commissioning and managing of health services. This is something that we will continue to monitor in future reports, as their new role takes form.

For two NHS services – ambulance services and hospital accident and emergency departments – satisfaction levels have increased substantially in recent years. We asked about NHS ambulance services for the first time in 2008, when six in ten (61 per cent) indicated they were "very" or "quite" satisfied. By 2010 this proportion has risen by seven percentage points, to 68 per cent. Satisfaction with hospital accident and emergency departments has been measured at regular intervals since 1999, when slightly more than half (53 per cent) were satisfied. After reaching a low point of 43 per cent in 2002 it has risen fairly consistently – back to its original level in 2008 (53 per cent) and reaching 61 per cent in 2010, an increase of eight percentage points.

For these services, we do not have data for 2009, meaning we can't pinpoint precisely when the changes took place (it is certainly possible that as with our other measures, the main change had already happened by 2009, with little movement since), but regardless of this, the fast pace of increase is notable. These services were subject to waiting time targets introduced by Labour, and there is separate evidence that this resulted in real improvements (Department of Health, 2010). Although our data do not allow us to examine the link between satisfaction and waiting times for these particular services, we know from previous reports (Appleby and Robertson, 2010) that views on waiting times are closely linked to overall satisfaction levels. The fact that the Coalition has abandoned certain elements of the targets[2] therefore raises a question about whether this trend is set to continue or not.

Table 9.1 Satisfaction with NHS services, 1996–2010

	96	99	01	03	05	07	08	09	10
GPs									
% very/quite satisfied	77	76	71	72	74	76	77	80	77
Dentists									
% very/quite satisfied	52	53	53	52	45	42	42	48	51
Inpatients									
% very/quite satisfied	53	58	51	52	50	49	51	59	59
Outpatients									
% very/quite satisfied	52	56	50	54	61	60	61	67	68
Diagnostic services									
% very/quite satisfied	n/a	n/a	n/a	n/a	n/a	n/a	n/a	72	75
NHS Direct									
% very/quite satisfied	n/a	n/a	n/a	27	32	33	38	44	42
Accident and emergency services									
% very/quite satisfied	n/a	53	43	n/a	51	51	53	n/a	61
Ambulance services									
% very/quite satisfied	n/a	n/a	n/a	n/a	n/a	n/a	61	n/a	68
Base	1761	3143	2188	2293	3193	3078	3358	3421	3358

n/a = not asked

We have seen that while general satisfaction with the way in which the NHS is run nowadays is at its highest ever level, having increased significantly since 2009, the picture in relation to individual health services is more mixed. One factor which could potentially influence an individual's satisfaction with a particular service is the length of time which they, or those they know, have to wait to receive it. This is an issue to which the Labour administration paid particular attention and where the coalition government had begun to discuss and implement change at the time of data collection in the summer of 2010. It is to this topic that we turn next.

Waiting times – public expectations and perceptions

The Labour government focused considerable energy and resources on reducing waiting times, with significant tangible outcomes.[3] However, one of the Coalition's first policies in relation to the NHS was to abolish or revise specific targets relating to waiting times, with the intention of removing perceived bureaucracy and interference in the work of health professionals. In June 2010, the Coalition cut two long-standing waiting time targets – for a patient to see a family doctor within 48 hours and for the period from hospital referral to start of treatment to last less than 18 weeks.[4] The intention was also expressed for the maximum waiting time in accident and emergency units of four hours to be removed the following year (this target was in fact revised in June 2010 and replaced with a set of quality indicators in April 2011). By June 2011, there was already some evidence that patient waiting times had increased, although this development cannot necessarily be directly attributed to the removal of the waiting time targets (Department of Health, 2011).

Although it is highly unlikely that the abolition of the targets would have impacted on actual waiting times by the time of data collection for the 2010 survey, it is worth reviewing public expectations about waiting times at this time, as these constitute a baseline against which to measure the long-term impact of these targets being dropped. Moreover, an increase in waiting times could impact on attitudes to the NHS more generally; multivariate analysis of the 2009 data revealed that perceptions about waiting times are strongly linked to levels of satisfaction, with those who think that waiting times have improved being significantly more likely to be satisfied with the NHS (Appleby and Robertson, 2010).

To examine this issue, we start by considering how long people expect to wait when they have an NHS appointment, asking about the following scenarios:

Suppose you had a back problem and your GP referred you to a hospital out-patients' department. From what you know or have heard, please say whether you think you would get an appointment within three months?

And please say whether you think when you arrived, the doctor would see you within half an hour of your appointment time?

Figure 9.2 shows that expectations about waiting times have become more positive over the past decade, having remained relatively constant for most of the 1990s. In 1993, 45 per cent thought that they would ("definitely" or "probably") get an appointment at a hospital outpatients' department within three months; by 2010 this figure had risen dramatically to 73 per cent. Much of this increase occurred during the past four years, with just 50 per cent expressing this view in 2006. Expectations have also become more favourable about the likelihood of being seen promptly by the doctor. In 1993, just 30 per cent thought they would be seen within half an hour of the appointment time, a proportion which had increased to 54 per cent by 2010.

Expectations about waiting times have become more positive over the past decade, having remained relatively constant for most of the 1990s

The first scenario described above specifically relates to the target introduced by Labour for the elapsed time between being referred to hospital and an appointment to take no longer than 18 weeks. Considering the high public confidence we have found (almost three in four believe that the target would be met), the coalition government will need to watch carefully how their reforms affect public expectations.

Figure 9.2 Expectations about waiting times for NHS appointments, 1993–2010

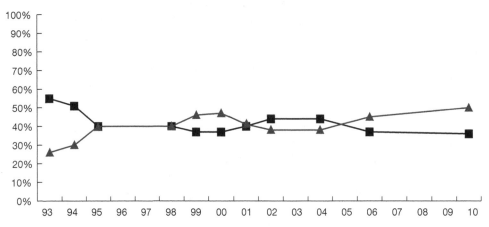

■ *Would get hospital outpatient appointment in 3 months*
▲ *Doctor would see you within half an hour of appointment time*

The data on which Figure 9.2 is based can be found in the appendix to this chapter

Public expectations on waiting times are currently far more positive than in the past. But that doesn't tell us whether people perceive NHS performance on waiting times to have improved or not. To examine this, we asked respondents how much better or worse they think waiting times for a range of services have been getting over the last five years. Table 9.2 demonstrates that on each measure, the proportion who feel that waiting times have improved over the past five years has increased over the past decade. The most marked changes have occurred in relation to hospital appointments. In 1995, 17 per cent thought the time most people have to wait to get operations in NHS hospitals had got better over the past five years; by 2010, this proportion had more than doubled (39 per cent). The picture is similar in relation to views about waiting times for outpatients' appointments. When it comes to GP appointments, the increase is less marked. In 1995 28 per cent thought that waiting times in a GP's surgery had got better compared to 36 per cent now. Notably, while perceptions for each measure have improved over time, our measures for 2009 and 2010 are very similar – possibly suggesting this long-term rise in perceptions of NHS performance is at an end.

36%

think that waiting times in a GP's surgery have got better compared to 28 per cent in 1995

Table 9.2 Views on improvements in NHS waiting times in past five years, 1995–2010

% agree that has been getting "much better" or "better" over last five years	95	01	08	09	10
The time most people wait to get operations in NHS hospitals	17	11	31	n/a	39
The time most people wait to get out-patients' appointments in NHS hospitals	17	12	28	37	36
The time most people wait at a GP's surgery before their doctor sees them	28	23	34	39	36
The time most people would have to wait between being referred by their GP for hospital treatment and that treatment starting	n/a	n/a	n/a	36	37
Base	2399	2188	3358	3421	3297

We have seen that public expectations about waiting times and NHS performance in this area over time have greatly improved over the last few years. It seems likely that these changes are in response to the real improvements in waiting times that were a feature of the Labour administration. Clearly, we would anticipate a time-lag between the implementation of change and its impact on public attitudes and expectations. Nevertheless, it will be important to monitor these trends in the coming years, to assess the impact of the coalition government's removal and revision of key waiting time targets on public attitudes to this issue. And as we know from *The 27th Report* (Appleby and Robertson, 2010), positive views about waiting times are strongly correlated with satisfaction about the NHS overall, meaning that any downturn in the former might well impact on public levels of satisfaction with the NHS.

Conclusions

Public satisfaction with the NHS is at an all-time high, continuing an upwards trend that started a decade ago. Alongside that, people's expectations and perceptions about waiting times for various NHS services are far more positive than they were at the turn of the century. We have also seen rapid increases in satisfaction with accident and emergency services in the last two years.

However there are some signs that the positive trends in attitudes towards the NHS seen in the last decade may be stalling. Satisfaction levels for specific NHS services, such as GPs, inpatient and outpatient services have seen little change since 2009, having increased substantially in recent years. And while there has been a fast rate of increase in perceptions of improvement about waiting times in recent years, the

 There are some signs that the positive trends in attitudes towards the NHS seen in the last decade may be stalling

levels have stagnated since 2009. Perhaps this is in part related to the fact that this was a general election year with a change of government – with public debates about the different parties' policies on public services being relatively high profile. Or it may be that after such considerable improvements over time, levels are reaching a ceiling beyond which it's unlikely they will improve much further.

The impact of the coalition government's policies on the public's experiences of the NHS is something we can monitor in future years. Nevertheless, as we have seen with perceptions about waiting times, it seems clear that the public do notice real changes in service delivery, meaning that any perceived decline in the quality of services or speed with which they can be accessed has considerable potential to shift satisfaction downwards – given the very substantial degree to which it rose under Labour.

What is clear is that we have a public who are very happy with the NHS and have high expectations about service delivery, and that will be challenging for the government to maintain as NHS reforms begin to take effect.

Notes

1. In their analysis of 2009 data, Appleby and Robertson (2010) found that levels of satisfaction with the NHS were similar in England, Scotland and Wales, with the exception of improvements over the last five years, despite the different policies and spending in the three countries. This chapter presents results for Britain; data for England only does not change the trends reported in any meaningful way.

2. Specifically, the four hour waiting target for accident and emergency departments has been replaced by a set of clinical quality indicators, one of which relates to total time in the department. For the ambulance service, the waiting time target for the most seriously ill patients has been retained.

3. For example, the median wait for an inpatient admission in England fell from 13.4 weeks in 1997 to around 4.2 weeks in 2009 (Department of Health, 2010).

4. The NHS constitutional right for the period from hospital referral to start of treatment to last less than 18 weeks remains in place. Separately, the revised NHS Operating Framework for 2010/11, published in June 2010, removed central performance management of this target by the Department of Health.

References

Appleby, J. and Robertson, R. (2010), 'A healthy improvement? Satisfaction with the NHS under Labour', in Park, A., Curtice, J., Clery, E. and Bryson, C. (eds.) (2010), *British Social Attitudes: the 27th Report – Exploring Labour's Legacy*, London: Sage

Department of Health (2010), *Historic waiting times data*, available at www.dh.gov.uk/en/Publicationsandstatistics/Statistics/Performancedataandstatistics/HospitalWaitingTimesand ListStatistics/index.htm

Department of Health (2011), NHS referral to treatment waiting time statistics, June 2011, available at www.dh.gov.uk/en/Publicationsandstatistics/Publications/PublicationsStatistics/DH_129408

Acknowledgements

The National Centre for Social Research is grateful to the Department of Health for their financial support which enabled us to ask the questions reported in this chapter, although the views expressed are those of the author alone.

Appendix

The data for Figure 9.1 are shown below.

Table A.1 Satisfaction with the NHS, 1983–2010

	83	84	86	87	89	90	91	93
Overall satisfaction								
Very/quite satisfied	55	51	40	40	37	37	40	44
Very/quite dissatisfied	26	30	40	40	46	47	41	38
Base	*1761*	*1675*	*3100*	*2847*	*3029*	*2797*	*2918*	*2945*

	94	95	96	97	98	99	00	01	02
Overall satisfaction									
Very/quite satisfied	44	37	36	34	42	46	42	39	40
Very/quite dissatisfied	38	45	50	50	36	33	39	41	41
Base	*3469*	*3633*	*3620*	*1355*	*3146*	*3143*	*3426*	*2188*	*2287*

	03	04	05	06	07	08	09	09	10
Overall satisfaction									
Very/quite satisfied	44	43	48	49	51	58	64	64	70
Very/quite dissatisfied	37	37	31	34	30	25	19	19	18
Base	*2293*	*3199*	*3193*	*2143*	*3078*	*3358*	*3421*	*3421*	*3358*

The data for Figure 9.2 are shown below.

Table A.2 Expectations about waiting times for NHS appointments, 1993–2010

	93	94	95	98	99	00	01	02	04	06	10
What would happen if you had a back problem and doctor referred you to hospital outpatients department											
Would get hospital outpatient appointment in 3 months	55	51	40	40	37	37	40	44	44	37	36
Doctor would see you within half an hour of appointment time	26	30	40	40	46	47	41	38	38	45	50
Base	*2945*	*3469*	*3633*	*3146*	*3143*	*3426*	*2188*	*2287*	*3199*	*2143*	*3358*

10. Childhood
Growing up in Britain

International reports suggest the UK has not been as successful as other developed nations in promoting children's well-being. The media and some politicians appear to endorse a gloomy view of modern childhood; does the public share their pessimism?

While a majority think Britain is a good country to grow up in, only a minority think children are happier now than they were a decade ago. Contrary to popular belief, the views of older people are not always the most negative.

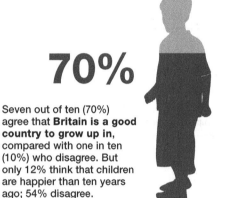

70%

Seven out of ten (70%) agree that **Britain is a good country to grow up in**, compared with one in ten (10%) who disagree. But only 12% think that children are happier than ten years ago; 54% disagree.

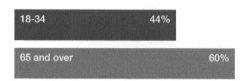

| 18-34 | 44% |
| 65 and over | 60% |

People aged 65 and over are more likely than 18–34 year olds to think Britain is a good place to grow up in (81% and 60% respectively agree). But older people are also more likely than younger adults to think that children are less happy now than a decade ago (60% and 44%).

....

A majority of adults think most young people are well-behaved. A majority, nevertheless, think that standards of behaviour were better in the past.

61%

think most young people are well behaved

Six out of ten (61%) think most **young people are responsible and well-behaved**; only one in five (21%) disagree. Older people are more likely to agree (69%) than young adults (45%).

| Agree | 28% |
| Disagree | 63% |

However, six out of ten (63%) disagree with the idea that **young people's behaviour is "no worse than in the past"**, compared with 28% who agree.

Author: Elizabeth Clery*

There are many reasons why the lives of children growing up in Britain today might be judged better than those of their parents and grandparents. They can expect to avoid disability or limiting illness and live longer than previous generations (Office for National Statistics, 2010a & 2010b). They live in households where disposable income per head is, on average, much higher and they are more likely to live in a warm 'decent' home. They can choose between more age-appropriate books than ever before, and they have access to sources of information, communication and entertainment that were unimaginable for previous generations (Cambridge Primary Review, 2010).

Schoolchildren when questioned about their lives mostly say they are happy, have good friends and are positive about their schools (Chamberlain *et al.*, 2010). Yet this is far from the whole story, as witnessed by an enduring political and media debate about children and the quality of modern childhood. Arguably the most damning contribution came in 2007, when the UK was placed bottom of a league table for child well-being across 'rich' countries, published by the United Nations Children's Fund, UNICEF. This compared countries on indicators of relative poverty, education, family and peer relationships, risk-taking behaviour and health (UNICEF, 2007). Since much of the data used had been collected around five years earlier, there was mild relief in Britain when an updated report, using data from the middle of the decade, placed the UK 19th out of 24 countries on children's material well-being, 13th on education and 11th on health – though only 21st using an overall indicator of equality in child well-being (UNICEF, 2010).

Following the 2010 General Election, the incoming coalition government showed interest in trying to improve the UK's performance. It established a Childhood and Families Taskforce, to be attended by the Prime Minister, Deputy Prime Minister and senior ministers, with a remit to co-ordinate policies for improving children's quality of life. This was expected to consider issues as varied as flexible parental leave, support for disabled children, helping children through family breakdown, helping communities to access play facilities and tackling the unwelcome sexualisation of children in marketing. However, little has been heard of the taskforce since the announcement and the government has appeared coy about its work or how often it has met (Mahadevan, 2011).

Against this background, we examine what the adult public thinks it is like growing up in Britain today. The questions we asked were first included in 2007 and 2008 with funding from the former Department for Children, Schools and Families (now the Department for Education) and we repeated a number of them in the 2010 survey. In this chapter we find out whether people think Britain[1] is a good country for children to grow up in and whether children fare better or worse here now than ten years ago. We also discover how far they agree that young people today are responsible and well-behaved and if they think behaviour is any worse than in the past. We begin with the overall balance of views, but go on to investigate the opinions held by different groups – notably, young adults, older people, parents and people living without dependent children.

....

* Elizabeth Clery is a Research Director at the *National Centre for Social Research* and a Co-Director of the *British Social Attitudes* survey series.

Exploring these attitudes will tell us whether people tend to be more optimistic about childhood than its generally gloomy portrayal by government and in the media,[2] or whether they, too, share a mood of pessimism and unease.

Childhood in Britain

We begin by considering whether the view that the UK performs relatively poorly on child well-being is reflected in public attitudes towards childhood in Britain. In 2010, we asked respondents for the first time to indicate whether they agree or disagree with the following statement:

Overall Britain is a good country for children to grow up in

The fact that we do not specify a comparison means that people may have stated their views with different reference groups in mind – including poorer countries than the industrialised nations assessed in the latest UNICEF report on inequalities in well-being (UNICEF, 2010). Nevertheless, the answers – presented in Table 10.1 – suggest that the public generally take a positive view. Seven in ten respondents agree Britain is a good country for children to grow up in, while around two in ten neither agree nor disagree. Just one in ten respondents disagree with this view.

Table 10.1 Attitudes to Britain as a country to grow up in

Overall Britain is a good country for children to grow up in	%
Agree	70
Neither agree nor disagree	17
Disagree	10
Base	*2791*

Even without knowing what comparisons people are making when agreeing to the statement, their broad assessment is clearly at odds with widely-publicised assessments that the UK is not performing well. However, to discover how far views are uniformly positive or vary, we next examine what the public thinks about a number of specific childhood issues and how these have changed over time.

7in10

respondents agree Britain is a good country for children to grow up in

Attitudes to childhood

Respondents' knowledge of childhood in other countries is bound, in most cases, to be limited. But no such qualification applies to questions about childhood in Britain itself, where they can draw on their own upbringing and their experiences as parents, or as members of the community, aware of other people's children. To ensure comparison with a common point in time, we asked respondents in 2010 to think back 10 years and say whether they agreed or disagreed with each of the following statements:

Children today are happier than children were 10 years ago

Children today are under more pressure from adverts than children were 10 years ago

Children today have better educational opportunities than children had 10 years ago

It is less safe for children today to play outside than it was 10 years ago

Their responses are compared in Table 10.2 with those obtained in 2008 when the same questions were asked. The results demonstrate that the public's perceptions of childhood and how this is changing are more nuanced than might be supposed from the large majority who agree that Britain is a good country to grow up in.

We can also see how perceptions differ markedly depending on the aspect of childhood being discussed; so it is not simply the case that a fixed proportion of the public regard childhood as having improved in the past decade, while the remainder think it has worsened. Overall, as in 2008, people think three of the four aspects of childhood we asked about have grown worse in the last decade. While just over half disagree that children are happier now than they were 10 years ago, the proportion saying this has declined by five percentage points since the previous survey. Nevertheless, the proportion of adults who positively agree that children are happier than 10 years ago remains low at 12 per cent. When it comes to children playing outside, the proportion agreeing they are less safe than 10 years ago rises above six out of ten, although this, too, is rather lower than in the previous survey. The percentage in active disagreement is, conversely, five percentage points higher than in 2008, at 23 per cent. This contrasts with an altogether stronger and less changing consensus that children are under more pressure from adverts now than 10 years ago, where 85 per cent agree and just seven per cent disagree.

The question where most people acknowledge there has been a positive improvement over the last 10 years concerns education. Around three-fifths agree that children have better educational opportunities today than a decade ago, while less than a fifth

The public's perceptions of childhood and how this is changing are more nuanced than might be supposed

disagree. Similar proportions were identified in 2008. This finding accords with other *British Social Attitudes* data showing that public attitudes to school-based education have become more positive in the past 10 years. For example, in *The 27th Report* we found that the proportion of the public who felt secondary schools were doing well preparing young people for work, teaching the 'three Rs' and bringing out pupils' natural abilities had increased significantly since the mid-1990s (Clery and Low, 2010).

Table 10.2 Attitudes to childhood, 2008 and 2010

	2008	2010
Children today are happier than children were 10 years ago	%	%
Agree	10	12
Neither agree nor disagree	29	31
Disagree	59	54
Children today are under more pressure from adverts than children were 10 years ago	%	%
Agree	83	85
Neither agree nor disagree	9	7
Disagree	6	7
Children today have better educational opportunities than children had 10 years ago	%	%
Agree	61	59
Neither agree nor disagree	20	20
Disagree	17	18
It is less safe for children today to play outside than it was 10 years ago	%	%
Agree	69	64
Neither agree nor disagree	12	12
Disagree	18	23
Base	*3393*	*3297*

People's positive views about improving educational opportunities over the past decade contrast with their prevailing pessimism about the direction of change in the pressures on children from advertising, children's safety playing outside and their overall happiness. But attitudes on these specific questions are not necessarily inconsistent with a general impression that Britain is a good country for children to grow up in. People could hold this positive view yet still feel that British childhood is not as good as it used to be in various key respects. The data reported above also give no indication of the extent to which people feel these aspects of childhood in Britain have deteriorated in a decade. Looking at the modest movement in attitudes that has taken place since 2008 towards a more optimistic stance, we can, at least, be sure that negative opinion on the four chosen issues has not hardened. In other words, the 2010 findings cannot be interpreted as evidence of a downward trend in public confidence concerning the quality of childhood.

In 2010, respondents were also asked whether they agreed or disagreed that:

Young people in this area do not have enough constructive things to do in their spare time

Sixty per cent of respondents agreed with this statement – a decline of six percentage points from the proportion who stated the same in 2007, when the question was first asked. This short-term change adds weight to a hypothesis that public attitudes to childhood, even when they show continuing concern, have not been getting any more pessimistic. But does this distinction still apply when it comes to people's view of today's children and young people – and more specifically the way that they behave?

Attitudes to children and young people

We asked respondents whether they agreed or disagreed with a range of statements about children and young people. In designing these questions, we recognised that respondents would be likely to hold different views about children of different ages and developmental stages, from infancy through to late adolescence. We chose to focus our questions on 10–19 year olds and advised respondents that:

*For the next few questions, I'd like you to think in particular about people aged between **10 and 19**. So when I use the term young people, **10 to 19** is the broad age group I'm referring to.*

People were then asked to indicate how far they agreed or disagreed with each of the following statements:

The behaviour of young people today is no worse than it was in the past

Girls are more badly behaved than boys nowadays

Most young people are responsible and well-behaved

Their responses are presented in Table 10.3 alongside views obtained in the 2008 survey when the same questions were asked. The first important point to note is that a majority of the public (61 per cent) agree that most young people are responsible and well-behaved – and that this is slightly higher than the proportion recorded three years earlier. The percentage that disagrees has, meanwhile, declined somewhat from 25 per cent to 21 per cent.

61%

think most young people are well behaved

Nevertheless, the data indicate a widely-held perception that standards of behaviour are not as high as "in the past". Slightly less than three in ten agree that young people's behaviour is no worse today, but more than six out of ten disagree. Again, we can see evidence of a modest shift in recent years towards a more positive view of the way that young people's behaviour has changed over time. This provides further evidence that, while the majority of the public still think many aspects of childhood have deteriorated, rather more adults express optimism about children and young people than a few years ago.

Table 10.3 Attitudes to children, 2008 and 2010

	2008	2010
The behaviour of young people today is no worse than it was in the past	%	%
Agree	24	28
Neither agree nor disagree	7	8
Disagree	69	63
Girls are more badly behaved than boys nowadays	%	%
Agree	41	40
Neither agree nor disagree	33	32
Disagree	25	27
Most young people are responsible and well-behaved	%	%
Agree	57	61
Neither agree nor disagree	17	17
Disagree	25	21
Base	*3393*	*3297*

However, it is instructive to observe how opinions about the behaviour of girls compared with boys are not only very mixed, but also little changed in three years. Four in ten agree with the proposition that girls are more badly behaved than boys nowadays, while three in ten neither agree nor disagree and slightly fewer than three in ten disagree. These views appear to fly in the face of the evidence that young women are less likely to commit crime than young men, commit less serious offences and also tend to stop offending at an earlier age (Smith, 2010). Even so, evidence from the middle of the last decade that teenage girls in Britain are more likely to drink alcohol regularly than in other European countries (Currie et al., 2008) attracted considerable media attention, fuelling concerns that young women are increasingly involved in a hard-drinking, anti-social 'ladette' culture. This may help to explain why such a large minority of the public think girls are more badly behaved than boys.

The influence of age and parenthood
Childhood is a topic where – exceptionally in social policy – everyone has personal experience on which to base their opinions. But to what extent do views change when

people are no longer young themselves, or do not have children living at home with them? Previous *British Social Attitudes* surveys have produced compelling evidence that people with direct or recent experience of an area tend to view it more positively. For example, in 2009, those who had recently used NHS services expressed greater levels of satisfaction with them (Appleby and Robertson, 2010) and parents of school-age children rated the performance of schools more positively than non-parents (Clery and Low, 2010). Is this also true of adults with the most recent experiences of childhood and children?

Perhaps surprisingly, the picture that emerges from the 2010 survey is unclear. There are almost no significant differences between the attitudes of parents caring for dependent children and other members of the public – suggesting that current experience of childhood from the standpoint of a parent does not result in attitudes that differ much from those of adult society as a whole. The only exception concerns behaviour, where parents of dependent children are less likely to accept that girls' behaviour is worse than boys. Not only do 30 per cent disagree, but another 37 per cent say they neither agree nor disagree. It may be that parents' experience of their children's friends as well as their own families reduce their capacity or willingness to generalise about children's behaviour. Even so, 32 per cent of current parents concur that girls' behaviour is worse than boys, aligning themselves with 40 per cent of non-parents who take this view.

Distinctions between the views expressed by younger and older adults are much more marked, but not always in predictable ways. As shown in Figure 10.1, the views that older people hold about childhood are not universally more positive or negative than those of younger people. Older age groups are much more likely to agree that Britain is a good country to grow up in. Eight in ten (81 per cent) people aged 65 years and above express this view, compared to six in ten (60 per cent) of those aged 18–34. Yet despite being positive about Britain as a place for children to grow up, older people are more negative than others about children's happiness over time. Sixty per cent of people aged 65 and over – and almost as high a proportion of 50–64 year olds – disagree that children are happier today than they were ten years ago, compared to 44 per cent in the youngest age group.

When we examine attitudes to young people's spare time, older age groups revert to adopting a more positive position. While 66 per cent of those aged 18–34 agree that young people do not have enough constructive things to do in their spare time, the proportion among those aged 65 years or over falls to 55 per cent. It is, perhaps, not difficult to imagine that the oldest age group, observing the rapid expansion in availability of computers, books and other leisure opportunities might be less inclined than younger adults to think that children lack constructive things to do.

The views that older people hold about childhood are not universally more positive or negative than those of younger people

Figure 10.1 Attitudes to childhood and children, by age

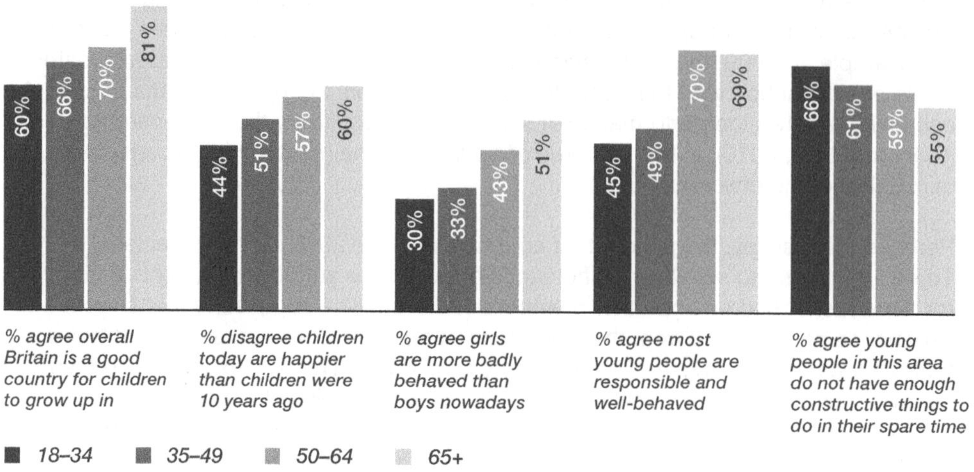

Bar chart:

- **% agree overall Britain is a good country for children to grow up in**: 18–34: 60%, 35–49: 66%, 50–64: 70%, 65+: 81%
- **% disagree children today are happier than children were 10 years ago**: 18–34: 44%, 35–49: 51%, 50–64: 57%, 65+: 60%
- **% agree girls are more badly behaved than boys nowadays**: 18–34: 30%, 35–49: 33%, 50–64: 43%, 65+: 51%
- **% agree most young people are responsible and well-behaved**: 18–34: 45%, 35–49: 49%, 50–64: 70%, 65+: 69%
- **% agree young people in this area do not have enough constructive things to do in their spare time**: 18–34: 66%, 35–49: 61%, 50–64: 59%, 65+: 55%

Legend: ■ 18–34 ■ 35–49 ▨ 50–64 ▨ 65+

The data on which Figure 10.1 is based can be found in the appendix to this chapter

In relation to children and young people's behaviour, very similar proportions of younger and older respondents agree that young people's behaviour today is no worse than it has been in the past. But, rather surprisingly, we find that respondents aged 50 and over are much more likely than 18–34 year olds to endorse the view that most young people are responsible and well-behaved. Seven in ten of those in the oldest age groups support this view, compared to less than half of those aged 18–34 years. It might be argued that those who were most recently children themselves have more experience of the way that today's children and young people behave, leading to less positive assessments. On the other hand, young adults might also be thought to have a stronger incentive than older people to put a positive gloss on their own childhood behaviour when comparing it with their even more youthful successors.

The waters are further muddied by the evidence that older people are much more likely than younger age groups to believe that girls' behaviour is nowadays worse than boys. In particular, where only 30 per cent of 18–34 year olds think this is the case, as many as 51 per cent of those aged 65 and over agree. This may be because expectations of girls' behaviour were very different in the period when the oldest age groups were growing up – and that what is construed as acceptable today was then viewed negatively. It is also possible that older people have also been more strongly influenced by negative media portrayals of girls' behaviour. Overall, however, we can see that the differences and distinctions between the attitudes to childhood held by older and younger adults are complex and may merit closer investigation in future.

The adult public's view of childhood and children is in many ways a less negative one than that presented by policy makers and the media

Clearly, however, it is quite wrong to suppose that older age groups, just by dint of being furthest removed from childhood, view children and growing up in Britain more negatively than younger age groups.

Conclusions

As The Children's Society's *Good Childhood Inquiry* (Layard and Dunn, 2009) observed in its assessment of children's lives in modern Britain, "There are causes to celebrate *and* causes to worry". Others, too, have contrasted the concerns that adults often express about childhood, with evidence that the vast majority of children and young people say their lives are happy and tend to take an optimistic view of the future (Cambridge Primary Review, 2010: pp. 53–62). Yet we can now see that the adult public's view of childhood and children is in many ways a less negative one than that presented by policy makers and the media, and certainly more nuanced. While a number of aspects of childhood and children are widely viewed as having deteriorated in the past decade, the data we have collected in recent years does not suggest we are witnessing a long-term slide into pessimism in these areas. Whatever their specific concerns, most people view Britain as a good country for children to grow up in.

Attitudes to childhood turn out to be less influenced by whether people are currently caring for dependent children – a somewhat unexpected finding that may merit further investigation across a wider range of topics. But it is also interesting to discover that while older people tend to hold distinctive views about children's lives, these do not run in any single direction – positive or negative.

The well-being of children and families was identified as a priority by the coalition government at an early stage in its administration, but it remains to be seen what substantive outcomes may emerge from this – and how these may influence the public's attitudes to childhood in the future.

Notes

1. While the UNICEF studies and the government's Children and Families Taskforce focus on children in the UK, our findings are for Britain and exclude Northern Ireland.

2. A recent statistical review provides evidence that young people themselves feel the media present an unduly negative view of their age group. Almost eight out of ten 16 and 17 year olds agree that the media usually make young people out to be worse than they really are. A similar proportion feel that most attention is given to a minority of troublemakers, rather than young people who are making positive contributions to society. (Department for Education, 2011).

References

Appleby, J. and Robertson, R. (2010), 'A healthy improvement? Satisfaction with the NHS under Labour', in Park, A., Curtice, J., Clery, E. and Bryson, C. (eds.) (2010), *British Social Attitudes: the 27th Report – Exploring Labour's Legacy*, London: Sage

Cambridge Primary Review (2010), *Children, their World, their Education. Final report and recommendations of the Cambridge Primary Review*, London: Routledge

Chamberlain, T., George, N., Golden, S., Walker, F. and Benton, T. (2010), *TellUs4 National Report*, London: Department for Children, Schools and Families

Clery, E. and Low, N. (2010), 'One school of thought? Reactions to education policy' in Park,

A., Curtice, J., Clery, E. and Bryson, C. (eds.), *British Social Attitudes: the 27th Report – Exploring Labour's Legacy*, London: Sage

Currie, C., Nic Gabhainn, S., Godeau, E., Roberts, C., Smith, R., Currie, D., Picket, W., Richter, M., Morgan, A. and Barnekow, V. (eds.) (2008), *Inequalities in Young People's Health: HBSC International Report from the 2005/06 Survey*, Edinburgh: University of Edinburgh Child and Adolescence Health Research Unit, for World Health Organization at www.education.ac.uk/cahru

Department for Education Youth Research Team, Young People Today – Statistics on Young People's Lives, July 2011, available at www.education.gov.uk/childrenandyoungpeople/ youngpeople/positive%20for%20youth/b0077531/positive-for-youth-discussion-papers

Layard, R. and Dunn, J. (2009), *A Good Childhood. Searching for Values in a Competitive Age*, London: Penguin

Mahadevan, J. (2011), 'Government blasted over childhood taskforce silence' *Children & Young People Now*, 8 February 2011

Office for National Statistics (2010a), *Health expectancies at birth and at age 65, United Kingdom, 2006–08*, London: London: Office for National Statistics

Office for National Statistics (2010b), *Life expectancy at birth and at age 65 by local areas in the United Kingdom, 2007–09*, London: Office for National Statistics

Piachaud, D. (2007), *Freedom to be a Child: commercial pressures on children*, London: Centre for Analysis of Social Exclusion, London School of Economics

Smith, D.J. (2010), 'Time trends in youth crime and in justice system responses' in Smith, D.J. (ed.), *A New Response to Youth Crime*, Cullompton: Willan

UK Children's Commissioners (2008), *UK Children's Commissioners' Report to the UN Committee on the Rights of the Child*, London: 11 Million

UNICEF (2007), *Child Poverty in Perspective: an overview of child well-being in rich countries*, Innocenti Report Card 7, Florence: UNICEF Innocenti Research Centre

UNICEF (2010), *The Children Left Behind: a league table of inequality in child well-being in the world's rich countries*, Innocenti Report Card 9, Florence: UNICEF Innocenti Research Centre

Acknowledgements
The *National Centre for Social Research* is grateful to the Department for Education for their financial support, which enabled us to ask the questions reported in this chapter, although the views expressed are those of the author alone.

Appendix
The data for Figure 10.1 are shown below.

Table A.1 Attitudes to childhood and children, by age

	Age			
	18-34	35-49	50-64	65+
% agree overall Britain is a good country for children to grow up in	60	66	70	81
Base	569	802	718	697
% disagree children today are happier than children were 10 years ago	44	51	57	60
% agree girls are more badly behaved than boys nowadays	30	33	43	51
% agree most young people are responsible and well-behaved	45	49	70	69
% agree young people in this area do not have enough constructive things to do in their spare time	66	61	59	55
Base	676	943	814	857

11. Child poverty
Fewer children in poverty: is it a public priority?

The coalition government has maintained Labour's target to eradicate child poverty by 2020 and has identified a number of key causes, including family breakdown. Do this target and diagnosis reflect public priorities and views?

Most people accept child poverty in Britain exists and do not expect it to fall. There is disagreement about why children live in poverty, although the most popular explanations support the government's view.

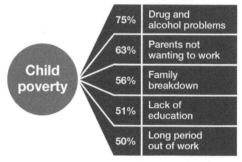

51%

think child poverty will increase in the next 10 years.

Four in ten (43%) say there is "some" child poverty in Britain; another third (36%) think there is "quite a lot" Around half (51%) think **child poverty will increase in the decade ahead**.

Among the **many reasons given for child poverty**, the most frequently cited are parents having drug and alcohol problems (75%), parents not wanting to work (63%), family breakdown (56%), lack of education among parents (51%) and parents being out of work for a long time (50%).

An overwhelming majority support action to reduce child poverty, with most people seeing this as a task for central and local government.

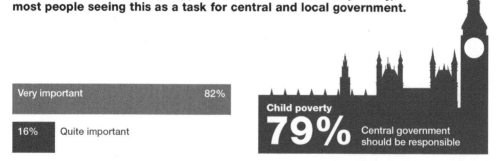

Eight in ten (82%) consider it **"very important" to reduce child poverty in Britain**, while another 16% think it is "quite important".

Eight in ten (79%) say central government should be **responsible for reducing child poverty**. But large minorities say people living in poverty including parents (46%) or their friends and relatives (32%) should be responsible.

Author: Elizabeth Clery*

Reducing child poverty has been a prominent government concern for more than a decade. Yet little is known about the public's attitudes to poverty specifically as it affects children. This includes people's views regarding the level of child poverty, what causes it and the extent to which eliminating it should be a government priority. Using answers to questions developed for the 2009 *British Social Attitudes* survey we are able to fill a notable gap in existing evidence.

During its 13 years in power the Labour government maintained a strong focus on reducing child poverty in Britain, encapsulated in Tony Blair's pledge in March 1999 to "eradicate" it by 2020. This commitment was accompanied by intermediate targets. Using the relative measurement of children in households with less than 60 per cent of median income before housing costs, the government's aim was to reduce the level of child poverty by a quarter by 2004/05 and a half by 2010/11. Although the first of these was missed by a considerable margin,[1] Labour went on to establish four separate targets for reducing child poverty by 2020/21 in the Child Poverty Act 2010. The legislation received cross-party support and a focus on child poverty has been maintained by the Coalition, whose 'Programme for Government' included a commitment to the 2020 target (Cabinet Office, 2010).

The development of reduction strategies has led to considerable debate about the causes of child poverty and how it should be measured. The Coalition has argued that Labour's targets, based on relative household income, are "poor proxies for achieving the eradication of child poverty" (House of Lords, 2010). An independent review that the new government commissioned from the Labour MP Frank Field called for a new index of children's 'life chance' measurements (Field, 2010). The Coalition has, meanwhile, placed its emphasis on tackling family breakdown, drug and alcohol addiction, limited education and skills, debt and worklessness as perceived causes of child poverty (Department for Education and Department for Work and Pensions, 2011).

The *British Social Attitudes* survey has regularly measured attitudes to poverty, but specific questions on child poverty were included for the first time in 2009. We begin by presenting up-to-date data on public attitudes to poverty in general; an important context in which to understand attitudes to child poverty in particular. Turning to child poverty, we examine the public's assessment of the current levels of child poverty, how this has changed and how it might change in the future. We then look at the public's understanding of the causes of child poverty and, finally, consider whether reducing child poverty is a priority for the British public and how far people think the responsibility lies with government. We conclude by assessing how far the current government's approach mirrors public perceptions and priorities in the period just before they came to power and the implications of this.

Attitudes to poverty

The public holds mixed views about the level of poverty in Britain and what causes it. That much is already apparent from responses to questions that the *British Social Attitudes* survey includes about the extent of poverty.

....

* Elizabeth Clery is a Research Director at the *National Centre for Social Research* and a Co-Director of the *British Social Attitudes* survey series.

Respondents are regularly asked a sequence of questions to gain their perceptions of the level of poverty in Britain and how it is changing:

*Some people say there is very little **real** poverty in Britain today. Others say there is quite a lot. Which comes closest to **your** view, that there is very little real poverty in Britain, or, that there is quite a lot?*

Over the last ten years, do you think that poverty in Britain has been increasing, decreasing or staying at about the same level?

*And over the **next** ten years, do you think that poverty in Britain will increase, decrease, or, stay at about the same level?*

Looking at the responses in Table 11.1 we can see that in 2009 almost six in ten consider there is "quite a lot" of poverty in Britain, while just under four in ten say there is "very little". Almost half think poverty has increased in the last ten years, while around one in three maintain it has stayed at the same level. Little more than one in ten think poverty has decreased over the previous decade. Looking ahead ten years, people take similar stances – with 56 per cent expecting poverty to increase, 29 per cent to remain the same and 11 per cent to decline. The survey also asks:

Why do you think there are people who live in need?

Because they have been unlucky?

Because of laziness or lack of willpower?

Because of injustice in our society?

It's an inevitable part of modern life?

Looking again at Table 11.1 we see there is no overriding explanation that people accept as the answer to this. While almost four in ten view living in need as inevitable in modern life, slightly less than three in ten attribute it to laziness or a lack of willpower. Around two in ten point to injustice in society while slightly more than one in ten think people live in need because they have been unlucky.

6 in 10

say there is "quite a lot" of poverty in Britain

Table 11.1 Perceptions of poverty, 1986–2009

	86	89	94	00	03	06	09
Perceived levels of poverty in Britain today	%	%	%	%	%	%	%
Very little	41	34	28	35	41	45	39
Quite a lot	55	63	71	62	55	52	58
Over the last 10 years ...	%	%	%	%	%	%	%
...poverty has increased	51	50	67	36	35	32	48
...poverty has decreased	15	16	6	20	19	23	14
...poverty has stayed the same	30	31	24	38	39	39	34
Over the next 10 years ...	%	%	%	%	%	%	%
...poverty will increase	44	44	54	41	46	44	56
...poverty will decrease	12	16	10	18	13	16	11
...poverty will stay the same	36	34	32	35	33	35	29
Why do people live in need?	%	%	%	%	%	%	%
Unlucky	11	11	15	15	13	10	12
Laziness/lack of willpower	19	19	15	23	28	27	26
Injustice in society	25	29	29	21	19	21	19
Inevitable in modern life	37	34	33	34	32	34	38
Base	*1548*	*1516*	*1167*	*3426*	*3272*	*3240*	*2267*

Table 11.1 also shows long-term trends. Looking at these in the 2008 *British Social Attitudes* report, Taylor-Gooby and Martin concluded that the share of the population who think poverty is prevalent in Britain increased until the mid-1990s, then fell back. The same was true of the proportion who thought poverty had increased over the previous decade. However, the proportion who expected it to increase or diminish in the next 10 years showed much less fluctuation (Taylor-Gooby and Martin, 2008). The data for 2009 shown in Table 11.1 reveal significant changes in all these trends. The 58 per cent of respondents who say there is "quite a lot" of poverty is six percentage points higher than in 2006 and reverses a downward trend that began in 1994. Likewise, 48 per cent say poverty has increased in the past decade – an increase of 16 percentage points since 2006. In addition, the future outlook is less positive than at any time since the survey began, with a majority (56 per cent) believing poverty will increase in the next 10 years – a 12 percentage point increase since 2006.

It is worth noting that the surveys for 1994 and 2009 were both conducted at, or close to, a time of economic recession when the public could be expected to show heightened public awareness of economic hardship. This may go some way to explain people's pessimism about poverty. Yet despite a more negative outlook concerning current and future levels of poverty, people's perceptions about the causes of "living in need" have remained relatively stable over two decades. There has, however, been a seven percentage point increase since 1986 in the proportion who blame "laziness or a lack of willpower". The proportion who cite "injustice in our society" has, conversely, declined by six percentage points over the same period.

Attitudes to child poverty

One reason for asking specific questions on child poverty in 2009 was to discover how far the public views child poverty in the same way as general poverty, or whether they hold different perceptions and expectations.[2] The data presented in Table 11.2 show that the responses regarding child poverty are, in fact, very similar to those regarding poverty in general. Most people – around four in five – think there is a considerable amount of child poverty in Britain. This is made up of 36 per cent who think there is "quite a lot" and 43 per cent who say there is "some" child poverty. Less than one in five think there is "very little" or no child poverty.

Our respondents were presented with more detailed answer categories for child poverty than for poverty in general and this means the replies are not directly comparable. However, people's assessments of how child poverty levels have changed in the past, and are likely to change in the future, are almost identical to those in relation to poverty overall. Almost half think that child poverty has increased over the last 10 years and around half think it will increase during the next ten years. Little more than one in 10 respondents in each case think that child poverty has decreased in the last 10 years or will decrease in the decade ahead.

Table 11.2 Perceptions of child poverty, 2009

Perceived levels of child poverty in Britain today	%
None/very little	18
Some	43
Quite a lot	36

Over the last 10 years ...	%
...child poverty has increased	46
...child poverty has decreased	12
...child poverty has stayed the same	35

Over the next 10 years ...	%
...child poverty will increase	51
...child poverty will decrease	14
...child poverty will stay the same	29

Base	*3421*

Although the public's views about the likelihood of child poverty being reduced are clearly more negative than those expressed by government policy makers, they are not necessarily more realistic. Statistics for 2009/10 showed that 20 per cent of children were living in UK households with less than 60 per cent of median net disposable income, before taking account of housing costs – the main measurement of child poverty adopted by Labour. This represented a fall of two percentage points since 2008/09 and six percentage points since 1998/09 (Department for Work and Pensions, 2011). On this definition, at least, it seems that most people assess recent trends in the level of child poverty incorrectly.

However, it is entirely possible that sections of the public understand child poverty in different terms to government and define it in different ways. The way that attitudes vary by income adds weight to this theory. While 85 per cent of those in the highest income quartile think there is quite a lot or some child poverty in Britain, the same is true of 74 per cent of those with incomes in the lowest quartile. These figures suggest that people with higher incomes tend to locate the boundary between poverty and non-poverty at a higher point than those who are, themselves, living on relatively low incomes – perhaps because of different perceptions about what constitutes an acceptable standard of living.

A question included in the *British Social Attitudes* survey in 2001 and 2008 supports this view. It asks:

Of every 100 children under 16 in Britain, about how many do you think live in poverty?

As we can see in Figure 11.1 there is widespread disagreement about the answer. In 2001, more than three in ten (34 per cent) thought that this figure was below 20 per cent. Around one in five (21 per cent) placed it in the 20–29 per cent bracket – which was closest to the government's own figures. Four in ten respondents thought that over 30 but less than 50 per cent of children in Britain are living in poverty (41 per cent), while a considerable minority (18 per cent) believed the figure was 50 per cent or more.

This suggests that a sizeable proportion of the public are more negative in their views about the extent of child poverty than the government. However, by 2008 assessments had become rather more optimistic with a larger minority (42 per cent) thinking that less than 20 per cent of children are in poverty.

A sizeable proportion of the public are more negative in their views about the extent of child poverty than the government

Figure 11.1 Perceptions of the proportions of children in Britain in poverty, 2001 and 2008

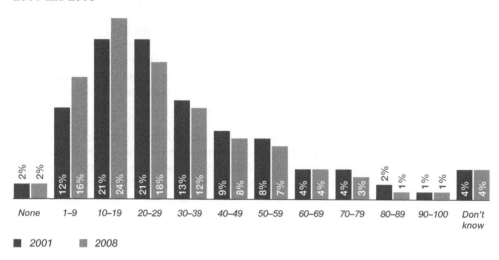

	None	1–9	10–19	20–29	30–39	40–49	50–59	60–69	70–79	80–89	90–100	Don't know
2001	2%	12%	21%	21%	13%	9%	8%	4%	4%	2%	1%	4%
2008	2%	16%	24%	18%	12%	8%	7%	4%	3%	1%	1%	4%

■ 2001   ■ 2008

The data on which Figure11.1 is based can be found in the appendix to this chapter

The causes of child poverty

To explore views on the causes of child poverty in Britain, we presented people with a list of possibilities and asked them to identify those they considered relevant, including what they viewed as the main reason. From Table 11.3, which shows the different reasons that were shown to respondents, it is apparent that no single factor is considered to cause child poverty. People, on average, select six different explanations from our list.

Nevertheless, more than half the respondents endorse four of the possible reasons for children living in poverty. Having parents who "suffer from alcohol, drug abuse or another addiction" is the most popular explanation, selected by three in four. Around two in three think having parents who "do not want to work" is a cause; while slightly more than a half in each case pointed to "family breakdown or loss of a family member" or the fact that "parents lack education". These four explanations were, again, the most frequently chosen when respondents selected the main reason why children in Britain live in poverty. We saw earlier that views about why people in Britain are "living in need" are mixed. While the causes of child poverty considered here cannot be easily allocated to overriding categories (such as "injustice in our society" or "laziness or a lack of willpower"), the wide range and large number of responses selected by respondents indicate that the causes of child poverty are viewed as a combination of factors relating to parents, families and local areas, welfare policies and the structure of society as a whole. Interestingly, the four explanations most frequently chosen as the main reason why children in Britain live in poverty closely

4 in 5

there is near-universal support for reducing child poverty, with more than four in five saying it is "very important"

mirror four of the five key issues prioritised by the coalition government (see above). This suggests that while government assessments of the extent of child poverty may differ from the public's opinion, its rhetoric concerning causes has been broadly in line.

Table 11.3 Perceptions of reasons why children live in poverty in Britain, 2009

Reasons why children live in poverty in Britain	A reason	Main reason
	%	%
Their parents suffer from alcohol, drug abuse or other addiction	75	19
Their parents do not want to work	63	15
There has been a family breakdown or loss of a family member	56	10
Their parents lack education	51	10
Their parents' work doesn't pay enough	44	9
Their parents have been out of work for a long time	50	6
They live in a poor quality area	44	5
Because of inequalities in society	25	5
Social benefits for families with children are not high enough	19	4
There are too many children in the family	39	3
Their grand-parents were also poor – it has been passed down generations	21	3
They – or their parents – suffer from a long-term illness or disability	43	3
Their parents do not work enough hours	16	1
Their family suffers from discrimination	25	1
Their family cannot access affordable housing	31	1
Base	3421	3421

Items are ordered by the proportions of respondents who selected them as the main reason why some children in Britain live in poverty.

Reducing child poverty – a public priority?

In a further question, we asked people to say how important they thought it was to reduce child poverty in Britain. Table 11.4 shows there is near-universal support for reducing child poverty, with more than four in five saying it is "very important" and most others choosing "quite important". By cross-comparing data we find that 93 per cent of those who think there is "quite a lot" of child poverty in Britain, view its reduction as "very important", while even 66 per cent of those who feel there is "very little" child poverty say the same.

This suggests there should be strong public support for a national goal of eradicating child poverty by 2020. But to what extent do people feel it is the role of government to fulfil this task? Respondents were asked to say who they thought should be responsible for reducing child poverty in Britain. While it is apparent in Table 11.4 that people do not view one organisation as solely implicated, there is a wide consensus that it is a task for government. Almost four in five identify child poverty reduction as a central government responsibility (including Parliament and government departments) and six in ten think that local government is responsible. However, just under half think that those who live in poverty, including parents, hold a responsibility. Friends and relatives and charities are also cited, by around three in ten in each case.

As might be expected, there is evidence that people's perceptions of the causes of child poverty link to their views about who is responsible for its reduction. For example, the vast majority (86 per cent) of those who view inadequate social benefits as a cause also think government is responsible for reducing child poverty. People who feel that children are in poverty because their parents do not want to work are more likely than average to insist that people living in poverty, including parents, are responsible.

Table 11.4 Attitudes to importance of and responsibility for reducing child poverty, 2009

Attitudes to reducing child poverty

Importance of reducing child poverty in Britain	%
Very important	82
Quite important	16
Not very important	1
Not at all important	*

Groups responsible for reducing child poverty[+]	%
Central government (e.g. Parliament, government departments)	79
Local government (e.g. local councils)	60
People in poverty, including parents	46
Friends/relatives of people in poverty	32
Charities	28

Base	*3421*

Respondents had the option of identifying "all groups" as being responsible for reducing child poverty in Britain. Five per cent of respondents selected this option; for the purpose of this analysis, they have been assigned to each of the groups above.
[+] *Respondents were allowed to select as many answers as they liked; as a result their answers add up to more than 100%.*

Conclusions

The responses to the new questions on child poverty provide a baseline for monitoring public attitudes as the 2020 deadline for eradicating child poverty approaches. We can see that in some ways the government's focus on child poverty reflects public thinking. People agree that child poverty exists in Britain, often to a substantial degree, and view action to reduce it as important and as a role for central government. The public also shares the government's view that child poverty has multiple causes, among which they tend to emphasise parental problems. There is, however, considerable – and arguably excessive – pessimism about likely progress in tackling child poverty. Despite a continuing government focus, public attitudes show little faith in past, current or future intervention to achieve a reduction.

Notes

1. Progress against the government's target to halve the number of children in poverty by 2010/11 will not be known until spring 2012. Current estimates suggest the target will be missed by a considerable margin. See for example Brewer *et al.* (2006).

NatCen Social Research

2. To develop questions on child poverty for the *British Social Attitudes* survey, cognitive question testing was undertaken, to ascertain whether the questions being considered were meaningful and could easily be answered by the public. This exercise highlighted the fact that the public is able to consider and answer questions about child poverty as a concept distinct from that of general poverty (Blake *et al.*, 2009).

References

Blake, M., Clery, E., d'Ardenne, J. and Legard, R. (2009), *Cognitive testing: British Social Attitudes child poverty questions,* Department for Work and Pensions Research Report 574, available at http://research.dwp.gov.uk/asd/asd5/rports2009-2010/rrep574.pdf

Brewer, M., Joyce, R. and Sutherland, H. (2006), *Micro-simulating child poverty in 2010 and 2020,* Joseph Rowntree Foundation, available at http://www.jrf.org.uk/sites/files/jrf/9781859355091.pdf

Department for Education and Department for Work and Pensions (2011), *Tackling the causes of disadvantage and transforming families' lives*, available at https://www.education.gov.uk/publications/standard/publicationDetail/Page1/CM%208061

Department for Work and Pensions (2011), *Households below average income (HBAI) – First Release*, May 2011, available at http://statistics.dwp.gov.uk/asd/hbai/hbai2010/pdf_files/first_release_0910.pdf

Field, F. (2010), *The Foundation Years: preventing poor children becoming poor adults. The report of the Independent Review on Poverty and Life Chances*, London: Cabinet Office

House of Lords Debate 5 January 2010 vol 716, cols. 18-34

Taylor-Gooby, P. and Martin, R. (2008), 'Trends in sympathy for the poor' in Park, A., Curtice, J., Thomson, K., Phillips, M., Johnson, M. and Clery, E. (eds.), *British Social Attitudes: the 24th Report,* London: Sage

Acknowledgements

The *National Centre for Social Research* is grateful to the Department for Work and Pensions for their financial support which enabled us to ask the questions reported in this chapter. The views expressed are those of the author alone.

Appendix

The data for Figure 11.1 are shown below:

Table A.1 Perceptions of the proportions of children in Britain who live in poverty, 2001 and 2008

	2001	2008
Proportion of children in Britain who live in poverty	%	%
None	2	2
1%–9%	12	16
10%–19%	21	24
20%–29%	21	18
30%–39%	13	12
40%–49%	9	8
50%–59%	8	7
60%–69%	4	4
70%–79%	4	3
80%–89%	2	1
90%–100%	1	1
Don't know	4	4
Base	*3287*	*3364*

12. Religion
Losing faith?

How religious is the British public and how has this changed over time? Getting an accurate picture of the importance of religion in people's lives matters; not least because it influences the role of religion in policy making and public life, and helps guide the allocation of funding and resources.

There was much debate in the run-up to the census about how to measure 'religiosity'. The chapter examines levels of religious affiliation, whether someone was brought up in a religion, and whether they regularly attend religious services.

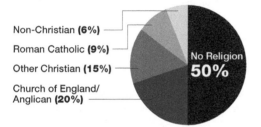

Non-Christian **(6%)**
Roman Catholic **(9%)**
Other Christian **(15%)**
Church of England/ Anglican **(20%)**
No Religion **50%**

14%
Attend weekly

Half (50%) do not regard themselves as **belonging to a particular religion**, while the largest proportion (20%) of religious affiliates belong to the Church of England. Nearly two-thirds (64%) of those aged 18–24 do not belong to a religion, compared with 28% of those aged 65 and above.

More than half (56%) of those who belong to or were brought up in a religion never **attend religious services or meetings**. Just 14% attend weekly.

Levels of religiosity have declined over the past three decades and are likely to decline further, mainly as a result of generational replacement.

One in three (31%) in 1983 did not belong to a religion, compared with one in two (50%) now. **The largest decline** has been in affiliation with the Church of England, which has halved since 1983 (from 40% to 20%).

This change – which is likely to continue – can be explained by **generational replacement**, with older, more religious, generations dying out and being replaced by less religious generations. There is little evidence that substantial numbers find religion as they get older.

1983
40%

2010
20%

Author: Lucy Lee*

We last closely examined religion in *The 26th Report*, contributing to the ongoing debates around how and why religious faith in Britain is changing, and what this means for public attitudes and social policy (Voas and Ling, 2010; McAndrew, 2010). This chapter updates some key elements of this earlier work, focusing particularly on the extent to which the British public is religious, how levels of religiosity vary, and how and why they have changed over the past three decades.

An accurate measure of religiosity in Britain is important for several reasons. We need to feel confident that we can accurately describe what Britain looks like, rather than accept the picture painted by religious or secular leaders. As recent debates around the census highlighted, measures of religiosity guide the allocation of time and money to religious groups and organisations (and consequently to their secular counterparts), and influence policies such as the support of faith schools and retention of bishops in the House of Lords. Understanding religiosity is also important because we know it underpins and influences a number of value and belief systems, whether by directly shaping political views (Andersen *et al.*, 2005), or informing attitudes through the influence of the social contexts people experience (Kotler-Berkowitz, 2001). Using *British Social Attitudes* data, McAndrew (2010) showed religiosity to be strongly linked with attitudes to a range of social issues; the most religious were more likely than others to be anti-abortion, support traditional gender roles and to believe premarital sex is wrong. So, changes in religiosity are likely to accompany and contribute to changes in attitudes to a range of issues.

However, measuring religiosity is not a straightforward exercise. In the run up to the 2011 census, a number of journalists, bloggers and campaigners publicised the disparity between the findings of the 2001 census and the corresponding *British Social Attitudes* survey. While the census reported that 72 per cent of the British population were Christian and 15 per cent of no religion, in that same year we found 43 per cent to be Christian and 41 per cent to be of no religion. The difference between the two results can be partly explained by question wording, the response options offered and the context in which the questions were asked.[1] In this chapter, we use a range of complementary measures of religious upbringing, affiliation and practice included in the *British Social Attitudes* survey to present an up-to-date and nuanced picture of religiosity in Britain, how this has changed and why.

How religious is the British public?
Religiosity can be measured in a number of ways – as testified by the aforementioned debate around the question wording used in the census and its implications for the data obtained. We cannot simply divide the public into the religious and non-religious; there will be varying levels and combinations of commitment and practice. Here, we utilise three long-standing *British Social Attitudes* questions, which measure distinct aspects of religious affiliation and practice.

....

* Lucy Lee is a Researcher at the *National Centre for Social Research* and a Co-Director of the *British Social Attitudes* survey series.

We measure religious affiliation using the following question:

Do you regard yourself as belonging to any particular religion?
IF YES: Which?

Table 12.1 shows how respondents answered this question in 2010. Half do not
belong to a religion, around one in five identify themselves as Church of England
or Anglican and around one in ten are Roman Catholic. Slightly less than one in
five belong to another type of Christian faith and around one in twenty belong
to a non-Christian religion.

Table 12.1 Religious affiliation

Religion which respondent belongs to	%
No religion	50
Church of England/Anglican	20
Other Christian	(15)
Christian – no denomination	9
Christian – specific denomination[2]	6
Roman Catholic	9
Non-Christian[3]	6
Base	*3297*

More often than not, religious belief is initiated in childhood. To ascertain the extent to
which the British public in 2010 has been brought up in a religion, we asked:

In what religion, if any, were you brought up?
PROBE IF NECESSARY: What was your family's religion?

Overall, 79 per cent of the British public describe themselves as having been brought
up in a particular religion. In Table 12.2 we cross-analyse responses to this question
with people's current religious affiliation, reported above. Clearly, being brought up in
a religion has a major impact on religious affiliation later in life. Around half of those
brought up as Anglican/Church of England still affiliate with this religion, though two-
fifths now follow no religion. Those who were brought up in a non-Christian faith or in
Roman Catholicism are far more likely to affiliate with their original religion; this was
the case for almost nine in ten of those brought up in a non-Christian religion and

50%   do not affiliate to a religion

six in ten of those brought up Roman Catholic. Despite this, those who were brought up without a religion are far less likely to shift from this position later in life – almost 19 out of 20 of those who were not brought up in a religion do not have a religious affiliation today. It is clear that the religion one was brought up in has a strong impact on religious affiliation later in life.

Table 12.2 Current religious affiliation, by religious upbringing

	Which religion brought up in				
	Church of England/ Anglican	Roman Catholic	Other Christian	Non-Christian	No religion
Current religious affiliation	%	%	%	%	%
Church of England/ Anglican	49	3	4	*	2
Roman Catholic	1	62	1	–	*
Other Christian	6	3	49	2	3
Non-Christian	1	*	1	87	*
No religion	43	32	44	10	94
Base	1279	447	765	147	628

Less than 0.5 per cent; – indicates zero

While around half of the public describe themselves as belonging to a religion, does this mean that a similar proportion actively practise their faith by attending religious services? If, and how far, is religious affiliation linked to religious practice? To assess this, we asked those who indicated they belong to and/or were brought up in a religion the following question:

Apart from such special occasions as weddings, funerals and baptisms, how often nowadays do you attend services or meetings connected with your religion?[4]

Their responses are presented in Table 12.3. Clearly, religious affiliation does not automatically translate into religious practice. Slightly more than half of those who belong to or were brought up in a religion never attend services or meetings connected with their religion. For the remainder of this group, practice varies widely – one in twenty attend religious meetings less than once a year while, at the opposite end of the spectrum, slightly more than one in ten attend at least weekly.

The religion one was brought up in has a strong impact on religious affiliation later in life

Table 12.3 Attendance at religious services or meetings

Level of attendance	%
Never	56
Less than annually	5
At least annually	15
At least monthly	9
At least weekly	14
Base	2680

Base: respondents who affiliate to a religion and/or were brought up in a religion

Is the propensity for those who belong to a religion to attend services and meetings the same for all religions, or are those who belong to particular religions more likely to attend than others? In Table 12.4 we cross-analyse attendance at religious services or meetings by religious affiliation. Those who affiliate to the Church of England/ Anglicanism are least likely to attend religious services; only around half ever attend and less than one in ten do so at least once a week. Attendance is considerably higher for followers of other religions; only slightly more than two in ten non-Christians never attend religious services, compared with around three in ten Roman Catholics or followers of other Christian faiths.

Table 12.4 Attendance at religious services/meetings, by religious affiliation

	Religious affiliation				
	Church of England/ Anglican	Roman Catholic	Other Christian	Non-Christian	No religion
Level of attendance		%	%	%	%
Never	48	29	34	23	88
Less than annually	7	5	5	4	3
At least annually	25	20	16	12	6
At least monthly	10	17	14	21	1
At least weekly	8	28	29	39	1
Base	719	287	495	152	1027

Base: respondents who affiliate to a religion and/or were brought up in a religion

We have seen that the British public cannot be easily divided into the 'religious' and 'non-religious' – the degree and nature of religiosity varies considerably. Across the public as a whole, 50 per cent do not affiliate with a religion, 18 per cent do affiliate but do not actively practise it (by attending services or meetings) and 30 per cent affiliate and actively practise. We next turn to consider how membership of these three broad groups differs across the population as a whole.

How does religiosity vary among the British public?

A number of groups are traditionally regarded as more religious than others – women compared with men, the old compared with the young, and the less well educated compared with the better educated. In addition, religiosity has been shown to link with support for particular political parties (Clements, 2010). In Table 12.5 we test these assumptions by comparing, across these characteristics, the proportions who are not religious, who belong to a religion but do not attend meetings, and who both belong to and practise a religion.

As expected, we see that men are slightly less likely than women to belong to a religion, while, among those who do belong, women are more likely than men to attend religious meetings. However, we also see that those with qualifications in the middle of the spectrum (CSE to A-level) are less religious than those at either end. While those at each end of the spectrum (no qualification/degree) are the most likely to affiliate with a religion, those with no qualifications are more likely than others to say they are religious but do not practise (27 per cent), and those with degree level qualifications are more likely than others to practise their religion (39 per cent). These findings do not completely support the assumption that the less well educated are traditionally more religious than the better educated, especially when it comes to religious practise. The larger differences, however, appear between older and younger age groups. Around two in three of the youngest age group (aged 18–24) do not belong to a religion, compared with less than one in three of the oldest age group (aged 65 years and over). A similar pattern is seen with religious attendance, with around four in ten respondents aged 65 years and over attending religious meetings, compared with slightly more than two in ten of the youngest age group.

56%

of those affiliating to a religion, or brought up in a religion, never attend religious services or meetings

Table 12.5 Religious affiliation and attendance, by demographic characteristics and party identification

		No religion	Religious but don't attend meetings	Religious and do attend meetings[5]	Base
All	%	50	18	30	3297
Sex					
Male	%	56	17	25	1442
Female	%	45	19	35	1855
Age					
18–24	%	64	10	24	230
25–34	%	57	14	28	446
35–44	%	60	11	28	637
45–54	%	51	18	30	557
55–64	%	47	21	30	563
65–97	%	28	31	39	857
Highest educational qualification					
Degree	%	48	12	39	643
A-level	%	55	14	30	780
O-level	%	58	17	25	537
CSE	%	56	21	20	183
No qualification	%	42	27	28	1129
Party identification					
Conservative	%	44	22	32	943
Labour	%	46	20	32	1011
Liberal Democrat	%	55	11	33	411
Other party	%	63	16	17	194
None	%	59	16	23	532

Religiosity also varies by party identification – the non-religious are the most likely to support a party other than the main three (63 per cent) or not to identify with a political party (59 per cent); they are least likely to support the Conservative party (44 per cent). Interestingly, despite a higher proportion of Conservative supporters belonging to a religion (54 per cent), levels of attendance at religious services are very similar for supporters of the three main political parties (around 32 per cent).

So, levels of religiosity vary markedly across the public and are strongly linked with age and, to a lesser degree, educational qualifications, sex and party identification. These links may provide clues as to how levels of religiosity have changed over time – and it is to this question that we turn to next.

How has religiosity changed over time?

Table 12.6 presents *British Social Attitudes* data on religious affiliation, which the survey has asked about since its inception in 1983. Looking back over the last three decades, we see major changes in the religiosity of the British public. One in three respondents in 1983 did not belong to a religion, compared with one in two now. This decline is largely accounted for by falling affiliation with the Church of England/Anglicanism; the proportion who follow this religion has halved across the lifetime of the study. Adherence to other Christian religions has remained relatively stable, while the share of the population who belong to non-Christian religions has risen – largely as a result of immigration to Britain after the Second World War (Voas and Ling, 2010). We can also see in Table 12.6 that the proportion of the population brought up in a religion has declined by nine percentage points in the last 15 years. Finally, we can look at patterns of attendance among people who affiliate or were brought up in a religion. There is a core of people who attend religious meetings at least weekly or monthly, the levels of which have remained relatively unchanged over the last 20 years. Similarly, the proportion of those who attend less than once a year remains stable. There has been some slight change, however, with those attending "at least annually", six percentage points down on levels for 1990, which is likely to have contributed to the slight rise in the proportion reporting they "never" attend.

Table 12.6 Religious affiliation and attendance, 1983–2010

	83	90	95	00	05	10	Change 83–10
Affiliation	%	%	%	%	%	%	
Church of England/Anglican	40	37	32	30	26	20	-20
Roman Catholic	10	9	9	9	9	9	-1
Other Christian	17	14	15	16	18	15	-2
Non-Christian	2	3	3	5	6	6	+4
No religion	31	36	40	40	40	50	+19
Base	*1761*	*2797*	*3633*	*3426*	*4268*	*3297*	
							95–10
Brought up in a religion	%	%	%	%	%	%	
	n/a	n/a	88	88	86	79	-9
Base	*n/a*	*n/a*	*3633*	*3418*	*4268*	*3287*	
							90–10
Attendance	%	%	%	%	%	%	
Never	n/a	49	55	55	58	56	+7
Less than annually	n/a	6	4	4	5	5	-2
At least annually	n/a	21	19	17	15	15	-6
At least monthly	n/a	10	9	9	8	9	-1
At least weekly	n/a	12	13	13	11	14	+2
Base	*n/a*	*2682*	*3333*	*3048*	*3800*	*2680*	

n/a = not asked
Base for 'Attendance': respondents who affiliate to a religion and/or were brought up in a religion

Why are we less religious than we used to be?

How can we explain this decline in religiosity? Here, we focus on the decline in religious affiliation, which we have seen is strongly influenced by being brought up in a religion, and links to levels of religious attendance. Does the decline in religious affiliation result from a lifecycle effect (with each individual generation's attitudes following a particular pattern throughout their lifecycle), a period effect (with a particular event or way of thinking affecting all or some of society at a particular point in time) or a generation or cohort effect (with more religious generations dying and being replaced by less religious ones)?

To explore these possibilities, we grouped respondents into nine 'generations' and considered their levels of religious affiliation at four points in time. This analysis is presented in Table 12.7. The first point to note is that there is no evidence of a lifecycle effect – that is, as people grow older they become more or less religious. Non-affiliation remains relatively stable as each generation ages; for example, 30 per cent of those born between 1936–1945 did not follow a religion in 1983 (when they were aged 38–47 years), compared with 31 per cent in 2010 (when they were aged 65–74 years).

Could the decline in religious affiliation be attributed to a period effect? At a time of plummeting trust in politicians and banks (Curtice and Park, 2010), might public cynicism have extended to religious bodies, perhaps spurred on by scandals within the church, such as the sex abuse scandal in the Roman Catholic Church in Ireland? There is some evidence of a decline in religious affiliation between 2000 and 2010, particularly for those generations currently aged in their mid-30s to mid-60s. This trend is likely to be very recent, as it has not been identified in previous work on this topic, and therefore merits further investigation.

However, by far the most marked differences occur between cohorts – indicating that the decline in religious affiliation in Britain has primarily been brought about by generational replacement. In 1983, for example, 55 per cent of those born between 1956 and 1965 (then aged 18–27) did not belong to a religion, compared with 12 per cent of those born before 1915 (then aged 68+). By 2010, 65 per cent of the youngest generation (born between 1986 and 1992 and then aged 18–24) did not belong to a religion, compared with 24 per cent of the oldest generation (born between 1926 and 1935 and then aged 75+[6]). The result of continual generational replacement is that, overall, the proportion of the population who does not belong to a religion continues to rise. These findings broadly reflect the conclusions of other studies which investigate the causes of the decline in religious affiliation in other European countries (see for example Voas, 2009).

Non-affiliation remains relatively stable as each generation ages

Table 12.7 No religious affiliation, cohort analysis, 1983–2010[7]

	1983	1990	2000	2010
% not belonging to a religion				
All	31	36	40	50
Cohort		**(age in brackets)**		
1986–1992	n/a	n/a	n/a	65 (18–24)
1976–1985	n/a	n/a	59 (18–24)	57 (25–34)
1966–1975	n/a	54 (17–24)	53 (25–34)	60 (35–44)
1956–1965	55 (18–27)	47 (25–34)	46 (35–44)	51 (45–54)
1946–1955	39 (28–37)	40 (35–44)	39 (45–54)	47 (55–64)
1936–1945	30 (38–47)	32 (45–54)	27 (55–64)	31 (65–74)
1926–1935	24 (48–57)	25 (55–64)	21 (65–74)	24 (75–94)
1916–1925	20 (58–67)	23 (65–74)	17 (75–94)	n/a
1915 or earlier	12 (68+)	19 (75–94)	n/a	n/a

n/a = not asked

What do our findings mean for the future? We cannot, of course, rule out the possibility that a major event might affect people's relationship with religion. But on the basis of our findings it seems likely that the ongoing decline in religious affiliation (and consequently religious attendance) will continue. This reflects the fact that each generation is less likely than its predecessor to be born into religious families, and that this lack of religiosity tends to remain with an individual as they get older.

Conclusions

Britain is becoming less religious, with the numbers who affiliate with a religion or attend religious services experiencing a long-term decline. And this trend seems set to continue; not only as older, more religious generations are replaced by younger, less religious ones, but also as the younger generations increasingly opt not to bring up their children in a religion – a factor shown to strongly link with religious affiliation and attendance later in life.

What does this decline mean for society and social policy more generally? On the one hand, we can expect to see a continued increase in liberal attitudes towards a range of issues such as abortion, homosexuality, same-sex marriage, and euthanasia, as the influence of considerations grounded in religion declines. Moreover, we may see an

65%

of 18–24 year olds do not affiliate to a religion, compared with 55% of the same age group (18–27) in 1983

increased reluctance, particularly among the younger age groups, for matters of faith to enter the social and public spheres at all. The recently expressed sentiment of the current coalition government to "do" and "get" God (Warsi, 2011) therefore may not sit well with, and could alienate, certain sections of the population.

Notes
1. The difference between the proportions of the population identified as belonging to a religion by the 2001 census and *British Social Attitudes* can be partly explained by question wording: the census asks respondents "What is your religion?" – implying that the respondent has one – while the *British Social Attitudes* survey asks "Do you regard yourself as belonging to any particular religion?" The difference may also be due to the response options offered; with the census listing the major world religions, and *British Social Attitudes* listing specific denominations; respondents answering the former would be most likely to see this as a question concerned with 'cultural classification' rather than religion (Voas and Bruce, 2004). Finally, the context of the questions is significant, with the census question following one on ethnicity, arguably causing 'contamination' of responses (*ibid.*).

2. "Other Christian – specific denomination" includes Baptist, Methodist, Presbyterian/Church of Scotland, Free Presbyterian, Brethren, and United Reform Church (URC)/Congregational.

3. "Non-Christian" includes Hindu, Jewish, Islam/Muslim, Sikh, Buddhist, and Other non-Christian. Due to small base size we cannot break this group down further for subgroup analysis.

4. Answer options are: *Once a week or more, less often but at least once in two weeks, less often but at least once a month, less often but at least twice a year, less often but at least once a year, less often than once a year, never or practically never, varies too much to say.*

5. 'Religious and do attend meetings' includes anyone who attends, however infrequent – that is, any of: *Once a week or more, less often but at least once in two weeks, less often but at least once a month, less often but at least twice a year, less often but at least once a year, less often than once a year.*

6. In fact this age category only includes those aged 75–94, so as to fit with the years specified in the left-hand column; there were three people aged 95 in the sample. When the 95 year olds are included in the 75–94 age group, this brings the percentage of those saying "No religion" down to 23 per cent, but this is largely due to rounding (the difference is 0.2 per cent).

7. The bases for Table 12.7 are as follows:

	1983	1990	2000	2010
All	1761	2797	3426	3297
1986–1992	n/a	n/a	n/a	229
1976–1985	n/a	n/a	277	446
1966–1975	n/a	336	614	637
1956–1965	298	512	715	557
1946–1955	357	560	521	563
1936–1945	286	456	501	497
1926–1935	289	382	432	357
1916–1925	261	330	359	n/a
1915 (or earlier)	264	207	n/a	n/a

n/a = not asked

Various corrections have been made to Table 12.7, for example, while those in the 1966–1975 cohort would be aged 15–24 years old in 1990, there were no 15 or 16 year olds in the sample.

References
Andersen, A., Tilley, J. and Heath, A. (2005), 'Political knowledge and enlightened preferences: party choice through the electoral cycle', British Journal of Political Science, **35**: 285–302

Census 2011 available at www.ons.gov.uk/ons/guide-method/census/2011/the-2011-census/2011-census-questionnaire-content/index.html

Census Campaign available at census-campaign.org.uk/2011/

Clements, B. (2010) 'Religious Affiliation and Political Attitudes: Findings from the British Election Study 2009/10', available at www.brin.ac.uk/news/?p=481

Baroness Warsi, University of Leicester, Sir Sigmund Sternberg lecture, 20 January 2011, available at www.sayeedawarsi.com/2011/01/university-of-leicester-sir-sigmund-sternberg-lecture/

Curtice, J. and Park, A. (2010), 'A tale of two crises: banks, the MPs' expenses scandal and public opinion', in Park, A., Curtice, J., Clery, E., and Bryson, C. (eds.), British Social Attitudes: the 27th Report – Exploring Labour's Legacy, London: Sage

Kotler-Berkowitz, L. (2001), 'Religion and voting behaviour in Great Britain: a reassessment', British Journal of Political Science, **31(3)**: 523–555

McAndrew, S. (2010), 'Religious faith and contemporary attitudes' in Park, A., Curtice, J., Thompson, K., Phillips, M., Clery, E. and Butt, S. (eds.), British Social Attitudes: the 26th Report, London: Sage

Voas, D. (2009), 'The Rise and Fall of Fuzzy Fidelity in Europe' in European Sociological Review, **25(2)**: 155–168

Voas, D. and Bruce, S. (2004), 'The 2001 census and Christian identification in Britain', Journal of Contemporary Religion, **19(1)**: 23–28

Voas, D. and Ling, R. (2010), 'Religious faith and contemporary attitudes' in Park, A., Curtice, J., Thompson, K., Phillips, M., Clery, E. and Butt, S. (eds.), British Social Attitudes: the 26th Report, London: Sage

Appendix I
Technical details of the survey

In 2010, the sample for the *British Social Attitudes* survey was split into three sections: versions A, B and C, each made up a third of the sample. Depending on the number of versions in which it was included, each 'module' of questions was put to one of the following: the full sample (3,297 respondents), a random third, or two-thirds. The structure of the questionnaire can be found at www.natcen.ac.uk/bsaquestionnaires.

Sample design
The *British Social Attitudes* survey is designed to yield a representative sample of adults aged 18 or over. Since 1993, the sampling frame for the survey has been the Postcode Address File (PAF), a list of addresses (or postal delivery points) compiled by the Post Office.[1]

For practical reasons, the sample is confined to those living in private households. People living in institutions (except for those in private households at such institutions) are excluded, as are households whose addresses were not on the PAF.

The sampling method involved a multi-stage design, with three separate stages of selection.

Selection of sectors
At the first stage, postcode sectors were selected systematically from a list of all postal sectors in Great Britain. Before selection, any sectors with fewer than 500 addresses were identified and grouped together with an adjacent sector; in Scotland all sectors north of the Caledonian Canal were excluded (because of the prohibitive costs of interviewing there). Sectors were then stratified on the basis of:

- 37 sub-regions
- population density, with variable banding used, in order to create three equal-sized strata per sub-region
- ranking by percentage of homes that were owner-occupied.

Two hundred and twenty-six postcode sectors were selected, with probability proportional to the number of addresses in each sector.

Selection of addresses
Thirty addresses were selected in each of the 226 sectors or groups of sectors. The issued sample was therefore 226 x 30 = 6,780 addresses, selected by starting from a random point on the list of addresses for each sector, and choosing each address at a fixed interval. The fixed interval was calculated for each sector in order to generate the correct number of addresses.

The Multiple-Occupancy Indicator (MOI) available through PAF was used when selecting addresses in Scotland. The MOI shows the number of accommodation spaces sharing one address. So, if the MOI indicates more than one accommodation space at a given address, the chances of the given address being selected from the list of addresses would increase so that it matched the total number of accommodation spaces. The MOI is largely irrelevant in England and Wales, as separate dwelling units (DU) generally appear as separate entries on PAF. In Scotland, tenements with many flats tend to appear as one entry on PAF. However, even in Scotland, the vast majority (99.7%) of MOIs had a value of one. The remainder were incorporated into the weighting procedures (described below).

Selection of individuals

Interviewers called at each address selected from PAF and listed all those eligible for inclusion in the *British Social Attitudes* sample – that is, all persons currently aged 18 or over and resident at the selected address. The interviewer then selected one respondent using a computer-generated random selection procedure. Where there were two or more DUs at the selected address, interviewers first had to select one DU using the same random procedure. They then followed the same procedure to select a person for interview within the selected DU.

Weighting

The weights for the *British Social Attitudes* survey correct for the unequal selection of addresses, DUs and individuals and for biases caused by differential non-response. The different stages of the weighting scheme are outlined in detail below.

Selection weights

Selection weights are required because not all the units covered in the survey had the same probability of selection. The weighting reflects the relative selection probabilities of the individual at the three main stages of selection: address, DU and individual. First, because addresses in Scotland were selected using the MOI, weights were needed to compensate for the greater probability of an address with an MOI of more than one being selected, compared to an address with an MOI of one. (This stage was omitted for the English and Welsh data.) Secondly, data were weighted to compensate for the fact that a DU at an address that contained a large number of DUs was less likely to be selected for inclusion in the survey than a DU at an address that contained fewer DUs. (We use this procedure because in most cases where the MOI is greater than one, the two stages will cancel each other out, resulting in more efficient weights.) Thirdly, data were weighted to compensate for the lower selection probabilities of adults living in large households, compared with those in small households.

At each stage the selection weights were trimmed to avoid a small number of very high or very low weights in the sample; such weights would inflate standard errors, reducing the precision of the survey estimates and causing the weighted sample to be less efficient. Less than one per cent of the sample was trimmed at each stage.

Non-response model

It is known that certain subgroups in the population are more likely to respond to surveys than others. These groups can end up over-represented in the sample, which can bias the survey estimates. Where information is available about non-responding households, the response behaviour of the sample members can be modelled and the results used to generate a non-response weight. This non-response weight is intended to reduce bias in the sample resulting from differential response to the survey.

The data was modelled using logistic regression, with the dependent variable indicating whether or not the selected individual responded to the survey. Ineligible households[2] were not included in the non-response modelling. A number of area-level and interviewer observation variables were used to model response. Not all the variables examined were retained for the final model: variables not strongly related to a household's propensity to respond were dropped from the analysis.

The variables found to be related to response were: Government Office Region (GOR), dwelling type, condition of the area, relative condition of the address and whether there were entry barriers to the selected address.

Table A.1 The final non-response model

Variable	B	S.E.	Wald	df	Sig.	Odds
Govt Office Region			72.6	10	0.00	
North East	0.03	0.12	0.08	1	0.78	1.03
North West	0.10	0.10	1.00	1	0.32	1.10
Yorks. and Humber	-0.15	0.10	2.25	1	0.13	0.86
East Midlands	0.04	0.10	0.16	1	0.68	1.04
West Midlands	-0.23	0.10	5.46	1	0.02	0.80
East of England	-0.14	0.10	2.14	1	0.14	0.87
London	-0.41	0.09	20.67	1	0.00	0.66
South East	-0.22	0.09	5.93	1	0.01	0.81
South West	-0.02	0.10	0.06	1	0.81	0.98
Wales	0.34	0.12	7.65	1	0.01	1.41
Scotland	(baseline)					
Barriers to address						
No barriers	0.55	0.09	39.04	1	0.00	1.73
One or more	(baseline)					
Relative condition of the address			57.97	2	0.00	
Better	0.80	0.11	54.3	1	0.00	2.22
About the same	0.34	0.09	15.62	1	0.00	1.40
Worse	(baseline)					
Condition of the area			18.33	2	0.00	
Mainly good	0.22	0.13	3.11	1	0.08	1.25
Mainly fair	0.03	0.12	0.06	1	0.81	1.03
Mainly bad	(baseline)					
Dwelling type			16.65	5	0.01	
Semi-detached house	0.13	0.06	5.09	1	0.02	1.14
Terraced house	0.08	0.06	1.52	1	0.22	1.08
Flat – purpose built	0.06	0.10	0.34	1	0.56	1.06
Flat – conversion	-0.28	0.14	4.04	1	0.04	0.76
Other	-0.37	0.21	2.94	1	0.09	0.69
Detached house	(baseline)					
Constant	-0.55	0.18	9.16	1	0.00	0.58

The response is 1 = individual responding to the survey, 0 = non-response
Only variables that are significant at the 0.05 level are included in the model
The model R2 is 0.02 (Cox and Snell)
B** is the estimate coefficient with standard error **S.E.

*The **Wald**-test measures the impact of the categorical variable on the model with the appropriate number of degrees of freedom **df**. If the test is significant (**sig.** < 0.05), then the categorical variable is considered to be 'significantly associated' with the response variable and therefore included in the model.*

The model shows that response increases if there are no barriers to entry (for instance, if there are no locked gates around the address and no entry phone) and if the general condition of the address is the same or better than other addresses in the area. If addresses in the area are generally good this also increases response. Response is also higher for addresses in Wales, but lower for those in London and also for those in a flat or maisonette conversion. The full model is given in Table A.1.

The non-response weight was calculated as the inverse of the predicted response probabilities saved from the logistic regression model. The non-response weight was then combined with the selection weights to create the final non-response weight. The top one per cent of the weight were trimmed before the weight was scaled to the achieved sample size (resulting in the weight being standardised around an average of one).

Calibration weighting

The final stage of weighting was to adjust the final non-response weight so that the weighted sample matched the population in terms of age, sex and region.

Table A.2 Weighted and unweighted sample distribution, by GOR, age and sex

	Population	Unweighted respondents	Respondents weighted by selection weight only	Respondents weighted by un-calibrated non-response weight	Respondents weighted by final weight
Govt Office Region	%	%	%	%	%
North East	4.4	4.8	4.3	4.4	4.4
North West	11.4	12.4	5.9	10.8	11.4
Yorks. and Humber	8.8	9.0	8.4	9.2	8.8
East Midlands	7.4	8.4	8.4	7.9	7.4
West Midlands	9.0	8.8	3.5	9.2	9.0
East of England	9.6	9.8	4.4	10.3	9.6
London	12.9	9.3	10.4	11.6	12.9
South East	14.0	12.8	5.2	13.5	14.0
South West	8.8	9.5	7.9	9.3	8.8
Wales	5.0	5.7	11.1	4.7	5.0
Scotland	8.8	9.5	9.9	9.2	8.8
Age & sex	%	%	%	%	%
M 18–24	6.2	3.1	4.3	4.5	6.2
M 25–34	8.3	5.4	5.9	6.0	8.3
M 35–44	9.2	8.1	8.4	8.5	9.2
M 45–54	8.5	7.8	8.4	8.6	8.5
M 55–59	3.6	3.4	3.5	3.5	3.6
M 60–64	3.7	4.2	4.4	4.2	3.7
M 65+	9.1	11.7	10.4	10.2	9.1
F 18–24	5.9	3.9	5.2	5.2	5.9
F 25–34	8.1	8.1	7.9	8.0	8.1
F 35–44	9.3	11.2	11.1	11.1	9.3
F 45–54	8.7	9.1	9.9	9.8	8.7
F 55–59	3.8	4.6	4.7	4.6	3.8
F 60–64	3.9	4.9	4.6	4.5	3.9
F 65+	11.7	14.5	11.2	11.2	11.7
Base	*46,920,219*	*3421*	*3421*	*3421*	*3421*

Only adults aged 18 and over are eligible to take part in the survey, therefore the data have been weighted to the British population aged 18+ based on the 2009 mid-year population estimates from the Office for National Statistics/General Register Office for Scotland.

The survey data were weighted to the marginal age/sex and GOR distributions using raking-ratio (or rim) weighting. As a result, the weighted data should exactly match the population across these three dimensions. This is shown in Table A.2.

The calibration weight is the final non-response weight to be used in the analysis of the 2010 survey; this weight has been scaled to the responding sample size. The range of the weights is given in Table A.3.

Table A.3 Range of weights

	N	Minimum	Mean	Maximum
DU and person selection weight	3297	0.55	1.00	2.21
Un-calibrated non-response weight	3297	0.40	1.00	2.68
Final calibrated non-response weight	3297	0.35	1.00	4.09

Effective sample size
The effect of the sample design on the precision of survey estimates is indicated by the effective sample size (neff). The effective sample size measures the size of an (unweighted) simple random sample that would achieve the same precision (standard error) as the design being implemented. If the effective sample size is close to the actual sample size, then we have an efficient design with a good level of precision. The lower the effective sample size is, the lower the level of precision. The efficiency of a sample is given by the ratio of the effective sample size to the actual sample size. Samples that select one person per household tend to have lower efficiency than samples that select all household members. The final calibrated non-response weights have an effective sample size (neff) of 2,602 and efficiency of 79 per cent.

All the percentages presented in this report are based on weighted data.

Questionnaire versions
Each address in each sector (sampling point) was allocated to either the A, B or C portion of the sample. If one serial number was version A, the next was version B and the third version C. Therefore, each interviewer was allocated 10 cases from each of versions A, B and C. There were 2,260 issued addresses for each version.

Fieldwork
Interviewing was mainly carried out between June and September 2010, with a small number of interviews taking place in October and November.

Fieldwork was conducted by interviewers drawn from the *National Centre for Social Research*'s regular panel and conducted using face-to-face computer-assisted interviewing.[3] Interviewers attended a one-day briefing conference to familiarise them with the selection procedures and questionnaires.

The mean interview length was 70 minutes for version A of the questionnaire, 69 minutes for version B and 75 minutes for version C.[4] Interviewers achieved an overall response rate of between 53.8 and 54.3 per cent. Details are shown in Table A.4.

Table A.4 Response rate[1] on *British Social Attitudes*, 2010

	Number	Lower limit of response (%)	Upper limit of response (%)
Addresses issued	6780		
Out of scope	649		
Upper limit of eligible cases	6131	100.0	
Uncertain eligibility	64	1.0	
Lower limit of eligible cases	6067		100.0
Interview achieved	3297	53.8	54.3
With self-completion	2791	45.5	46.0
Interview not achieved	2880	45.2	45.7
Refused[2]	2081	33.9	34.3
Non-contacted[3]	337	5.5	5.6
Other non-response	352	5.7	5.8

1 *Response is calculated as a range from a lower limit where all unknown eligibility cases (for example, address inaccessible, or unknown whether address is residential) are assumed to be eligible and therefore included in the unproductive outcomes, to an upper limit where all these cases are assumed to be ineligible (and are therefore excluded from the response calculation)*

2 *'Refused' comprises refusals before selection of an individual at the address, refusals to the office, refusal by the selected person, 'proxy' refusals (on behalf of the selected respondent) and broken appointments after which the selected person could not be recontacted*

3 *'Non-contacted' comprises households where no one was contacted and those where the selected person could not be contacted*

As in earlier rounds of the series, the respondent was asked to fill in a self-completion questionnaire which, whenever possible, was collected by the interviewer. Otherwise, the respondent was asked to post it to the *National Centre for Social Research*. If necessary, up to three postal reminders were sent to obtain the self-completion supplement.

A total of 506 respondents (15 per cent of those interviewed) did not return their self-completion questionnaire. Version A of the self-completion questionnaire was returned by 83 per cent of respondents to the face-to-face interview, version B of the questionnaire was returned by 86 per cent and version C by 85 per cent. As in previous rounds, we judged that it was not necessary to apply additional weights to correct for non-response to the self-completion questionnaire.

Advance letter
Interviewers were supplied with letters describing the purpose of the survey and the coverage of the questionnaire, which they posted to sampled addresses before making any calls.[5]

Analysis variables
A number of standard analyses have been used in the tables that appear in this report. The analysis groups requiring further definition are set out below. For further details see Stafford and Thomson (2006). Where there are references to specific question numbers, the full question text, including frequencies, can be found at www.natcen.ac.uk/bsaquestionnaires

Region
The dataset is classified by the 12 Government Office Regions.

Standard Occupational Classification
Respondents are classified according to their own occupation, not that of the 'head of household'. Each respondent was asked about their current or last job, so that all respondents except those who had never worked were coded. Additionally, all job details were collected for all spouses and partners in work.

With the 2001 survey, we began coding occupation to the new Standard Occupational Classification 2000 (SOC 2000) instead of the Standard Occupational Classification 1990 (SOC 90). The main socio-economic grouping based on SOC 2000 is the National Statistics Socio-Economic Classification (NS-SEC). However, to maintain time-series, some analysis has continued to use the older schemes based on SOC 90 – Registrar General's Social Class and Socio-Economic Group, though these are now derived from SOC 2000.

National Statistics Socio-Economic Classification (NS-SEC)
The combination of SOC 2000 and employment status for current or last job generates the following NS-SEC analytic classes:

* Employers in large organisations, higher managerial and professional
* Lower professional and managerial; higher technical and supervisory
* Intermediate occupations
* Small employers and own account workers
* Lower supervisory and technical occupations
* Semi-routine occupations
* Routine occupations

The remaining respondents are grouped as "never had a job" or "not classifiable". For some analyses, it may be more appropriate to classify respondents according to their current socio-economic status, which takes into account only their present economic position. In this case, in addition to the seven classes listed above, the remaining respondents not currently in paid work fall into one of the following categories: "not classifiable", "retired", "looking after the home", "unemployed" or "others not in paid occupations".

Registrar General's Social Class
As with NS-SEC, each respondent's social class is based on his or her current or last occupation. The combination of SOC 90 with employment status for current or last job generates the following six social classes:

I	Professional etc. occupations	
II	Managerial and technical occupations	'Non-manual'
III (Non-manual)	Skilled occupations	
III (Manual)	Skilled occupations	
IV	Partly-skilled occupations	'Manual'
V	Unskilled occupations	

They are usually collapsed into four groups: I & II, III Non-manual, III Manual, and IV & V.

Socio-Economic Group

As with NS-SEC, each respondent's Socio-Economic Group (SEG) is based on his or her current or last occupation. SEG aims to bring together people with jobs of similar social and economic status, and is derived from a combination of employment status and occupation. The full SEG classification identifies 18 categories, but these are usually condensed into six groups:

- Professionals, employers and managers
- Intermediate non-manual workers
- Junior non-manual workers
- Skilled manual workers
- Semi-skilled manual workers
- Unskilled manual workers

As with NS-SEC, the remaining respondents are grouped as "never had a job" or "not classifiable".

Industry

All respondents whose occupation could be coded were allocated a Standard Industrial Classification 2007 (SIC 07). Two-digit class codes are used. As with social class, SIC may be generated on the basis of the respondent's current occupation only, or on his or her most recently classifiable occupation.

Party identification

Respondents can be classified as identifying with a particular political party on one of three counts: if they consider themselves supporters of that party, as closer to it than to others, or as more likely to support it in the event of a general election. The three groups are generally described respectively as *partisans, sympathisers* and *residual identifiers*. In combination, the three groups are referred to as 'identifiers'. Responses are derived from the following questions:

Generally speaking, do you think of yourself as a supporter of any one political party? [Yes/No]

[If "No"/"Don't know"]
Do you think of yourself as a little closer to one political party than to the others? [Yes/No]

[If "Yes" at either question or "No"/"Don't know" at 2nd question]
Which one?/If there were a general election tomorrow, which political party do you think you would be most likely to support?

[Conservative; Labour; Liberal Democrat; Scottish National Party; Plaid Cymru; Green Party; UK Independence Party (UKIP)/Veritas; British National Party (BNP)/ National Front; RESPECT/Scottish Socialist Party (SSP)/Socialist Party; Other party; Other answer; None; Refused to say]

Income

Two variables classify the respondent's earnings (REarn) and household income (HHInc) on the questionnaire (see www.natcen.ac.uk/bsaquestionnaires). The bandings used are designed to be representative of those that exist in Britain and are taken from the Family Resources Survey (see http://research.dwp.gov.uk/asd/frs/). Four derived variables give deciles and quartiles of these variables. They are [REarnD], [REarnQ], [HHIncD] and [HHIncQ] and are calculated based on deciles/quartiles of individual earnings and household incomes in Britain as a whole.

Attitude scales
Since 1986, the *British Social Attitudes* surveys have included two attitude scales, which aim to measure where respondents stand on certain underlying value dimensions – left–right and libertarian–authoritarian.[6] Since 1987 (except 1990), a similar scale on 'welfarism' has been asked. Some of the items in the welfarism scale were changed in 2000–2001. The current version of the scale is listed below.

A useful way of summarising the information from a number of questions of this sort is to construct an additive index (Spector, 1992; DeVellis, 2003). This approach rests on the assumption that there is an underlying – 'latent' – attitudinal dimension which characterises the answers to all the questions within each scale. If so, scores on the index are likely to be a more reliable indication of the underlying attitude than the answers to any one question.

Each of these scales consists of a number of statements to which the respondent is invited to "agree strongly", "agree", "neither agree nor disagree", "disagree" or "disagree strongly".

The items are:

Left–right scale
- Government should redistribute income from the better off to those who are less well off. *[Redistrb]*
- Big business benefits owners at the expense of workers. *[BigBusnN]*
- Ordinary working people do not get their fair share of the nation's wealth. *[Wealth]*[7]
- There is one law for the rich and one for the poor. *[RichLaw]*
- Management will always try to get the better of employees if it gets the chance. *[Indust4]*

Libertarian–authoritarian scale
- Young people today don't have enough respect for traditional British values. *[TradVals]*
- People who break the law should be given stiffer sentences. *[StifSent]*
- For some crimes, the death penalty is the most appropriate sentence. *[DeathApp]*
- Schools should teach children to obey authority. *[Obey]*
- The law should always be obeyed, even if a particular law is wrong. *[WrongLaw]*
- Censorship of films and magazines is necessary to uphold moral standards. *[Censor]*

Welfarism scale
- The welfare state encourages people to stop helping each other. *[WelfHelp]*
- The government should spend more money on welfare benefits for the poor, even if it leads to higher taxes. *[MoreWelf]*
- Around here, most unemployed people could find a job if they really wanted one. *[UnempJob]*
- Many people who get social security don't really deserve any help. *[SocHelp]*
- Most people on the dole are fiddling in one way or another. *[DoleFidl]*

- If welfare benefits weren't so generous, people would learn to stand on their own two feet. [WelfFeet]
- Cutting welfare benefits would damage too many people's lives. *[DamLives]*
- The creation of the welfare state is one of Britain's proudest achievements. *[ProudWlf]*

The indices for the three scales are formed by scoring the leftmost, most libertarian or most pro-welfare position as 1, and the rightmost, most authoritarian or most anti-welfarist position, as 5. The "neither agree nor disagree" option is scored as 3. The scores to all the questions in each scale are added and then divided by the number of items in the scale, giving indices ranging from 1 (leftmost, most libertarian, most pro-welfare) to 5 (rightmost, most authoritarian, most anti-welfare). The scores on the three indices have been placed on the dataset.[8]

The scales have been tested for reliability (as measured by Cronbach's alpha). The Cronbach's alpha (unstandardised items) for the scales in 2010 are 0.81 for the left–right scale, 0.81 for the welfarism scale and 0.73 for the libertarian–authoritarian scale. This level of reliability can be considered 'good' for the left–right and welfarism scales and 'respectable' for the libertarian–authoritarian scale (DeVellis, 2003: 95–96).

Other analysis variables
These are taken directly from the questionnaire and to that extent are self-explanatory (see www.natcen.ac.uk/bsaquestionnaires). The principal ones are:

- Sex (Q. 48)
- Age (Q. 45)
- Household income (Q. 1141)
- Economic position (Q. 703)
- Religion (Q. 909)
- Highest educational qualification obtained (Q. 1033)
- Marital status (Qs. 143–149)
- Benefits received (Qs. 1096–1114)

Sampling errors
No sample precisely reflects the characteristics of the population it represents, because of both sampling and non-sampling errors. If a sample were designed as a random sample (if every adult had an equal and independent chance of inclusion in the sample), then we could calculate the sampling error of any percentage, p, using the formula:

$$s.e.\ (p) = \sqrt{\frac{p(100 - p)}{n}}$$

where n is the number of respondents on which the percentage is based. Once the sampling error had been calculated, it would be a straightforward exercise to calculate a confidence interval for the true population percentage. For example, a 95 per cent confidence interval would be given by the formula:

$$p \pm 1.96 \times s.e.\ (p)$$

Clearly, for a simple random sample (srs), the sampling error depends only on the values of p and n. However, simple random sampling is almost never used in practice, because of its inefficiency in terms of time and cost.

As noted above, the *British Social Attitudes* sample, like that drawn for most large-scale surveys, was clustered according to a stratified multi-stage design into 226 postcode sectors (or combinations of sectors). With a complex design like this, the sampling error of a percentage giving a particular response is not simply a function of the number of respondents in the sample and the size of the percentage; it also depends on how that percentage response is spread within and between sample points.

The complex design may be assessed relative to simple random sampling by calculating a range of design factors (DEFTs) associated with it, where:

$$DEFT = \sqrt{\frac{\text{Variance of estimator with complex design, sample size } n}{\text{Variance of estimator with srs design, sample size } n}}$$

and represents the multiplying factor to be applied to the simple random sampling error to produce its complex equivalent. A design factor of one means that the complex sample has achieved the same precision as a simple random sample of the same size. A design factor greater than one means the complex sample is less precise than its simple random sample equivalent. If the DEFT for a particular characteristic is known, a 95 per cent confidence interval for a percentage may be calculated using the formula:

$p \pm 1.96 \times \text{complex sampling error } (p)$

$= p \pm 1.96 \times DEFT \times \sqrt{\dfrac{p(100 - p)}{n}}$

Calculations of sampling errors and design effects were made using the statistical analysis package STATA.

Table A.5 gives examples of the confidence intervals and DEFTs calculated for a range of different questions. Most background variables were fielded on the whole sample, whereas many attitudinal variables were asked only of a third or two-thirds of the sample; some were asked on the interview questionnaire and some on the self-completion supplement.

Table A.5 Complex standard errors and confidence intervals of selected variables

Classification variables	% (p)	Complex standard error of p	95% confidence interval	DEFT	Base
Q. 823 Party identification (full sample)					
Conservative	28.6	1.1	26.6–30.8	1.361	*3297*
Labour	29.6	0.9	27.9–31.5	1.133	*3297*
Liberal Democrat	13	0.7	11.6–14.6	1.278	*3297*
Q. 533 Housing tenure (full sample)					
Owns	67.7	1.4	64.8–70.4	1.753	*3297*
Rents from local authority	9.8	0.9	8.1–11.7	1.749	*3297*
Rents privately/HA	21.6	1.1	19.5–23.9	1.544	*3297*
Q. 909 Religion (full sample)					
No religion	49.9	1.2	47.6–52.2	1.331	*3297*
Church of England	19.6	0.9	17.9–21.5	1.309	*3297*
Roman Catholic	9.1	0.6	7.9–10.4	1.264	*3297*
Q. 968 Age of completing continuous full-time education (full sample)					
16 or under	49.9	1.5	47.0–52.8	1.685	*3297*
17 or 18	18.8	0.9	17.2–20.5	1.257	*3297*
19 or over	25.8	1.3	23.4–28.4	1.679	*3297*
Q. 248 Home internet access (full sample)					
Yes	80.1	0.9	78.4–81.8	1.240	*3297*
No	19.9	0.9	18.2–21.6	1.240	*3297*
Q. 899 Urban or rural residence (full sample)					
A big city	9.8	1.1	7.7–12.3	2.193	*3297*
The suburbs or outskirts of a big city	26.3	1.9	22.8–30.2	2.433	*3297*
A small city/town	42.9	2.4	38.3–47.7	2.747	*3297*
Country village	18.1	1.9	14.6–22.2	2.867	*3297*
Farm/home in the country	2.3	0.4	1.7–3.3	1.545	*3297*

Table A.5 Complex standard errors and confidence intervals of selected variables (continued)

Attitudinal variables (face-to-face interview)	% (p)	Complex standard error of p	95% confidence interval	DEFT	Base
Q. 353 Benefits for the unemployed are... (full sample)					
...too low	23.5	1.0	21.6–25.4	1.288	3297
...too high	53.9	1.1	51.7–56.2	1.300	3297
Q. 461 How serious a problem is traffic congestion in towns, cities (full sample)					
A very serious problem	12.3	0.7	10.9–13.9	1.308	3297
A serious problem	30.2	0.9	28.6–32.0	1.079	3297
Not a very serious problem	39.8	1.0	37.8–41.9	1.192	3297
Not a problem at all	17.2	0.8	15.6–18.9	1.259	3297
Q. 541 If you had a free choice would you choose to rent accommodation, or would you choose to buy? (full sample)					
Would choose to rent	13.6	0.9	12.0–15.3	1.426	3297
Would choose to buy	85.9	0.9	84.1–87.5	1.439	3297
Q. 296 Would you say that someone in Britain was or was not in poverty if they had enough to buy the things they really needed, but not enough to buy things most people take for granted? (full sample)					
Was in poverty	21.4	1.0	19.5–23.4	1.375	3297
Was not	77.1	1.0	75.0–79.0	1.374	3297

Attitudinal variables (self-completion)

	% (p)	Complex standard error of p	95% confidence interval	DEFT	Base
A51a Government should redistribute income from the better off to those who are less well off (full sample)					
B28a Agree strongly	8.7	0.7	7.4–10.1	1.276	2791
C32a Agree	26.5	1.0	24.6–28.4	1.174	2791
Neither agree nor disagree	27.6	1.0	25.7–29.6	1.152	2791
Disagree	28.9	1.1	26.9–31.1	1.234	2791
Disagree strongly	6.5	0.6	5.4–7.7	1.252	2791
B28 Which of these statements comes closest to your view about general elections? (1/3 sample)					
It's not really worth voting	17.6	1.6	6.5–10.6	1.106	921
People should vote only if they care who wins	20.1	1.6	4.7–8.1	1.077	921
It's everyone's duty to vote	60.8	1.9	17.7–24.1	1.222	921

Table A.5 Complex standard errors and confidence intervals of selected variables (continued)

Attitudinal variables (self-completion)	% (p)	Complex standard error of p	95% confi-dence interval	DEFT	Base
C22a Do you personally think it is wrong or not wrong for a woman to have an abortion if there is a strong chance of serious defect in the baby? (1/3 sample)					
Always wrong	8.3	1.0	6.5–10.6	1.106	921
Almost always wrong	6.2	0.9	4.7–8.1	1.077	921
Wrong only sometimes	20.7	1.6	17.7–24.1	1.222	921
Not wrong at all	51.6	2.0	47.5–55.6	1.236	921
A36a People should be able to travel by plane as much as they like (1/3 sample)					
Agree	63.9	1.7	60.4–67.2	1.104	928
Neither agree nor disagree	18.5	1.5	15.7–21.6	1.162	928
Disagree	12.5	1.2	10.3–15.1	1.122	928

The table shows that most of the questions asked of all sample members have a confidence interval of around plus or minus two to three per cent of the survey percentage. This means that we can be 95 per cent certain that the true population percentage is within two to three per cent (in either direction) of the percentage we report.

Variables with much larger variation are, as might be expected, those closely related to the geographic location of the respondent (for example, whether they live in a big city, a small town or a village). Here, the variation may be as large as six or seven per cent either way around the percentage found on the survey. Consequently, the design effects calculated for these variables in a clustered sample will be greater than the design effects calculated for variables less strongly associated with area. Also, sampling errors for percentages based only on respondents to just one of the versions of the questionnaire, or on subgroups within the sample, are larger than they would have been had the questions been asked of everyone.

Analysis techniques

Regression
Regression analysis aims to summarise the relationship between a 'dependent' variable and one or more 'independent' variables. It shows how well we can estimate a respondent's score on the dependent variable from knowledge of their scores on the independent variables. It is often undertaken to support a claim that the phenomena measured by the independent variables *cause* the phenomenon measured by the dependent variable. However, the causal ordering, if any, between the variables cannot be verified or falsified by the technique. Causality can only be inferred through special experimental designs or through assumptions made by the analyst.

All regression analysis assumes that the relationship between the dependent and each of the independent variables takes a particular form. In *linear regression*, it is assumed that the relationship can be adequately summarised by a straight line. This means that a one percentage point increase in the value of an independent variable is assumed to have the same impact on the value of the dependent variable on average, irrespective of the previous values of those variables.

Strictly speaking the technique assumes that both the dependent and the independent variables are measured on an interval-level scale, although it may sometimes still be applied even where this is not the case. For example, one can use an ordinal variable (e.g. a Likert scale) as a *dependent* variable if one is willing to assume that there is an underlying interval-level scale and the difference between the observed ordinal scale and the underlying interval scale is due to random measurement error. Often the answers to a number of Likert-type questions are averaged to give a dependent variable that is more like a continuous variable. Categorical or nominal data can be used as *independent* variables by converting them into dummy or binary variables; these are variables where the only valid scores are 0 and 1, with 1 signifying membership of a particular category and 0 otherwise.

The assumptions of *linear regression* cause particular difficulties where the dependent variable is binary. The assumption that the relationship between the dependent and the independent variables is a straight line means that it can produce estimated values for the dependent variable of less than 0 or greater than 1. In this case it may be more appropriate to assume that the relationship between the dependent and the independent variables takes the form of an S-curve, where the impact on the dependent variable of a one-point increase in an independent variable becomes progressively less the closer the value of the dependent variable approaches 0 or 1. *Logistic regression* is an alternative form of regression which fits such an S-curve rather than a straight line. The technique can also be adapted to analyse multinomial non-interval-level dependent variables, that is, variables which classify respondents into more than two categories.

The two statistical scores most commonly reported from the results of regression analyses are:

A measure of variance explained: This summarises how well all the independent variables combined can account for the variation in respondents' scores in the dependent variable. The higher the measure, the more accurately we are able in general to estimate the correct value of each respondent's score on the dependent variable from knowledge of their scores on the independent variables.

A parameter estimate: This shows how much the dependent variable will change on average, given a one-unit change in the independent variable (while holding all other independent variables in the model constant). The parameter estimate has a positive sign if an increase in the value of the independent variable results in an increase in the value of the dependent variable. It has a negative sign if an increase in the value of the independent variable results in a decrease in the value of the dependent variable. If the parameter estimates are standardised, it is possible to compare the relative impact of different independent variables; those variables with the largest standardised estimates can be said to have the biggest impact on the value of the dependent variable.

Regression also tests for the statistical significance of parameter estimates. A parameter estimate is said to be significant at the five per cent level if the range of the values encompassed by its 95 per cent confidence interval (see also section on sampling errors) are either all positive or all negative. This means that there is less than a five per cent chance that the association we have found between the dependent variable and the independent variable is simply the result of sampling error and does not reflect a relationship that actually exists in the general population.

Factor analysis

Factor analysis is a statistical technique which aims to identify whether there are one or more apparent sources of commonality to the answers given by respondents to a set of questions. It ascertains the smallest number of *factors* (or dimensions) which can most economically summarise all of the variation found in the set of questions being analysed. Factors are established where respondents who give a particular answer to one question in the set, tend to give the same answer as each other, to one or more of the other questions in the set. The technique is most useful when a relatively small number of factors are able to account for a relatively large proportion of the variance in all of the questions in the set.

The technique produces a *factor loading* for each question (or variable) on each factor. Where questions have a high loading on the same factor, then it will be the case that respondents who give a particular answer to one of these questions tend to give a similar answer to the other questions. The technique is most commonly used in attitudinal research to try to identify the underlying ideological dimensions that apparently structure attitudes towards the subject in question.

International Social Survey Programme

The *International Social Survey Programme* (ISSP) is run by a group of research organisations, each of which undertakes to field annually an agreed module of questions on a chosen topic area. Since 1985, an *International Social Survey Programme* module has been included in one of the *British Social Attitudes* self-completion questionnaires. Each module is chosen for repetition at intervals to allow comparisons both between countries (membership is currently standing at 48) and over time. In 2010, the chosen subject was Environment, and the module was carried on the A version of the self-completion questionnaire (Qs. 1a–23b).[9]

Notes

1. Until 1991 all *British Social Attitudes* samples were drawn from the Electoral Register (ER). However, following concern that this sampling frame might be deficient in its coverage of certain population subgroups, a 'splicing' experiment was conducted in 1991. We are grateful to the Market Research Development Fund for contributing towards the costs of this experiment. Its purpose was to investigate whether a switch to PAF would disrupt the time-series – for instance, by lowering response rates or affecting the distribution of responses to particular questions. In the event, it was concluded that the change from ER to PAF was unlikely to affect time trends in any noticeable ways, and that no adjustment factors were necessary. Since significant differences in efficiency exist between PAF and ER, and because we considered it untenable to continue to use a frame that is known to be biased, we decided to adopt PAF as the sampling frame for future *British Social Attitudes* surveys. For details of the PAF/ER 'splicing' experiment, see Lynn and Taylor (1995).

2. This includes households not containing any adults aged 18 and over, vacant dwelling units, derelict dwelling units, non-resident addresses and other deadwood.

3. In 1993 it was decided to mount a split-sample experiment designed to test the applicability of Computer-Assisted Personal Interviewing (CAPI) to the *British Social Attitudes* survey series. CAPI has been used increasingly over the past decade as an alternative to traditional

interviewing techniques. As the name implies, CAPI involves the use of laptop computers during the interview, with interviewers entering responses directly into the computer. One of the advantages of CAPI is that it significantly reduces both the amount of time spent on data processing and the number of coding and editing errors. There was, however, concern that a different interviewing technique might alter the distribution of responses and so affect the year-on-year consistency of *British Social Attitudes* data.

Following the experiment, it was decided to change over to CAPI completely in 1994 (the self-completion questionnaire still being administered in the conventional way). The results of the experiment are discussed in *The 11th Report* (Lynn and Purdon, 1994).

4. Interview times recorded as less than 20 minutes were excluded, as these timings were likely to be errors.

5. An experiment was conducted on the 1991 *British Social Attitudes* survey (Jowell *et al.*, 1992) which showed that sending advance letters to sampled addresses before fieldwork begins has very little impact on response rates. However, interviewers do find that an advance letter helps them to introduce the survey on the doorstep, and a majority of respondents have said that they preferred some advance notice. For these reasons, advance letters have been used on the *British Social Attitudes* surveys since 1991.

6. Because of methodological experiments on scale development, the exact items detailed in this section have not been asked on all versions of the questionnaire each year.

7. In 1994 only, this item was replaced by: Ordinary people get their fair share of the nation's wealth. *[Wealth1]*

8. In constructing the scale, a decision had to be taken on how to treat missing values ("Don't knows", "Refused" and "Not answered"). Respondents who had more than two missing values on the left–right scale and more than three missing values on the libertarian–authoritarian and welfarism scales were excluded from that scale. For respondents with just a few missing values, "Don't knows" were recoded to the midpoint of the scale and "Refused" or "Not answered" were recoded to the scale mean for that respondent on their valid items.

9. See www.natcen.ac.uk/bsaquestionnaires.

References
DeVellis, R.F. (2003), *Scale Development: Theory and Applications*, 2nd edition, Applied Social Research Methods Series, 26, Thousand Oaks, Calif.: Sage

Jowell, R., Brook, L., Prior, G. and Taylor, B. (1992), *British Social Attitudes: the 9th Report*, Aldershot: Dartmouth

Lynn, P. and Purdon, S. (1994), 'Time-series and lap-tops: the change to computer- assisted interviewing', in Jowell, R., Curtice, J., Brook, L. and Ahrendt, D. (eds.), *British Social Attitudes: the 11th Report*, Aldershot: Dartmouth

Lynn, P. and Taylor, B. (1995), 'On the bias and variance of samples of individuals: a comparison of the Electoral Registers and Postcode Address File as sampling frames', *The Statistician*, **44**: 173–194

Spector, P.E. (1992), *Summated Rating Scale Construction: An Introduction*, Quantitative Applications in the Social Sciences, 82, Newbury Park, Calif.: Sage

Stafford, R. and Thomson, K. (2006), *British Social Attitudes and Young People's Social Attitudes surveys 2003:*, Technical Report, London: National Centre for Social Research

Subject index